URBAN POLITICAL SYSTEMS
A FUNCTIONAL ANALYSIS OF METRO TORONTO

NUMBER SEVEN: METROPOLITAN POLITICS SERIES

URBAN
POLITICAL SYSTEMS

A FUNCTIONAL ANALYSIS OF
METRO TORONTO

BY HAROLD KAPLAN

COLUMBIA UNIVERSITY PRESS
New York and London   1967

To ABIGAIL *and* HARRIET

ACKNOWLEDGMENTS

I wish to thank the Research Advisory Committee of the Central Mortgage and Housing Corporation, York University, and particularly the Canadian Council on Urban and Regional Research for financing my research on Canadian urban politics.

For their advice, encouragement, and constructive criticism, I am also indebted to Alan Armstrong, Guy Bourassa, Lionel Feldman, Albert Rose, Wallace S. Sayre, John Saywell, and Douglas Verney.

Toronto, Ontario   HAROLD KAPLAN
August, 1967

CONTENTS

TABLES

FIGURES

METROPOLITAN POLITICS SERIES

WALLACE S. SAYRE, EDITOR

Urban Political Systems: A Functional Analysis of Metro Toronto is the seventh in a series of studies to be published under the auspices of the Department of Public Law and Government of Columbia University. The metropolitan study program, in which this series has its origin, was begun in 1957 with the support of a grant from the Ford Foundation. The committee supervising the program and serving as editors of the initial volumes in the series were Wallace S. Sayre, Richard E. Neustadt, David B. Truman, and William N. Cassella Jr.

Volumes which have already been published are:

Urban Renewal Politics: Slum Clearance in Newark
   Harold Kaplan
Federal Metropolitan Politics and the Commuter Crisis
   Michael N. Danielson
Community Leadership: The Regional Plan Association of New York
   Forbes B. Hays
Politics of Zoning: New York 1916–1960
   Stanislaw J. Makielski Jr.
Neighborhood Groups and Urban Renewal
   J. Clarence Davies III
Metropolitan Transportation Politics and the New York Region
   Jameson W. Doig

URBAN POLITICAL SYSTEMS
A FUNCTIONAL ANALYSIS OF METRO TORONTO

CHAPTER I

THE USES AND LIMITS
OF FUNCTIONAL THEORY

This book represents an attempt to integrate general theory and a specific research problem. Behind such an attempt is the belief that social scientists should be mainly concerned with linking broad theory to the concrete phenomena of social life. I am far from satisfied with the integration of theory and data achieved in this study, but my attempt may be of use to other political scientists interested in both theory and research. However feeble the integrating ability of a particular author is, I would still maintain that such attempts at integration are preferable to theorizing without benefit of data or describing without benefit of theory.

The research topic of this study is the municipality of Metropolitan Toronto, an unusual experiment in the federation of municipal governments in a metropolitan area. The research problem I initially set for myself was to describe the political structure of this metropolitan government and to relate this structure to the rapidly growing body of literature on American urban politics. Thus, while this study presents data on a single case, the approach and goals of the research are primarily comparative. My purpose, moreover, is less to evaluate and prescribe than to analyze, although I do consider how one would go about gauging the success of the Metro system.

The general theory I attempt to apply and assess, usually referred to as "structural functionalism," has been given its most elaborate definition by the sociologist Talcott Parsons. Other sociologists, like Robert Merton, and political scientists, like Gabriel Almond, have developed their own brand of functionalism. The term "functionalism," when used without any further qualification or identification, will refer to the works of Parsons; the other brands of functionalism will be explicitly linked to their authors.

A general theory like functionalism is less a set of substantive explanations of phenomena than it is a collection of interrelated definitions, categories, and questions. Functional theory is mainly a research strategy, primarily a group of suggestions about which are the more relevant questions to ask and which would be the more illuminating concepts to employ. Like any strategy it should be judged by its results. The major questions to be asked of this, and any other, general theory are whether it organizes data into a coherent whole in an efficient manner, whether it accounts for or explains the data as well as any other current theory, and whether it helps clarify any traditional problems of explanation in the social sciences. Logical and semantical analyses of a general theory may point up ambiguities, inconsistencies, or internal contradictions; but the most effective critique of any research strategy is a demonstration that it does not do the job expected of it—that it does not explain certain phenomena or does not explain them as well as some other theory does.[1]

The exact utility of functional theory can be demonstrated, and at the same time circumscribed, only by applying the theory to concrete research problems. Through this process of application the theory itself changes, as certain concepts are seen to be irrelevant or less useful and are dropped or modified. I do not assume that functionalism holds the key to all future political analysis. My only assumption is that Parsons' ideas hold great promise as conceptual guides to certain types of political research and that this promise deserves further exploration.

In this study Metro Toronto is treated as one case of a more general species called "urban political systems." My concern is with the utility of functional theory not only in the study of this one case but in the study of all urban political systems. Ideally one would want to include in such an assessment urban political systems drawn from a number of nations and cultural types. Unfortunately the literature on urban political systems is adequate only for American cities. Much of my analysis will involve comparisons between Metro Toronto and American cities, with occasional references to other Canadian cities on which I have begun research.[2]

I began collecting data on Metro Toronto before deciding to apply functional theory. My particular research interest, which determined my criteria of relevance in assembling the data, was the roles of the legislators, administrators, parties, and interest groups in the policy-making process. I later decided that functionalism was the most useful general approach because of the economy with which it permitted me to summarize my data. More than this, functional theory encouraged me to pose new questions, seek additional data on certain questions, and rearrange my data along lines that had not initially occurred to me. I decided to make a virtue out of necessity. I had collected the data not with a general theory in mind but with the interests and perspectives frequently employed by political scientists studying the policy-making process. It seemed to me that this study could demonstrate how functional theory clarifies a research problem selected independently of that theory and how functionalism adds some new dimensions to the study of the policy-making process.

Ideally, there should be no clash between the theoretical and descriptive purposes of this study. Functionalism should add to one's understanding of Metro, and the data on Metro should help reveal what in functionalism is useful and not useful for urban political analysis. In practice, however, one is frequently torn between including only the data necessary for a theoretical exposition of the system and including as much of the Metro story as one knows. My decision to pursue the first course will probably rob the study of much of its color and disappoint those students of urban government who are more interested in Metro than in functional theory.

[3]

The remainder of this chapter discusses what functionalism is, what its utilities and disutilities for political science are, and what changes I would make in the Parsonian framework. In one respect this chapter's purpose is to define the concepts that will be applied to the Metro system in succeeding chapters. In addition, since my views on the utilities of functionalism were products of the study more than initial assumptions, this introductory chapter may be seen as summarizing my conclusions on the relevance of functionalism to urban political analysis. These conclusions are based not only on the Metro data but also on my interpretation of the literature on American city politics.

Functional Theory

The basic argument of this chapter is that functionalism can be of great use in the study of urban political systems, provided that some limitations of the functional approach are first recognized and some modifications in the approach made. Before turning to these limitations and modifications, a brief outline of Parsons' theory and some indications of its general utilities are in order.

Basic Concepts. Parsons suggests that politics, like any other area of human behavior, might be usefully described as the operation of one or more social systems, analogous in structure and performance to biological or physical systems.[3] Parsons considers functionalism a general theory because it can be used to analyze an entire society or the economic, religious, political, and consanguineal segments of society. In the political realm the same mode of analysis could be applied to a nation, a province or state, an interest group, the Metro system, or some part thereof like the Metro School Board or the Toronto Transit Commission.

A system consists of a collection of individuals who interact on a regular basis and who agree on certain values. The agreement on values may have resulted from the regular interaction or may have given rise to it. The system will develop norms, or common beliefs, about what constitutes appropriate behavior for system members. The exact behavior expected of individuals in typical interaction situations, and the behavior that the individual can expect of others involved in this situation, are called roles. Roles, as specific prescriptions, will reflect the more general norms of the system. Thus, "equality" is a value of most Western societies, the notion that all individuals deserve equal treatment by the courts regardless of their social positions is a norm of these societies, and the roles that reflect these norms are the exact forms of behavior expected of judges, attorneys, and other participants in a trial situation.

According to functional theory, the analysis of a system should begin by identifying the content of the major roles in that system. Thus, functionalism is mainly interested in routinized or institutionalized behavior—behavior that is recurrent and governed by normative expectations. In fact, Parsons describes the content of a role not in terms of the incumbent's behavior but in terms of the normative expectations surrounding the incumbent. A system is viewed as a network of interrelated roles.

In addition to describing the content of these roles, functional theory is interested in how particular individuals are recruited for the major roles, what gratifications the individual receives from his role and what his motive for playing the role is, how well role performance meets role expectations, how individuals are taught the substance of their roles, and how well the values implicit in the roles accord with the general values of the system —that is, how internally consistent the system is.

When large areas of behavior are controlled by norms and role prescriptions, when the individual internalizes the values of the system and considers them sacred or not open to question, and when the individual is motivated to perform his role in the manner expected of him, that system may be said to be well integrated. Integrated systems are also internally consistent systems, in which the behavior expected of members embodies or lives up to the general values of the system. To phrase it differently, a social system is essentially a set of expectations about what individuals should do in certain situations; a particular system is integrated to the extent that the actual behavior of members meets these expectations. Typically, integrated systems strive to preserve their structures unchanged, resisting demands for change, punishing rebels or deviants, and minimizing the impact of environmental changes. No system is perfectly integrated. In any given system there will always be ambiguous norms, areas of behavior not covered by norms, internal inconsistencies, and some members who are not satisfied with their roles. The nonintegrated or poorly integrated parts of the system are the loopholes through which social change occurs, although these loopholes are not the only channels of change. Integration, in summary, is a matter of more or less; but every system must attain some minimal degree of integration to survive.

There is another sense in which Parsons uses the word "integration." Implicit in the idea of system is the notion that changes in one part of the organism affect the other parts. Functional theory encourages the researcher to examine entire systems, since they are integrated wholes. There is a theoretical affinity between functionalists and configurationists, who see a consistent thread running through the various segments of a single society.[4] In examining one part of a system, one should be aware of how that part reflects the overall ethos of the system. One should also be concerned with the relevance of the part to the whole, particularly how that part affects the stability and continuance of the whole.

More recently, Parsons has emphasized the notion that society may be thought of as a hierarchy of subsystems.[5] The crucial question to ask about any subsystem is how it relates to subsystems that stand above it and below it in the hierarchy. Parsons' stress on the points of articulation between subsystems demonstrates his continuing interest in the interrelation of a system's parts.

Parsons posits certain functional imperatives, or certain tasks that every system must undertake if it is to survive. Among the functional imperatives of all self-sustaining systems are provisions for recruiting new members and teaching them the norms and roles of the system, minimizing or managing internal conflict and tension, adapting the system to the demands of the physical and social environment, mobilizing the members for attainment of the system's goals, and maintaining the solidarity of the system or the personal commitment of individuals to the collectivity. Because these functions are essential to the system's survival, one may evaluate particular systems on the basis of how well they meet these needs, that is, how well they provide for their own continuance. Particular practices, roles, or norms may be classified according to whether they are functional or dysfunctional to the meeting of these basic needs. Typical roles will emerge in all systems in response to the functional requirements of survival. For example, Parsons notes the frequent emergence of one role that tends to the internal problems of the system (allocating resources, mobilizing behavior behind the system's goals) and another role that focuses on the system's foreign policy, that is, on mediating between the system and its environment.

Parsons' notion of functional imperatives is meant to apply primarily to self-sufficient systems and probably can be best utilized in the study of nation-states. Within a nation, the different functional requirements may be met by different subsystems, e.g., socialization by the family, and maintenance of solidarity by religious institutions. The political institutions of a nation are more concerned with mobilizing behavior behind the system's goals and meeting the demands of the national system's environment than with socialization or maintenance of solidarity. But each subsystem must perform all of these functional imperatives for itself if it is to survive or operate successfully. Even political systems must recruit new members, teach them political norms, and develop emotional symbolism or other devices to preserve the loyalty of the citizenry. The notion of functional imperatives, like most aspects of functional theory, is supposed to be applicable to many levels of analysis—to political institutions as well as to the entire society, to particular political subsystems like Metro Toronto as well as to the entire Canadian political system. Thus, one should distinguish between a subsystem's contribution to the functional needs of the larger system—a contribution which may be specialized—and a subsystem's efforts to solve its own functional problems—an effort which must be comprehensive. The former is contingent on the latter.

Parsons' classification of system is based on the orientation of the major roles in each system. Roles are categorized on the basis of whether they are assigned to individuals or achieved by them (the ascription–achievement continuum), whether role obligations are directed toward individuals or toward nonpersonal tasks (diffuseness–specificity), whether roles permit expressions of personal feeling (affectivity–neutrality), and whether roles dictate that other persons are to be treated on the basis of their social position or on the basis of generalized criteria unrelated to social position (particularism–universalism). The rise of urban, industrial societies has meant a growing emphasis on achieved, specific, neutral, and universal roles.

Some of Parsons' recent formulations emphasize that the social system may be seen as a series of exchanges between its component parts.[6] Each subsystem in a society has a product or output, which forms its contribution to the overall functioning of the society. The outputs of one subsystem form the inputs of another. The outputs of political subsystems, whether it be the Metro government, the federal government, or the entire Canadian political subsystem, consist of authoritative decisions or public policies. These decisions relate mainly to the allocation of costs and benefits, the adaptation of the society to environmental changes, the management of internal conflict, and the mobilization of behavior in support of the society's goals. The raw materials for these policy outputs, the so-called inputs, include the natural and financial resources at the subsystem's command, the support of subsystem members, and the demands made upon the subsystem. These demands to some extent emanate from the members' expectations about the subsystem's performance, expectations which the subsystem itself helped create. In one sense, then, the demand-inputs constitute pressure on the subsystem leaders to live up to the subsystem's norms and values. Demands may also emanate from other subsystems and thus serve as the vehicles through which a subsystem adjusts to its environment.

The extent to which a subsystem or system meets the demands of its members will greatly influence the members' motivation to continue playing roles in the system. In order to survive, a system must provide inducements sufficient to evoke some minimal degree of membership support. A rough equilibrium exists when the inducements evoke just the degree of support desired by the system's leaders. Those systems desiring only limited membership support need only provide limited inducements; in these cases equilibrium may occur at a relatively low level of membership commitment to the system. A political system faces serious problems when it lacks the resources to meet most of the demands made of it, when the demands are internally inconsistent, and when the demand-inputs far exceed the support-inputs. Another perennial problem of political leaders is the conflict between the demands of a system's membership and the demands of a system's environment.

(Use of the terms "system" and "subsystem" depends on one's level of analysis. If the purpose of the study is to examine all of Canadian society, Canada is the "system," and the religious, economic, and political institutions are "subsystems." If one is examining all of Canadian politics, the federal government or local governments are "subsystems." In this study I shall refer to Metro Toronto as a political "system," to parts of Metro Toronto, like the cabinet or the Metro Council, as "subsystems," and to Ontario government as the "larger system" of which Metro is a part.)

The Varieties of Functionalism. Parsons' contribution might be further clarified by indicating how his theories differ from other forms of functional analysis. In my view, the hallmarks of Parsonian functionalism are its reliance on concepts drawn from the main sociological tradition, its attempt to study whole systems, and its attempt to describe systems in terms of a set of basic needs or problems.

The term "functional analysis" sometimes has been used to describe statements about social causation. To say that one phenomenon is a function of another phenomenon is to say that the two are causally related. Similarly, if we equate the functional significance of a phenomenon with its impact on the rest of the society, we are again making a simple causal statement. If defined in this manner, "functionalism" does not constitute a new or distinctive approach.[7]

To add to the confusion over definition, "functional analysis" is sometimes equated with the entire sociological approach. Thus, Robert Merton, who usually is very careful in his use of terms, calls his analysis of deviant behavior "functional" because he traces such behavior to social structural causes rather than to individual or psychological causes.[8] To define "functionalism" in this way is to equate it with almost all of current sociology, economics, and political science. Furthermore, it should be made clear that most of Parsons' concepts—role, norm, social control, integration, and so on—are not his inventions but are the working tools of most sociologists. Parsons' synthesis of the classical sociological tradition is a hallmark of his approach but is not the sum and substance of his contribution.[9]

The essence of Parsons' functionalist approach, it seems to me, is the attempt to define certain basic requisites for the survival and success of social systems and to see the structure of a system as a set of mechanisms that attempt to fulfill these requisites. This approach owes a considerable debt to anthropological functionalists like Malinowski and Radcliffe-Brown.[10] But Parsons does not assume, as Malinowski did, that every form of institutionalized behavior meets some basic need of the social system. Nor is it assumed that explaining the functional significance of a phenomenon is an alternative to explaining its origins or causes. Functionalism, in its more recent version, need not exclude diachronic analysis.

[10]

The crucial difference between Parsons and Merton is the former's interest in macro-analysis and the latter's preference for middle-range theory. Parsons begins with the overall features of a system and then proceeds to a discussion of the parts; his beginning point is a list of functional requisites. Merton begins with a single phenomenon and then traces its functional consequences. Merton is more willing to recognize diversity and weak integration in a system, which probably reinforces his preference for dealing with parts of systems rather than systems as wholes.

To restate an earlier point, I shall use the term "functionalism" to denote Parsons' brand of functionalism. Merton's type of functionalism, where it differs from Parsons', will be specifically linked to the author's name.

Functional Theory and Political Science

The Uses of Functionalism in Political Analysis. Functionalism is of use to political scientists partly because it embodies the sociological model of human behavior. The concepts that make up this model—e.g., norm, status, role, socialization, social control, deviation, and integration—have been used with considerable effectiveness by sociologists in studying a wide range of social phenomena. These research results, and the failure of political science to develop an equally comprehensive, explicit, and empirically oriented model, constitute at least a *prima facie* case for applying sociological concepts to political analysis. There are advantages, both for incisive description and systematic theory building, in seeing political science as the study of a particular type of social system. Power, which has been the central focus in political science, might be usefully seen as an attribute of a particular role in a social system—a role largely defined by the norms of that system and the expectations of other system members. The social structural approach permits us to distinguish the recurrent forms of behavior from the unique and incidental. Such an approach diverts the attention of political scientists from a narrative of events to the delineation of forms and processes.[11]

Second, functionalism encourages political scientists to relate a particular research topic to the broader social environment—to explore the points of articulation between a given process or subsystem and the larger social system of which it is a part. Rather than select a controllable, neatly defined research topic and then exhaust the internal aspects of that topic, the researcher is led by the functional approach to study entire political systems or, if he is examining some part of a system, to trace the relevance of that part for the larger system. In short, Parsons' macroscopic approach is as important a contribution as his sociological model of behavior.

Third, the classification of political systems on the basis on how and by whom certain systemic needs are performed permits the political scientist to abandon formal, institutional bases for comparison. For this reason Parsons has had considerable impact on political scientists studying comparative government, particularly those comparing Western and non-Western systems.[12]

Finally, while it is true that the original Parsonian formulation did not provide an elaborate theory of social change, this approach naturally lends itself to theories of social change.[13] Political scientists have used aspects of Parsons' framework in considering questions of nation building and political development. Concern with the structure of entire political systems naturally provokes questions about why systems appear, develop, stagnate, or decline and why different types of systems emerge in different locales. Functionalism does not provide substantive answers to these traditional questions in historical and comparative analysis, but the approach does permit such inquiries to be made again with some new conceptual tools.

Functionalism, Conflict, and Power. Critics of Parsonian functionalism have noted Parsons' heavy emphasis on integration and the small role that conflict plays in his theories. Parsons is concerned primarily with how systems establish norms and roles that minimize or manage conflict. As Lewis Coser has noted, Parsons is a modern Hobbes, interested in how order and stability emerge from disorganization and dissension.[14]

Functionalism's emphasis on integration, although admittedly one-sided, does serve as a useful antidote to what I shall call the "war theory of politics."[15] For over a generation many American political scientists have held, implicitly or explicitly, that conflict is the essence of politics and that political behavior could best be studied in terms analogous to war, international diplomacy, or competitive sports. Power is viewed as the central concept in political science and is defined as the imposition of one's will on others. Since power is distributed unequally, the political scientists' major task is to trace the distribution of power in particular systems. Individual actors are treated as contestants or claimants. Most of their behavior is alleged to be tactical, that is, directed toward the furtherance of their particular goals and the frustration of their competitors. This approach, then, directs attention to the political resources that each of the claimants has at his command and the skill with which he uses these resources. Public policy decisions in democracies are treated as the outcome of conflict, with the substantive result generally representing a compromise among the demands of the major claimants. Bargaining and negotiation become the crucial methods of resolving conflicts.

The analogous model for this approach, although rarely made explicit, appears to be the economic market, operating under conditions of imperfect competition or oligopoly. Political man, carefully calculating risks, influence, and votes, appears to be a direct offspring of economic man. Political entrepreneurs pursue their own special goals in the absence of any general consensus on goals or any central coordination of the market processes. Political resources (time, skill, expertise, money) replace economic resources. Influence replaces money as the basic currency of transactions. The negotiated compromise replaces contractual agreements or purchases.

The politics-as-conflict theory has utilities of its own but in several respects it is less successful than functionalism. The politics-as-conflict school never satisfactorily explains what holds systems together. It neglects the fact that conflict must occur within the context of some consensus on fundamentals. If there were no consensus, there would be no system. As William Mitchell has argued in his application of Parsonian theory to the American political system, American political scientists have tended to take for granted the overall stability of the American system and to focus on the competitive aspects. As a result these political scientists never explained the sources of stability and cohesion.[16]

The politics-as-war approach, it seems to me, confuses a general theory with the characteristics of one political system. This approach emerged from studies of the American political system —hence the emphasis on open-ended pluralism, overt conflict, negotiation and compromise, and piecemeal decision making. The limits of this approach in comparative analysis, particularly in the study of non-Western systems, has contributed to the political scientists' recent interest in sociological models.[17]

Since many areas of political behavior can be reduced to normative control or become matters of consensus, politics is not always the study of conflict. The goals of the political system may often be to mobilize behavior behind a common goal. To use Parsons' phrases, power has both productive and allocative aspects. In one respect power is a resource of the entire system, to be used in pursuing the system's goals, coping with environmental challenges, and solidifying the members' support for the system. This is the productive aspect of power. But power also is a resource unevenly distributed among the members of the system. This is its allocative aspect. The politics-as-war approach looks only at the allocative aspect of power. It also assumes that politics is a sum-zero game, in which the particular aspirations of the system's members are directly in conflict and in which accretions in power for one actor involve a diminution in power for some other actor. Emphasis on the distributive aspects of power and on politics as a sum-zero game, Parsons argues, elevates a secondary phenomena to the central position in one's analysis.[18]

But Parsons can be criticized for focusing almost exclusively on the productive aspects of power. He treats the goals of a system as given—since a system is by definition a collection of individuals agreed on certain values—and emphasizes how behavior is mobilized and coordinated to attain those goals. Thus, Parsonian functionalism is mainly interested in the implementation or administration of already established goals. There is little recognition of the process by which political systems consciously set goals or the likelihood that some of these goals will reflect the wishes of some members more than others.

In the following study of Metro Toronto, goal definition will take precedence over goal implementation. The Metro system's policy output will be viewed as a means of coping with the environment, maximizing internal support for the system, and asserting the values of particular groups within the system. We wish to know how much consensus and dissensus there is over the political system's goals, and which members influence policy outputs more than other members. In other words, the relative importance of the productive and allocative aspects of power will be the subject of empirical inquiry, not a matter for *a priori* determination at the outset of the study.

The Normative Integration of Political Systems. The institutionalization of values, norms, and roles is the focal point of functional analysis. But this orientation has its limits, as well as uses, in the analysis of modern political systems. Parsons is mainly interested in the process whereby individuals internalize (or consecrate) certain standards of judgment and canons of behavior. In modern political systems, however, the norms governing behavior are not as extensive, explicit, or sacred as the Parsonian general model suggests. In such political systems, but particularly in liberal democratic systems, weak normative integration has been institutionalized.

In all rational–legal (or modern) societies, an attempt has

been made to separate the political order from the other segments of the society and to make the setting of goals a conscious and rational process. This attempt at separation necessitates divesting political values of some of their sacredness. If planned, purposeful change is to be institutionalized, the things to be changed—the policies or goals of the system and to some extent its political structure—cannot be viewed with the same awe that moral and religious norms evoke. Modern societies accept a degree of conscious self-direction in politics that would be unthinkable in the more sacred areas of the society. Modern states have more to do with the instrumental than the expressive aspects of the social system.

More specifically, the liberal democratic values attempt to further divest politics of its expressive or sacred character. Individual citizens are exhorted to be rational and calculative in the formation of their political opinions and the use of their votes. There is a large area of legitimate conflict. It is considered appropriate for individuals and groups to pursue their particular (nonconsensual) goals. Most of the norms that govern political behavior in this type of system are negative; they set an outer limit to the tactics employed in this pursuit of particular goals, by indicating those forms of behavior that the system will not tolerate. Of course democracy, the nation itself, and other aspects of the democratic system may remain sacred; but the liberal values, by warning against an uncritical approach to one's government and by attempting to institutionalize skepticism, place limits to the extent of this sacred sphere. Moreover, democratic political systems play a less significant role in socialization and social control than do totalitarian states. In societies with democratic polities, the integrative functions are more clearly the responsibility of nonpolitical institutions.

In the large scope permitted to the pursuit of self-interest and in the prevalence of largely negative norms, the democratic and market processes are similar. But neither the market model nor the normative-integration model *alone* can be made the basis for analyzing democratic political systems. The market approach ignores the areas of normative control. Parsons, on the other hand, shows little interest in the poorly integrated areas of social behavior or in the segments of society where dissension is permitted and sometimes encouraged. We may, of course, wish to study how the liberal, democratic norms emerged and how these values differ from other value systems.[19] But if we are more interested in how democratic systems operate and how one democracy differs from another, a theory that concerns itself with how norms are institutionalized and enforced can only provide a first step in the analysis.

Functionalism and Urban Political Systems. That Parsons' focus on the normative order has severe limits when applied to political analysis is even more apparent in the case of urban political systems. This point can be demonstrated by presenting some of the findings on the Metro Toronto system.

Metro Toronto did not approach the level of normative integration described in Parsons' general model. In Metro there was a minimal consensus on goals, values, or norms, outside of a consensus on the liberal, democratic values that pervade Canada and most Western democracies. Actors in Metro, for example, preferred debate to violence as a means of settling disputes, respected the products of the electoral and legislative processes, and accepted the legitimacy of differing viewpoints. Thus, Metro shared the normative standards of the nation but had no distinctive normative order of its own. There were no distinctive socialization and social control processes at work in the Metro system because there were no local norms to transmit or enforce.

Citizens accepted the legitimacy of the Metro system and obeyed its laws because these individuals were members of Canadian society. If citizens have not learned to obey local regulations intuitively, the senior governments will compel their obedience, even though the municipality is legally little more than a private corporation. A normative order was necessary to the Metro system's functioning but was not the responsibility of the Metro system itself. The functions that stand at the core of

Parsons' analysis were, from Metro's point of view, environmental inputs. These functions were performed for Metro by other segments of Canadian society.

Structural requisites for the operation of urban political systems were also provided by senior governments. Every political system must include provisions for recruiting individuals to fill roles and formal statuses, but not every system must develop its own recruitment mechanisms. Provincial law provided for, and carefully defined, the procedures by which Metro officials were appointed or elected.

The orientation of the Metro system's members to the system itself was instrumental or calculative. (This was probably true of the citizens as well as the political leaders, although the following chapters do not contain any evidence on public attitudes.) Metro was expected to provide certain services or payoffs and to do so in an efficient and inexpensive manner. Metro lacked an expressive sphere. The Metro leaders, unlike the national leaders, did not have emotional symbolism at their command to build diffuse support for the system. The members' support for the system *per se* was weak, and the commitment of the members to active involvement in the system's processes was limited and tentative. Many Metro politicians gauged their personal political success by their ability to leave the Metro system and enter federal or provincial politics.

In summary, Metro was a specialized or partial system that had more in common with voluntary associations in open, contractual societies than it had with Parsons' model of integrated systems. For this reason, concepts developed to study weakly integrated or specialized systems—like Truman's notion of the "mediate group," Merton's notion of the "segmental group," and Dahl's description of the "slack system"—are used extensively in this study.[20] The partial or segmental system controls only a small part of the behavior of its members, may lead the members only in areas deemed appropriate to that system, must compete for the members' attention and loyalty with a number of other systems, and cannot make extensive use of social control mechanisms without provoking a reduction in the members' commitment to the system. Since the sights of Parsonian functionalism are trained on isolated, self-sufficient systems, there is little room in this scheme for problems of multiple group membership and divided loyalties.[21]

Some reasons for the Metro system's failure to develop a normative order were unique to Metro. These reasons are examined in succeeding chapters. But it may also be true that urban political systems tend to be less integrated on a normative basis than their national counterparts. Local systems are even less involved than national systems in socialization, social control, and other integrative functions. The expressive aspects of politics are focused at the national level; national systems monopolize the drama and ritual of government. Within the realm of goal definition and implementation, moreover, urban political systems are responsible for those goals that stand on the lowest level of the society's hierarchy of values. For this reason, a political system can sooner tolerate weak normative integration and extensive conflict at the local level than at the national level. If local systems failed to perform their responsibilities adequately, the higher levels of government would simply assume more local responsibilities. No one need worry about weak integration leading to the collapse of local systems, since these systems borrow the legitimacy and stability of the national system.

In view of the local systems' emphasis on purely instrumental functions and less important goals, the members' calculative, tentative, and nonemotional attitude to such systems is not surprising. In fact, if local leaders were able to build strong, diffuse support for local systems, the integration of the national political system would be weakened. Thus, limited commitments and calculative orientations among members of local systems is functional to national unity.

In describing any political system, one must include a delineation of the key, institutionalized values; for without this area of normative control there would be no system. But in studying urban political systems—and other partial or segmental systems devoted to instrumental functions—these institutionalized values may provide little more than a background to the more central goal-setting process. The institutionalized values may be provided by other systems; but through its own goal-setting processes a system will determine its success in the larger environment.[22]

A Modified Functional Approach

Much of the functionalist approach to social phenomena can be used effectively in the study of political systems without adopting all the specific concepts contained in the Parsonian general model. In this section I suggest some modifications in Parsons' approach and in the next section apply this modified functional framework to a comparison of three types of urban political systems. The purpose of my revisions is to develop concepts that are useful in the study of segmental as well as highly integrated systems.

The following discussion may appear to be excessively preoccupied with the definition of terms. Such definitions are necessary because many phrases in functional theory contain multiple meanings and because I borrow some of Parsons' phrases but sometimes attach different meanings to them.

Systems. Political science may be defined as the study of certain types of social systems, and a social system may be defined as a relatively self-contained network of human interaction. It is assumed that, if a collection of individuals interact regularly over a period of time, certain stable forms of interaction will emerge. Rather than make their decisions in an *ad hoc* manner, the members will develop an overall orientation to the system and a notion of their appropriate behavior in the system. I shall call these regularities in behavior "roles," without assuming that roles emerge from the system's norms.

Defining a system in terms of behavioral regularities rather than institutionalized values does not entail the pursuit of a strict behaviorist approach, which would discuss only observable behavior and would reject any discussion of subjective factors. Behind a persistent form of behavior usually stands a stable attitude or orientation to the system. Parsons, it seems to me, is correct in arguing that social interaction cannot be understood without knowing something about the actor's frame of mind.[23] My point is that these subjective orientations need not consist of the internalized, almost sacred, values described by Parsons. The members' orientation to a system may be tentative, flexible, and calculative.

The term "equilibrium" will be used to indicate that roles exist—that there is some stability in the behavior of a collection of individuals. Individuals would probably resist threats to an equilibrium—so defined—but would not necessarily try to restore an equilibrium once it had been disturbed. We do not equate equilibrium with a high degree of normative integration; a system may stabilize, or reach an equilibrium, at a low level of normative integration.[24]

The degree of normative integration in real systems is left for empirical determination. Although some minimal degree of normative integration must be present in a system, or lent to a system by other systems, that minimal degree will vary considerably from one type of system to another. In a limited purpose system, very little integration would be necessary.[25] Thus, the norms of a system may structure only a small part of the members' behavior in the system. It is conceivable, for example, that the norms of a system merely set certain ground rules for conflict, that individuals come together in a system primarily to compete, and that a system is little more than an arena for the pursuance—and perhaps reconciliation—of special goals.[26]

System Analysis and Actor Analysis. If the role expectations of a system are not the only, or even the most important, referent points for the behavior of system members, one cannot avoid dealing with the problem of individual choice. Parsons builds his model from the top down. Once it is known what the values, norms, and role expectations of a system are, it is assumed that individuals will behave largely in accord with these systemic demands. In partially integrated systems, however, the individual will be faced with socially undefined or ambiguous situations, will have to create his own role, and, in defining a role, will have to choose among different values and demands. The expectations of other members may be more negative than positive; they may simply indicate what the members will not tolerate. In other instances, expectations may arise only after a pattern of behavior has been established and may still lack the compulsory quality that Parsons associates with role expectations. Because an individual occupant of a formal position usually behaves in a certain fashion, other members may come to expect that behavior of him and of succeeding occupants.

A partially integrated system, like Metro Toronto, must be described from the bottom up. We must first understand how individuals formed their basic orientation to the system and defined their role in the system, since the resulting structure is a composite of such individual decisions. Even after decisions are taken and a pattern is set, the process of individual redefinition continues. In Metro, for example, the new occupant of a formal position was not bound by the behavior of his predecessor and was free, within certain broad limits, to reconstruct his role.

Functional analysis, in other words, must proceed at two levels. In system analysis, one is primarily interested in assessing the consequences of actor behavior for the system's functional performance. At this level of analysis one may speak of "the system" as if it were an individual actor, who behaves in certain ways and who does or does not meet certain problems. In actor analysis, one examines how specific individuals made up their minds about the system and about their roles in it.[27]

What is meant by actor analysis can be illustrated by my discussion in chapter 8 of how Metro legislators defined their roles. The process of role definition is described by noting the referent points that served as guidelines for the Metro councilors' decisions on role (see Table 8.1).[28] Exactly how the councilors made up their minds is less important at this point than the fact that choice was involved. The values, norms, and role expectations of the Metro system, since they did not exist, did not serve as a referent point for the Metro councilors' decisions on role. The same may be said about the other Metro actors' decisions. The Metro chairman, however, *did* pattern his behavior in response to the functional needs of the Metro system, as he interpreted them.

Parsons might argue that the Metro councilor's patterned behavior was not a "role" at all but a "style" or "strategy." The problem with adhering to Parsons' definition of "role" is that this definition tells us little about the Metro actors or the Metro system. Using the Parsonian definition, the "role" of the Metro councilor would consist of those expectations that are directed at all legislators in liberal, democratic systems. But it is the councilor's more specific, patterned behavior—or "role," as I define it—that helped provide the Metro system with its distinctive structure.[29]

Contributions and Tasks. I have found it useful to divide the idea of function into several component concepts and to assign a different label to each concept. Parsons' concept of the problems that every system must solve, the functional imperatives, will be called the "functions" of a system. Some authors also speak of the functions that a system performs for other systems, particularly for the larger system of which it is a part. Here, I would suggest that we speak of a system's "contributions" to other systems. The system's own survival problem and its contributions to other systems, though distinct, are obviously related. In order to make any contribution, a system must solve its own functional problems. On the other hand, the inputs provided by other social units may greatly influence a system's ability to cope with its functional problems. One may define a system's "tasks" as the powers and goals formally assigned to that system. A system's contributions may equal, exceed, or fall short of its assigned tasks. Where contributions exceed tasks, we may speak of a system making unrecognized contributions.[30]

Political systems, as opposed to religious or economic systems, can best be defined in terms of the contributions that governments make to modern society. Such governments are more concerned with tension management, adaptation to the environment, and goal attainment than with socialization, social control, normative integration, and the expressive, symbolic aspects of the society. A political system, then, would be that part of a society that defines and enforces rules in a conscious and formal manner. This emphasis on conscious enforcement distinguishes the governmental process from informal, social control mechanisms. Emphasis on formal goal setting distinguishes government from those segments of society, like religion and the family, where rules are not consciously defined or revised.[31]

Parsonian analysis directs attention to the points of articulation between a system and all other systems with which it interacts. In the case of Canadian urban political systems, the interrelation of the urban and provincial systems is particularly important. The tasks of the municipal system are set by the province. If municipal units make any contributions, these contributions are made to the provincial systems. The failure of municipal systems to perform their assigned tasks, or a decline in the municipalities' contributions to the provincial systems, would produce a shift of more responsibility and power to the higher levels of government.[32]

Functions. Most of the functional imperatives discussed in the literature can be subsumed under two broad types of functions: adaptation to the physical and social environment, and maintenance of internal solidarity. The first might be called the "adaptive," "external," or "problem-solving" function; the second might be called the "internal" or "integrating" function. (Integration, in this context, does not necessarily mean the normative integration of which Parsons speaks.) These functions also provide one basis for classifying the orientations of system members. The adaptive leader will be oriented to problems perceived in the environment, to general value schemes that transcend the particular system, or to the demands of other systems.

The integrative leader will be more committed to the system itself than to any set of substantive goals, mainly interested in defending the *status quo* and forestalling the internal strain that might be induced by problem solving, or primarily dedicated to the mediation of conflicts that arise within the system. The adaptive leader often generates conflict; the integrative leader usually strives to minimize, smother, or arbitrate conflict. The adaptive leader will express dissatisfaction with the *status quo* and will attempt to thrust the system in certain directions; the integrative leader will support new policies reluctantly and, even then, will only support piecemeal changes in present policies. The adaptive leader's reference groups lie partly or largely outside the system. Viewing himself as a mediator between the system and other systems, the adaptive leader will urge the system to meet the expectations of other segments of the society. He is task-or-contribution oriented, using those phrases in the sense defined above. The integrative leader mediates between parts of the internal system. He sees to it that the system, in the process of meeting environmental demands, does not tear itself apart. Of course, these are ideal types. A specific actor may mix both orientations, although one will most likely predominate.[33]

"Integration," as I define it, is synonymous with the unity or solidarity of a system. Such unity may or may not have a normative basis. Perhaps integration can be more precisely defined by noting the external signs or indices used to gauge the degree of integration. Indices of normative integration are: 1) indications that members have developed a diffuse, noncalculative support for the system and that their loyalty to the system equals or outranks their loyalties to other systems; 2) the generation of distinctive norms and the appearance of socialization and social control mechanisms; and 3) a growing consensus on goals, a lessening degree of overt conflict, and a willingness to smother conflict in order to preserve the system.

But members may support a system merely because it is convenient or fulfills some limited utility for them. A system may win internal support and minimize internal conflict by skillfully manipulating payoffs. Thus, some minimal degree of unity may be attained without the appearance of diffuse support for the system and without the subjection of behavior to normative control. Some signs of nonnormative integration are: 1) the members' willingness to defend the system against wholesale change; 2) a rough satisfaction with the policy outputs of the system; and 3) a willingness to continue one's participation in the system.

This equation of integration with internal solidarity, and some of the specific indices cited above, can be found in the Haas and Deutsch studies of integration at the international level.[34] An advantage of this approach is that it treats normative integration, so heavily emphasized in Parsonian analysis, as one basis—but not the only basis—of solidarity in political systems. Another contribution of the Haas—Deutsch approach is the emphasis on integration as a process rather than a state of being. Pursuing this diachronic approach to integration, we are encouraged to assess the relative degree of integration in any particular system, to note the direction in which the system is moving, and to identify the factors that impede or encourage greater integration.

Normative integration may be viewed as a higher level of integration. A decline in the members' careful calculation of advantages and disadvantages and a growth in generalized support for the system would increase the problem-solving capacity of the system, while at the same time reducing the incidence of internal, overt conflict. In the presence of diffuse support, balances need not be struck in each particular policy decision. The system would have some credit to draw upon. Those members displeased with a particular policy decision would continue to support the system with the same intensity; their level of commitment would change only if the number of objectionable decisions continued and eventually surpassed a certain threshold. The elaboration of normative control settles the integration problem and permits the members to focus more directly on problem solving or adaptation. Thus, the transition from non-normative to normative integration is an important breakthrough for a political system.[35]

Over the long run, a system's success in the performance of one function will enhance its ability to perform the other. Raising the level of integration, as already noted, increases the adaptive potential of a system. Success in the environment, by enhancing the external reputation of the system and by producing an increased level of inputs by other systems, will make it easier for the integrative leaders of a system to preserve the members' commitments. To the extent that the two functions mutually interact, one may speak of systems being caught in a cycle of success or a cycle of failure.[36]

In the short run, however, tension between the integrative and adaptive functions—and conflict between actors who embody these different orientations—seems inherent in political systems. Of course, if all the members of a system were to demand the same solution and if that solution were to increase the system's adaptive level, there would be no conflict between the system's two imperatives. More often, problem solving, because it requires some rearranging of internal relations, expectations, and rewards, induces stress in the system and threatens the system's integration. This conflict between a system's two basic functions appears to be not only endemic but incapable of permanent solution.[37] A successful system strikes a temporary but necessarily unstable balance between the two needs. A system may fail because it overemphasizes problem solving and tries to move too fast, because it excludes certain groups from policy making, or because it fails to reconcile conflicts among the internal segments of the system. In these cases the integrative function was not adequately performed. A system may fail because it emphasizes internal harmony to the neglect of environmental demands. At the national level, such a breakdown in the adaptive function might prove disastrous. At the urban political level, the result probably would be a withdrawal by other systems of their supportive inputs and a decline in the relative importance of the urban unit. Deutsch calls this latter type of malfunctioning "closure"—the failure to accept and process vital information emanating from outside the system.[38]

The differentiation of roles along adaptive and integrative lines ensures that both imperatives are considered by the system. Thus, conflict between these two types of leaders is functional to the system's survival. It is important, therefore, that systems motivate different individuals to perform these two types of roles and ensure that the properly motivated individuals arrive at formal positions where they can effectively perform these roles. It is also important that the role occupants learn the skills necessary to perform these roles well.[39]

Activities. The term "function" is sometimes used by political scientists to denote types of behavior that recur in the policy-making processes of modern governments. For example, the Almond–Cohen studies of foreign policy refer to the following functions in the policy-making process: initiation, authorization, modification, vetoing, representation, communication, and advocacy.[40] Dividing the policy-making process into constituent types of behavior is a useful research strategy, but I propose to call these forms of behavior "activities" rather than "functions."

One way of compiling a list of activities is to ask what general kinds of behavior are indispensable to the official enactment of a policy proposal—that is, to apply the functionalists' concern with requisites to the policy-making process.[41] In all democratic systems, for example, enactment would probably require the initiation and definition of proposals; the creation of generalized understanding, sympathy, and support for the proposal both within and without the system; the relation of that proposal to the specific values and interests of groups in the system; and the construction of a specific majority in the enacting body.

I shall use these four types of behavior as a tentative list of policy-making activities. Each of the four types will be called an "activity," although each is really a category or collection of more specific actions. Thus, the majority-building or aggregating category might include logrolling, persuasion, compromise, intimidation, bribery, and other specific actions. A single act, like the publication of a study commission report, may fall into several of the above four categories. And the same action performed twice may each time be classified in a different category, depending on the purpose of the actor.

Although any of the above four activities may be performed with either an integrative or adaptive orientation, it is likely that adaptive actors would more often perform the issue-initiating and support-securing activities, while integrative leaders would more often perform the interest-articulating activity.

Although the above-defined activities may be generally indispensable in democratic policy making, not every one of these activities need be performed in every policy decision. If there is a consensus on some policy question in a particular system, there may be no need for the creation of generalized support or the construction of a specific majority. Control of the enacting body by a disciplined, majority party may eliminate the need to perform all four activities in each particular policy decision. My only assumption is that either there are compensating mechanisms, which make one or more activities dispensable in particular cases, or the enactment process will not be successfully completed.

The nonperformance of an activity in the absence of a compensating mechanism may be called a gap in the policy-making process. Since political systems must produce policy decisions in order to solve their own functional problems and to make contributions to other systems, policy-making gaps may hamper the long-range success of the system. The following cases illustrate some typical gaps in policy making:

1. The system includes members who perceive problems but lacks members with the skills required to formulate solutions. System members feel that "something should be done" but lack direction.
2. Proposals are approved without some of the affected individuals and groups being informed of the significance of these proposals. The result may be a rebellion against the proposals, once their implications are understood, or a withdrawal of support for the system by the discontented groups.
3. A proposed solution requires a sharp break with prevailing

policies, but none of the solution's supporters undertakes an educative campaign to make the solution seem less utopian or radical.

4. The enacting body may favor some solution to a problem but may remain deadlocked because no official undertakes the majority-building activity.

Gaps 1 and 3 would adversely affect the performance of the adaptive function, gap 2 would harm integration, and gap 4 might weaken the performance of both functions.

Any of the basic activities could be performed for a system by individuals who are not members of that system. One index of autonomy is the extent to which a system performs its own activities and provides its own compensating mechanisms.

This list of activities permits one to characterize the structure of a political system on the basis of which actors perform which activities (see Table 1.1). Influence over the outcome of a system's policies is synonymous with the performance of some activity in the policy-making process.[42] The role of a particular actor, or of the occupants of a particular formal position, may be summarized in terms of:

1. Scope of activities: How many activities does the actor attempt to perform?
2. Scope of policy interests: In how many different policy areas does the actor attempt to perform some activity?
3. Intensity of involvement: How regularly does the individual attempt to perform certain activities, and how much of his time, energy, skill, or money does he dedicate to his performance?
4. Skill: How well does the actor use the resources he has committed?
5. Functional orientation: Does the actor pursue his activities in order to increase the system's internal integration or its adaptation to environmental problems?

Thus, one may trace the minimal influence of a particular actor to his low aspirations (small scope, low intensity) or to his failure

[30]

to achieve high aspirations. Failure to realize one's aspirations may reflect inadequate skill or the actor's refusal to match broad scope with intense involvement. The greater influence of actors with one type of functional orientation—e.g., integrative—will explain why a system overemphasizes that one function.

In discussing influence, one should distinguish between the ability to influence outcomes through the performance of activities—which I shall call "specific influence"—and the ability to influence the way in which other actors define their roles in the system—which I shall call "pervasive influence." While focusing on the policy-making process, one should avoid equating "influence" with "specific influence."[43]

Comparative Urban Politics: An Application of the Framework

In the following pages the modified functional framework is applied to a comparison of the Metro system and two other types of urban political system. I hope, by this procedure, to highlight what is distinctive and what is not distinctive to the Metro system. An attempt will be made to explain Metro's distinctive features in the chapters that follow. Another purpose of the following exercise in comparative urban politics is to suggest that a functional approach offers a more complex and accurate way of characterizing urban systems that the frequently employed "elitist–pluralist" distinction.[44] Metro, for example, is "elitist" in some ways and "pluralist" in others. And many of Metro's basic features cannot be described in either "elitist" or "pluralist" terms.

The Business Elite System. In some large American cities and in a good number of small American cities and towns, political power is concentrated in the hands of perhaps thirty or forty of the community's leading businessmen.[45] Issues are raised and defined in the offices of the major business executives and are informally transmitted to the mayor and city council. The politicians almost always go along with the proposals of the businessmen. Moreover, no proposal initiated in the political sector can succeed without the approval of the business elite. Most citizens in the community appear to know who this elite is. Occasionally, a center of opposition may form around labor union officials, university people, and local welfare workers, but this liberal bloc is usually unimportant in community politics. On the whole, there is little overt conflict. Rarely are there electoral contests for local office. The business elite informally recruits candidates for local political office from the middle and lower-middle classes. The businessmen themselves rarely deign to hold political office. Not surprisingly, the policy outputs in this type of system reflect the values of business-oriented conservatism. The emphasis is on maintaining a healthy local climate for business and economic development.

The Broker Leadership System. The broker leadership system deserves a more elaborate description, because it is more complex and because it appears to be the dominant form of big-city politics in the United States.[46]

The hallmark of the broker leadership system is the pervasive and highly influential role of interest groups in policy making and the more passive role played by elected officials. Issues are generally raised and defined by private groups. The political officials put off a commitment on the issues, waiting to see what the alignment of groups on any particular issue will be and whether any decision at all will be required. Sometimes, the city politicians insist that the interest groups work out an informal accord on policy, to which the city council will add its formal ratification. There are occasional exceptions to this pattern, but as Banfield and Wilson conclude, "typically the civic groups propose and the political leaders acquiesce when they can do so without provoking excessive controversy."[47]

In any significant area of policy making there will be group conflict, with each group pressing to impose its values on public policy. The municipal politician sees himself as an arbiter or broker, in search of a policy compromise that will least offend a maximum number of interests. The mayor and city councilmen see policy making as a means of minimizing discontent and protecting themselves from political retaliation, not as a means of implementing long-range plans or comprehensive solutions to problems. As Banfield has argued, policy decisions in this type of system must be made on political rather than technical grounds; the decision maker must be more concerned with which groups are presenting the arguments than with the substantive merits of the arguments.[48]

The broker leadership system is antipathetic to long-range planning and to major innovations in policy. Official decisions usually represent compromises of the various group demands. In this type of system, bargaining is the essence of the policy-making process. Since policy decisions represent the outcomes of separate political battles, involving different alignments of interest, these decisions will not always be logically consistent. Policy outputs are products of a competitive market not of centralized planning.

The politician–broker, moreover, will insist on proceeding in a pragmatic fashion, handling issues only after serious grievances are voiced. He shuns any commitment to long-range policies because he cannot predict what future political alignments will be. The pace of decision making is slow. The politician will approach a final decision with considerable caution, hoping to muster a consensual majority in support of a particular decision before publicly committing himself. The politician–broker always prefers marginal rather than comprehensive changes in the *status quo*, since marginal changes disturb a smaller number of interests. If no workable compromise comes to mind, the politician–broker would rather put off the entire problem. Thus, the broker leadership system is often characterized by *immobilisme* or what Sayre and Kaufman, in speaking of New York City, refer to as "stasis."[49] One observer of American city politics concluded that "'the cards are stacked against the innovator.'"[50]

In many cities, alert, politically oriented public administrators also play a large role in initiating policy. To succeed in this pluralistic, competitive system, however, the administrator must construct a coalition of interests friendly to his department and its program. This strategy reinforces the tendency of each major policy area to become a semi-autonomous subsystem, each with its own distinctive alignment of groups and each with its distinctive group-administrator relationships. The urban political system becomes a holding company for self-contained centers of decision making.

A Functional Comparison. Table 1.1 summarizes the structures of the business elite, broker leadership, and Metro Toronto systems. The structure of a system is described in terms of which actors perform which activities. In the case of the majority-building activity, I further specify which techniques or tactics are most often used in each system. The actors considered are the occupants of formal positions.

Both the Metro and broker leadership systems might be called "pluralist," since a variety of different persons and groups participates in policy making. In both systems there is competition among different viewpoints within the decision-making elite. But in the Metro case there appears to be more consensus and less private-group and private-citizen participation in policy making. Most of Metro's policy-making process remains intragovernmental; that is, most of the important policy-making activities are performed by appointed or elected public officials. Support-securing and interest-articulating activities are performed less often in Metro than in broker leadership systems. There also is much less overt conflict in the Metro case. The majority-building activity is more consciously performed in both pluralist systems than in the business elite system; but persuasion, not bargaining, is the most frequently employed means of building specific majorities in the Metro system. In Metro many issues are resolved on the basis of arguments offered in legislative debate and are settled on the merits of the case. This fact should make us wary of equating pluralism with bargaining, compromise, and logroll-

TABLE I.I The Policy-Making Structures of Three Types of Urban Political Systems

Policy-Making Activities	Type of System		
	Business Elite	Broker Leadership	Metro Toronto
Issue initiation	Performed by business leaders	Performed usually by interest groups and sometimes by administrators	Performed by administrators and sometimes by Metro chairman
Creation of general support	Rarely performed	Performed by interest groups	Not always performed; performed by interest groups (the press) when at all
Interest articulation	Rarely performed	Performed by interest groups, legislators, and political parties; sometimes by administrators	Not always performed; performed by legislators and interest groups when at all
Construction of specific majorities	Rarely consciously performed	Performed by mayor, legislators, or interest groups	Performed by Metro chairman
Tactic of aggregation	Reliance on underlying consensus	Bargaining, logrolling, compromise	Persuasion within context of a parity in distribution of rewards

ing. Banfield's statement about governmental decisions having to be made on political grounds should not be transformed into a general law. To the extent that many issues in Metro Council are resolved by the plausibility of the arguments offered and without regard to integrative considerations, much of Metro Council's decision making may be said to be nonpolitical.

In all three systems most policy-making activities are performed by nonlegislative actors, although the councilors must appear at the final stage to either give or withhold their consent. In the buisness elite and broker leadership systems, many important activities are performed by nonofficial actors—by the business leaders in one case and by the interest groups in the other. In Metro the activities that lead up to legislative enactment are generally performed by public administrators and by a semi-administrative official, the Metro chairman. For this reason I refer to Metro as an "executive directed" or "executive centered" system.[51] If systems are to be distinguished on the basis of how important private, nongovernmental actors are in the making of public policy, Metro stands apart from both the elitist and broker leadership systems.

One may also compare these three systems by characterizing the roles pursued by the occupants of formal positions. The role of an occupant is defined by his intensity of involvement, scope of activity, and the other variables outlined above. A table presenting these comparisons is not included here. It was found that the crucial differences between the systems could be succinctly summarized in a few sentences and that the cumbersome table only obfuscated these crucial differences. In the following summary, emphasis is placed on how Metro departs from the broker leadership pattern. Since this pattern is prevalent in large American cities, Metro's departure from that pattern is more surprising than Metro's failure to develop a business elite.

In comparison to administrators in broker leadership systems, Metro's top-level administrators are more committed to solving general, environmental problems and less committed to the protection of departmental jurisdictions and the preservation of departmental routine. In other words, Metro administrators are more adaptive in their orientation and are less dedicated to the enhancement of the department's internal integration. But Metro administrators perform a smaller number of activities. The role of Metro department heads is confined to issue initiation, with the more political activities being left to the Metro chairman.

Yet Metro administrators appear to dominate the initiating activity far more than their counterparts in broker leadership cities.

The Metro chairman, like any political executive, must take integrative considerations into account, but the chairman is more committed to problem solving or adaptation than are the mayors in most broker leadership cities. The Metro chairman performs the majority-building activity far more consistently and intensely than does the mayor, but the chairman rarely resorts to support-securing and interest-articulating activities. Compared to the mayor, the chairman is more exclusively a legislative floor leader.

The one factor that most clearly distinguishes the Metro and broker leadership systems is the lesser involvement of Metro's interest groups and their smaller scope of activities.

Metro legislators and the city councilors in broker leadership systems are more alike than different; but Metro legislators appear to be even less involved in the system and even less committed to performing a variety of activities.

A Comparative Functional Assessment. The business elite system has a high potential for problem solving, although only solutions in line with the values of business-oriented conservatism are considered. A high degree of integration, perhaps even normative integration, exists, but only within a restricted segment of the community. The unity and solidarity of the ruling group has been attained by systematically excluding certain groups from participation or membership. The flaw in the system is its poor integrative performance, which over the long run could impair the system's problem-solving capacity as well. Because certain groups are excluded, there is always the threat of an electoral rebellion by the outsiders. Because only certain viewpoints are considered, problems and solutions that lie outside the ideology of the business elite will be ignored, perhaps with damaging results to the system's environmental success.

The achievements of the broker leadership system lie mainly in the integrative sphere. This system spreads participation widely

[37]

and incorporates a variety of viewpoints. Because of its flexibility and permeability, this system rarely permits grievances to build up. No particular group is systematically excluded from the policy-making process.

The failures of the broker leadership system are mainly adaptive failures. Because power is highly decentralized, the job of pulling the fragments together in order to enact policies is arduous and sometimes impossible. Broker leadership cities move ponderously or not at all to meet the demands of the environment and of other systems. If comprehensive solutions are being demanded by internal groups—for example, the demands of Negroes in most U.S. cities—this adaptive weakness will have negative repercussions for the political integration of the system. The more problem-oriented an internal group is, the less its satisfaction with the broker leadership system. This system also seems ill-equipped to protect the cities from a loss of authority. Adaptive failure at the local level has probably contributed to the tendency for more and more urban problems to be handled at the federal level.

On the other hand, most broker leadership cities have developed what might be called "compensating mechanisms": institutions or practices that provide for occasional innovation and that temporarily relieve the pressures for problem solving. In New York City periodic reform waves achieve this purpose. In Chicago an integrated party organization bridges the gap between separate centers of decision making and provides at least the institutional means for comprehensive problem solving. In some cities a skillful individual, serving as mayor or occupying one of the appointive, administrative positions, may construct a coalition of interests friendly to innovation in particular policy areas. Most of these mechanisms are either periodic or temporary. Rather than change the system, these occasional departures from the prevailing pattern make that pattern slightly more successful and hence more secure.[52]

A functional assessment of Metro will be deferred until the system has been described. It might only be noted at this point that, in terms of functional performance, Metro stands between the business elite and broker leadership systems.

Plan of the Study

The following three chapters describe the overall structure of Metro's policy-making system in the modified functional terms defined above. Chapter 2 begins by tracing the origins of Metro's formal structure and the initial points of articulation between the provincial, Metro, and municipal systems. This chapter also examines how Metro actors elaborated upon this formal structure and produced what I have called an "executive-directed" system. In chapters 3 and 4, I present a more detailed account of how this executive-directed system performed during Metro's first thirteen years. The emphasis in chapter 3 is on the structured relations that emerged among three pivotal actors—the Metro chairman, the Metro councilors, and the administrators—and on the sources of strain in these relations. Chapter 4 looks at the policy outputs emerging from this type of system and then assesses the structural modifications that resulted—and that may still result—from the 1962 change in Metro chairmen.

In chapter 5, the functional terms used to describe the overall system are applied to policy-making subsystems that operate more or less independently of the chairman–council–administrator network. (In chapter 8, another subsystem, the internal structure of the Metro council, is analyzed in these same terms.)

The theme of chapters 6 and 7 is the weak articulation between Metro's policy-making system and the issues and groupings that exist in the social community. An attempt is made to determine why Metro politics is "low pressure" or "slack"—why the interest groups, political parties, ethnic groups, and working-class groups do not challenge the executive-directed and middle-class dominated Metro system. In effect these chapters note some preconditions for the centralization of leadership in the executive branch. In chapter 7, the electoral process is analyzed in the same way that the policy-making process was analyzed in Table 1.1.

By considering the impact of pervasive influence and internalized values on policy outcomes, these two chapters also guard against too narrow a focus on events in the policy-making process.

Chapter 8, in examining how Metro councilors went about defining their legislative roles, expands upon the type of actor analysis and the problem of role definition mentioned earlier in this chapter. I also gauge the relevance of interaction within the legislative subsystem for this role-defining process.

The final chapter considers the problem of how one uses the functional approach to assess a system's performance and to prescribe reforms that would improve its performance. This theme leads to an account of the 1966 reorganization of the Metro system and to some predictions about the functional significance of these reforms.

CHAPTER 2

THE METRO SYSTEM: ORIGINS AND INITIAL DEVELOPMENT

The municipality of Metropolitan Toronto is a federation of thirteen municipalities, created by the Province of Ontario in 1953 to provide for the solution of certain region-wide problems. Metro Toronto was the first working example in North America of what has been called the "metropolitan federation plan." To reformers in both Canada and the United States, Metro Toronto represented a major breakthrough in the postwar drive for a reorganization of municipal governments in metropolitan areas. Since 1953, metropolitan federalism has been employed in the Winnipeg, Miami, and Nashville areas and has been seriously discussed in many other metropolitan areas.[1]

Origins and Environmental Inputs

The Socio-Economic Environment. The major nonpolitical inputs of the Metro political system were the problems associated with the development of a sprawling metropolitan area. Postwar metropolitan development in the Toronto area followed familiar North American lines.[2] There was a steady exodus of business firms and middle-class citizens from the central city to the suburbs and a steady immigration of lower-income families to the central city from elsewhere in the nation and from other countries. Independent suburban government had proliferated around the boundaries of the central city earlier in the century. By 1950, the Toronto metropolitan area, as defined by the federal census, included the City of Toronto and twelve suburban municipalities (see Figure 2.1).

These trends produced a familiar break in the social characteristics of City and suburban dwellers. Suburbanites generally were car-owning, home-owning, middle- and upper-class citizens; most of the City of Toronto's population consisted of wage-earning laborers in the lower- and lower-middle income brackets. Postwar population changes also affected the ethnic composition of the area and created new social distinctions between City and suburbs. The City of Toronto, which as late as 1945 was still a predominantly British, Protestant, middle-class city, absorbed large numbers of "New Canadians"—primarily Catholics from Eastern and Central Europe. By the early 1960s, the City's British-Protestant segment had shrunk to a bare majority of the population. The 1961 census revealed that almost one-third of the City's population had immigrated to Canada since 1946. Persons of Italian origin formed the largest non-British group in the City. Throughout this process of rapid demographic change, the suburbs retained their British–Protestant character. An exception was York Township, whose population resembled the City's in ethnic and religious characteristics.

None of these trends is new to North American metropolitan areas. The most distinctive feature of the Toronto area's development was the great rapidity of the social and economic changes. Between 1950 and 1965, the Toronto metropolitan area absorbed on the average of 50,000 new residents each year. The population of Toronto and the twelve suburbs was about 900,000 in 1945, had risen to approximately 1.8 million in 1965, and is expected by local planners to exceed 2.3 million in 1980. North York, a rural township of 25,000 in 1945, had acquired 350,000 residents by 1965 and had become the fifth largest municipality in Canada. (Population changes in the thirteen municipalities between 1953 and 1964 are summarized in Table 2.1.) Local planners attribute this rapid metropolitan growth to the increasing impor-

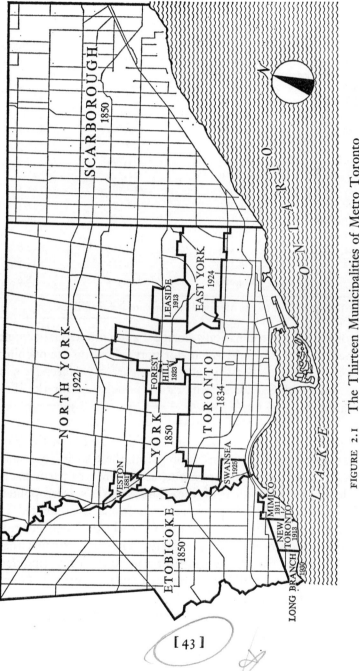

FIGURE 2.1   The Thirteen Municipalities of Metro Toronto

Source: Metropolitan Toronto, *Annual Report*, 1965

TABLE 2.1 Population Changes in the Thirteen Municipalities of Metro Toronto, 1953–1964

Municipality	1953	1964	Percentage Growth
Toronto	665,502	649,462	−2.4
North York	110,311	341,437	209.5
Scarborough	78,803	253,292	221.4
Etobicoke	70,209	195,700	178.7
York	100,463	128,281	27.7
East York	65,736	71,894	9.4
Forest Hill	17,719	22,771	28.5
Leaside	15,910	18,783	18.1
Mimico	12,301	18,590	51.1
New Toronto	11,190	12,689	13.4
Long Branch	9,140	11,656	27.5
Weston	8,374	10,454	24.8
Swansea	8,344	9,322	11.7
Total	1,174,002	1,744,311	48.6

Source: Data published by the Metropolitan Toronto Planning Board.

tance of the area as the nation's financial and commercial center, the emergence of Toronto as a major port following the opening of the St. Lawrence Seaway, and the apparent preference of a large segment of Canada's immigration population for the Toronto area.

The Local Political Response. Most political actors in the Toronto area perceived problems arising from these socio-economic changes. It seems reasonable to argue, as some Metro participants now do, that the rapidity of the Toronto area's metropolitan development created more severe dislocations than existed in most other metropolitan areas and made early political recognition of these dislocations more likely. The fact remains that earlier and more earnest searches for solutions to metropolitan problems were undertaken in this area than in any other Canadian metropolitan area.

At the local level, however, different parts of the metropolitan area defined the nature of the problems differently. The City officials worried about Toronto's increasing needs in urban renewal, public assistance, and public housing, at a time when the City's revenues from the property tax were declining and when the City's tax rate already was one of the highest municipal rates in Canada. The problem, according to the rapidly growing, outlying suburbs, was the inability of these municipalities to meet the service and capital-construction needs of a rapidly increasing suburban population. The outlying suburbs lacked sewers, watermains and reservoirs, roads, schools, and sidewalks. By 1950 the outstanding capital debt of several outlying suburbs had reached such heights that municipal officials were experiencing great difficulty in borrowing additional funds.

Between the three rapidly growing suburbs—North York, Scarborough, Etobicoke—and the City of Toronto lay a ring of smaller suburbs, whose urban development and capital-construction programs had been completed prior to World War II. These inner suburbs perceived few problems in the socio-economic environment. They faced neither the needs to accommodate additional population and build new facilities nor the need to renovate aging facilities. Tax rates in these suburbs were lower than in the City of Toronto, partly because these suburbs could rely on the City to provide certain services, like parks, hospitals, and libraries, for the entire metropolitan area. The degree of satisfaction with the *status quo* varied from one inlying suburb to another, depending on the suburb's industrial-residential assessment ratio. Suburbs with a below-average amount of industry and a large number of inexpensive homes had to levy higher rates. A suburb's tax rate also hinged on the size of its school-age population, since this determined the size of the education budget. Tax rates tended to be higher in the City, the outlying suburbs, and smaller suburbs like York and East York; the lowest rates in the area were levied by Leaside, Swansea, and New Toronto.

With these variations in the attitudes of the smaller suburbs noted, it generally is correct to say that postwar trends divided the metropolitan area into three camps—the City, the outlying, rapidly growing suburbs, and the inlying, fully developed suburbs. The first two blocs were more or less dissatisfied with the results of the metropolitan trends and felt that "something should be done."

That "something," according to most suburbs, proved to be a joint service area of the twelve suburban municipalities, permitting these suburbs to pool certain facilities and to cooperate in the provision of some services. The request for a joint service area was sent to the Ontario Municipal Board (OMB)—a provincial, quasi-judicial body with sweeping powers over municipalities, including the power to order changes in municipal boundaries or municipal governmental structure.

The City of Toronto sent a counterapplication to the OMB asking for permission to annex all of the inlying suburbs. The City had lost interest in annexation in the 1920s, when it became apparent that the City would have to finance comprehensive, construction programs in these outlying areas. Even in its 1950 application to the OMB, Toronto ruled out annexation of the three large suburbs, whose construction programs were still in the early stages. The City officials urged total amalgamation, or "one city for the entire metropolitan area," but wanted this metropolitan city to include only fully developed suburbs.

Some of the inlying suburbs responded to the Toronto application by becoming intransigent supporters of the *status quo*, while the other suburbs pressed ahead with their bid for a joint service area.

Impact of the American Metropolitan Reform Movement. American reformers, mainly social scientists and public administrators, had been trying for several decades to reorganize municipal governments in metropolitan areas.[3] Some form of region-wide government, it was argued, would permit municipal officials to meet problems that were regional in scope and would permit a more equitable distribution of costs and benefits in the metropolitan area. The solution offered usually was an annexation of the suburbs by the central city or, in case this first proposal proved politically unacceptable, a federation of the city and suburbs. This reform movement produced a large number of studies and proposals for change in American metropolitan areas but, with one or two exceptions, achieved little in the way of structural reform.

The American reform movement appeared to have no direct effect on the emergence of Metro Toronto. The joint service plan, which would have permanently divided the area into City and suburban sectors, ran counter to reformist ideas. The City's move for annexation would also have divided the metropolitan area by excluding the large, growing suburbs. There was no groundswell of opinion for a federated metropolitan government among public officials, citizens, or interest groups in any of the municipalities.

Whether the American reformers' prolonged discussion of the federation idea influenced OMB's decision to urge such a plan for the Toronto area is difficult to say. The board's report made no mention of American reform ideas. Moreover, most American reformers at that time seemed to prefer annexation to federation.

The Imposition of Reform. After long deliberation the OMB, in 1953, rejected both the joint service and annexation applications. It proposed instead that the thirteen municipalities of the Toronto area be joined in a metropolitan federation. The provincial cabinet next had to decide whether to secure legislative enactment of this plan.

The question facing the Ontario cabinet was whether a federation plan should be imposed on the Toronto area when none of the municipalities concerned had requested this plan. In fact, most of the municipalities in the area opposed the OMB proposal, the City because the proposal did not go far enough, the suburbs because the proposal went too far.

It should be made clear at the outset that respect for local home rule did not deter provincial politicians. Because the nineteenth-century crusade for local home rule was less significant in Canada than in the United States, Canadian provinces exert a far tighter and more pervasive control over their municipalities than do American states.[4] Canadian provinces, though certainly sensitive to the demands of municipalities, are prepared to rearrange municipal governmental structure and municipal boundaries in a much freer fashion than any American state government would contemplate. No American state government has been willing to approve a reorganization of governments in a metropolitan area unless the proposal were first requested and actively supported by the municipalities concerned. In many cases the state has required that metropolitan reform be approved by the voters in a metropolitan-wide referendum before the state will consider adding its assent. In the Toronto area, Ontario officials never seriously considered a referendum. Nor did they grant the municipalities concerned an unofficial veto power over proposed metropolitan reforms.

The leaders of the Ontario Conservative Party had mixed feelings about helping the Toronto area meet its metropolitan problems. The heart of the Conservative Party was rural and small-town Ontario. Many of the Cabinet ministers, hailing from other parts of the province and usually from smaller communities, were skeptical about the severity of the Toronto area's problems and about the need for special governmental arrangements in meeting these problems. The cabinet also had to contend with anti-Toronto sentiment throughout the rest of the province. There were frequently voiced fears about Toronto dominating provincial politics and receiving considerations at the provincial level that were not accorded to other large urban areas. The creation of a Metro Toronto government would only add to these fears and threse cries of special treatment.

But Ontario, in the 1940s and 1950s, was close to being a one-party province. The Conservatives did almost as well in the cities as in the nonurban areas. Toronto in particular had been for many years a Tory stronghold. Thus, the Ontario cabinet, while rural-based, was not as hostile or indifferent to urban problems as were many other rural-based governments in Canadian provinces and American states.[5]

The final decision to approve the OMB proposal was made by Premier Leslie Frost. The premier acted in large part out of respect for Lorne Cumming, the OMB chairman who had authored the federation plan, and Frederick Gardiner, a prominent Conservative who had agreed to serve as the first Metro chairman if the plan were to be instituted. Federalism at the metropolitan level appealed to Frost as a workable political compromise, which seemed to strike a middle ground between some suburban demands for "no change" and the City's demand for "total amalgamation." Retaining a multiplicity of governments in the area, moreover, would assure other parts of the province that a Toronto giant, capable of dominating provincial politics, was not being created.

The board's plan, with a few amendments added, passed the Ontario legislature in 1953, and Metro went into effect on July 1 of that year.

Provincial Inputs: Tasks and Formal Structure

Tasks. The central tasks of the new Metro government, as stipulated in the public pronouncements of the Ontario officials, were to meet certain region-wide problems that the municipalities separately could not deal with, to provide certain services more efficiently than the municipalities separately could provide, and to soften some of the glaring fiscal inequities in the area by providing for regional sharing of certain costs.

Metro also performed for the province the same unstated or implicit task that all municipal governments perform. Municipalities, I would contend, assist the provinces (or states) in meeting their adaptive and integrative needs by siphoning off and dealing with some of the lesser responsibilities of the provinces. Provincial officials respect local home rule partly out of deference to the liberal creed but also because the municipalities perform this useful task. If local autonomy were weakened or abolished, more issues would be injected into provincial politics, the provinces' functional problems would become more complicated, and the provincial systems would be less able to focus on the larger issues. This local task, while rarely verbalized either publicly or privately by provincial officials, is (in my view) intuitively understood by them.

Along with all other local governments, then, Metro was expected to remove certain issues from provincial politics; but Metro in particular was designed to remove the metropolitan reorganization issue from the provincial sphere. For five years prior to the creation of Metro, provincial officials had been subjected to pressures in favor of one or another metropolitan-reform proposal. Many politicians, in all parties, saw this issue as a distraction from the more crucial questions facing the province. The Metro scheme, it was hoped, would win the support of local actors, quiet the demands for further reforms, and remove this issue from Ontario politics for at least five or ten years.

Formal Structure. The Metro Toronto Act, also known as Bill 80, was designed to achieve a dual purpose: to give the Metro government enough powers to meet regional problems and promote greater financial equity, but at the same time to make a Metro government as acceptable to the municipalities as possible. The very notion of federation was favored because it created a regional government without changing municipal boundaries and without greatly disturbing the operation of municipal government. At the Metro level most decisions would be made by a 25-member Metro Council, whose membership would be composed largely of municipal officials serving *ex officio*. (The formal organization of Metro government is presented in Figure 2.2.) The Council was to have twelve suburban and twelve City of Toronto delegates. The suburban delegation would be composed of the mayor or reeve of each of the twelve suburban municipalities; the City's delegation would include the mayor, two city controllers, and one city alderman from each of the

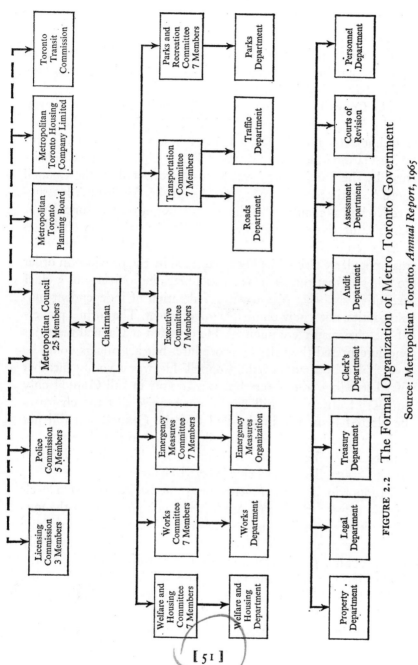

FIGURE 2.2 The Formal Organization of Metro Toronto Government

Source: Metropolitan Toronto, *Annual Report*, 1965

[51]

nine Toronto wards. Direct election to the Metro Council was considered and rejected by Ontario officials, who concluded that having municipal officials sit on the Council would make Metro more acceptable to the municipalities and would eliminate possible Metro-municipal conflict.

The Council was to have a presiding officer, called "chairman of the Metropolitan Council," initially appointed by the province but elected by the Metro Council in succeeding years. (Frederick Gardiner, a former reeve of Forest Hill, was named chairman by the province and was annually reelected by the Council until his retirement in 1961. City Controller William Allen succeeded him as chairman.) Bill 80, again out of respect for the sensibilities of the municipalities, made it clear that the chairman was not to be a mayor of Metro. The notion of having the chairman popularly elected had been rejected by the province in order to reiterate that the chairman was a presiding officer, not a chief executive, and that Metro was a federation of independent municipalities, not a new municipal government. The formal powers of the chairman were minimal. He presided at Council meetings and interpreted the rules of procedure, but his rulings could be overridden by a vote of the Council. He was a voting member of all standing committees but was to vote in full Council only in case of a tie vote. Bill 80 did not require that the chairman be elected from within the ranks of the Council and did not indicate whether a Metro councilor elected to the chairmanship had to resign his municipal office. Allen, however, did resign as city controller upon being elected chairman.

In apportioning governmental programs between the two levels of government, the Metro Act left as much power with the municipalities as possible and shifted to the Metro level only those powers necessary to deal with critical, regional problems. Only one program, public transportation, was shifted wholly to the Metro level; while important responsibilities, like police, fire, public health, libraries, and licensing, were left wholly at the municipal level.

To avoid conflicts between the two levels of government, many government programs were made areas of shared responsibility. Thus, Metro would be responsible for constructing and repairing expressway and major through-streets designated as "Metro roads," and the municipalities would retain jurisdiction over "local roads." Traffic control was divided in the same way, with the municipalities responsible for regulations on "local roads" and Metro responsible for regulations on expressways and "Metro roads." Bill 80 empowered Metro to construct and improve sewer and water-supply facilities in the area and to sell water on a wholesale basis to the municipalities, but the municipalities would act as retailers and sell the water to local residents and businesses. In some areas of shared responsibility, like public assistance, the powers left at the municipal level were far more important than the powers shifted to Metro. Bill 80 made Metro responsible for the hospitalization of indigents and the provision of homes for the aged, but all the other categories of welfare assistance were left with the municipalities.

In areas like zoning and land planning the major powers rested at the municipal level, while Metro acted as adviser, overseer, and technical assistant—somewhat analagous to the role played by the federal government in provincial programs it helps finance. The municipalities made all decisions on zoning and subdivisions and drew up official plans for the municipality; but the Metro Planning Board was to provide advice and warning, to draw up a Metro Official Plan, and to require that all local plans be brought into accordance with the Metro Plan. (Since a Metro Official Plan was never enacted, the Metro planners' influence over municipal decision making eventually rested less on the use of legal sanctions than on the Metro planners' ability to warn, persuade, negotiate with, and provide technical assistance to municipal officials.)

In education the federal–provincial analogy was again used: A Metro School Board would help finance education in the thirteen municipalities—and thus contribute to the regional sharing of costs—but substantive policy would still be set by the local boards. The Metro School Board was to consist of delegates named by and from the local boards.

In the fields of public housing and redevelopment, Bill 80 made provisions for parallel rather than cooperative programs. The municipalities retained their housing and redevelopment powers, and Metro was given all the powers of a municipality in these fields.

Metro's most important powers were in the area of public finance. The Metro Council was given authority to do all the borrowing for municipalities and independent boards in the area, thus permitting the outlying suburbs to benefit from the lower interest rates that Metro bonds probably would be able to secure. Metro, rather than imposing any direct tax, was to apportion its revenue needs among the thirteen municipalities in accordance with each municipality's share of total area assessment. To prevent a municipality from underassessing its properties in order to reduce its share of total assessment and its share of the tax burden, Metro was given full powers in the field of property assessment and was ordered to undertake an immediate reassessment of all property in the area on a uniform standard.

Bill 80, in distributing powers between the two levels of government, clearly suggested which problems deserved immediate Metro attention. The inability of the suburbs to borrow funds at reasonable interest rates, the inadequacy of suburban water and sewer facilities, the need for more expressways, and the suburban demand for new schools were all considered regional problems. The Metro government was given powers sufficient to cope with these matters. Public housing, redevelopment, public assistance, public health, police, fire, and land-use control were not viewed as critical regional problems or not viewed as regional problems at all. Of course, Metro Council would be free to reassess these priorities or to propose changes in the distribution of powers between Metro and the municipalities.

In summary, Bill 80 tried to reconcile two conflicting values: the desire to create a significant Metro government with powers to meet certain important regional needs and the desire to make such a government acceptable to the municipalities by interfering with municipal autonomy as little as possible. The result was a relatively unusual federal system, giving fewer powers to the "federal government" than either the Canadian or American federal systems do and requiring that federal legislators be recruited from the political cadre of the constituent governments.

The Municipal Systems. The structure of Metro government reflected not only the tasks assigned to that system by the province but also the values of the provincial system relating to the organization of all municipal governments.

The organization of municipalities in Ontario has been heavily influenced by the nineteenth-century liberal notion that local government is grassroots democracy at work. Municipal government has been kept close to the people through legislative supremacy and annual elections. All policy-making authority in Ontario communities is vested in the entire municipal council. These communities have what Americans would call "weak mayor" systems. At the same time, and perhaps paradoxically, important local programs have been vested in independent administrative agencies, in order to protect these programs from politics in the person of the municipal councilor. In summary, Ontario values on local government combine the nineteenth-century British liberal's faith in municipal government as a training ground for democracy with the nineteenth-century American Progressive's faith in nonpolitical boards.[6]

These values are reflected in the organization of municipal government in the Metro area. In 1953, the twelve suburban municipalities were governed by municipal councils, elected every year and varying in size from five in Long Branch to eight in North York. A reeve or mayor, elected at large, spoke for the municipality at ceremonial occasions, but he had little formal control over the administrative branch and little voice in setting municipal policy beyond his one vote in council.

Toronto, like Ottawa, Hamilton, and London, was governed by the board of control system. Toronto's City Council consisted of eighteen aldermen, two elected in each of nine wards; four controllers, elected at large; and a mayor, also elected at large. The mayor and the four controllers made up the City Council's executive committee, or board of control, with powers to supervise administrative agencies and draft policy proposals. In the aldermanic election each voter could indicate two choices, and the two candidates polling the largest number of votes in the ward were declared elected. Similarly, in the race for controller each voter had four choices, and the four candidates leading the poll were declared elected. The candidate for controller polling the largest number of votes became the City's chief budget officer. The Toronto plan reduced the power of the council to some extent but transferred that power to a five-man committee, not to the mayor. Within the board the mayor was merely one vote; he had no powers beyond those of a controller, and he was not even in charge of preparing the municipal budget.

The Metro Toronto Act left the organization of the thirteen municipal governments intact. According to the terms of the act, suburban municipalities were to be represented on Metro Council by their reeves or mayors. The twelve-man City delegation would consist of the mayor, the two controllers receiving the largest vote in the preceding election, and the nine aldermen topping the poll in their respective wards. There were only two major changes in the area's municipal governments during 1953–1965: the adoption by North York and Etobicoke of the board of control system, and the adoption by all the municipalities of a two-year term for elected local officials.

The authors of Bill 80 not only respected the values that lay behind the organization of municipal government in the Metro area but incorporated some of these values in the organization of Metro government. The insignificant powers of the Metro chairman demonstrated the province's continued belief in legislative supremacy at the local level. Moreover, provincial officials apparently concluded that members of Council would be unwilling to accept a chairman who had more powers at the Metro level than mayors and reeves had at the municipal level. Bill 80 also continued the tradition of vesting important responsibilities, like housing, planning, public transit, and education, in agencies more or less free of legislative control. (When Metro later expanded its powers by raising police and licensing programs from the municipal to the Metro level, these programs were also assigned to independent commissions.)

But Bill 80, by failing to provide for a mayor or board of control, went further than any municipal charter in the direction of minimal executive powers. Here, as in other matters, the province's purpose was to reassure the municipalities that Metro would be little more than a loosely organized federation. When Gardiner later constructed a Metro executive committee modeled after the boards of control, he brought the organization of Metro government closer to the plan used in most large Ontario cities.

The Development of an Informal Structure

Emergence of a "Leadership" Role. The development of a powerful Metro chairman is largely attributable to major gaps in the policy-making process left by the Metro Toronto Act. In Gardiner's terms there was no provision for "leadership." In functional terms the Metro Toronto Act failed to make any official responsible for issue-initiation, issue-definition, and majority-building activities. With final decisions being controlled by popularly elected legislators, it seemed reasonable to assume that the interest-articulation activity would be performed. The recruitment of Metro councilors from the municipal councils probably would enhance Metro's chances of winning municipal support. But the performance of change-producing activities was left to chance. The integrative function was stressed at the expense of the adaptive. The province apparently assumed that there would be a consensus among municipal officials on the nature of the metropolitan problems, that municipal officials could be relied upon to draft solutions, and that Council majorities would naturally form around some of these solutions.

There also were important gaps in the formal structure. No one was responsible for overseeing the operations of the administrative branch and no link was provided between the legislature and the administration. In all, the formal organization of Metro government was more appropriate to an international conference on disarmament than to a government responsible for goal determination and goal implementation over a period of time.

The first chairman, Gardiner, saw the shortcomings in the act and decided to step into the breach. He concluded—correctly, I think—that Metro could not meet the tasks assigned to it while retaining the organization of an *ad hoc* international conference. During Gardiner's tenure, the chairman became chief administrator, legislative floor leader, and intermediary between Council and administration. Metro councilors and the local press began to speak of "Gardiner's administration" and of "Gardiner's record in office."

Gardiner's role as legislative leader was strengthened when the Council acceded to his request and created an executive committee. This Executive Committee, established in the Council's 1953 procedural bylaw, was to have all the powers that boards of control had in municipal governments. The committee could award contracts, hire and fire staff, and initiate legal action on behalf of the full Council, all subject to later confirmation by the Council. The committee was empowered to prepare budgets, nominate department heads, nominate candidates for positions on independent boards, and approve all reports of standing committees before they were forwarded to the Council. Motions not approved by the Executive Committee could be introduced in Council only by a two-thirds vote, and recommendations of the committee on matters of personnel and finance could be amended only by a two-thirds vote. Originally the committee was to consist of five members: the Metro chairman and the chairmen of the Council's four standing committees.

Creation of the Executive Committee greatly reduced the importance of the other standing committees. These committees were now prohibited from communicating directly with the Council. The Executive Committee, moreover, soon began initiating proposals on any and all policy matters, ignoring the other standing committees, and sending executive-approved proposals directly to the Council. The effectiveness of the other standing committees was further impaired in 1955, when Council decided to strip the committee chairmen of their positions on the executive and to have Council itself elect Executive Committee members. In theory Metro's organization was highly decentralized. As shown in Figure 2.2, each department head was officially responsible to one of the standing committees. In reality a much more centralized structure emerged. The Executive Commitee became the *de facto* head of the administration, and Gardiner became the informal head of the Executive Committee.

Throughout the history of the Executive Committee, the principle of equal City and suburban representation was observed. After 1954, Council held separate votes in electing the City and suburban members of the committee, but all councilors voted in both elections.

The 1953 procedural bylaw did not add to the formal powers of the Metro chairman, aside from giving him a vote on the Executive Committee and naming him the presiding officer of that committee. (Of course the Toronto mayor had no greater authority in *his* board of control.) If the chairman could secure a majority for his proposals in this committee, however, he would be better able to muster a majority in the full Council. In practice Gardiner had little difficulty in securing committee backing, and Council rarely overturned Executive Committee recommendations.

Role Differentiation. Gardiner was convinced that the representative (or what I have called the integrative) function and the problem-solving (adaptive) function should be performed by different actors. The Metro councilors were more interested in maintaining a balance in Metro's payoffs to municipalities than in perceiving environmental problems; and Gardiner doubted whether the councilors had the expertise to define problems even if the inclination had been present. The answer to the system's needs, according to the chairman, was to recruit a cabinet of experts.

At an early session of the Council, Gardiner convinced the

legislators that the recruitment of administrative personnel could not be adequately performed by the entire Council and that this responsibility should be delegated to the chairman. Gardiner then recruited the department heads, insisting on skilled professionals rather than men with political backgrounds, but attempting wherever possible to name men from municipal governments in the area rather than outsiders. Many of these administrators accepted a Metro position out of respect for Gardiner and because they were led to believe that there would be minimal political interference in their work. This recruitment process helps explain why the department heads subsequently worked hand-in-glove with Gardiner and why an informal Metro cabinet made up of the chairman and the department heads emerged. According to the procedural bylaw, the department heads were responsible to standing committees of Council; in fact only Gardiner regularly interacted with the top-level administrators. This cabinet never met as a whole, but an administration position on issues was generally worked out by interdepartmental committees. The cabinet soon became the major source of policy proposals, and the chairman became the individual responsible for securing Council majorities in support of cabinet proposals.

It would be naive to argue that top-level administrators operated outside of politics. Several decades of research on "the politics of administration" has demonstrated that such administrators, while generally standing outside *partisan* politics, are deeply immersed in *policy-making* politics.[7] Public administrators often perform the same support-securing and conflict-resolving activities that politicians perform. But these basic truths should not preclude the possibility of administrators' playing a more restricted, though still influential, role in the policy-making process. The American pattern of the top-level administrator acting as independent political entrepreneur should not be enshrined as a general law.

Gardiner tried to shield the department heads from local demands and discouraged the administrators from seeking their own sources of local support. The cabinet's role in policy making, then, was confined to initiation and definition; the department heads did not attempt to secure interest-group or legislative support for their proposals. Gardiner also urged the department heads to make their recommendations on purely technical or professional grounds, without regard to the problems of political acceptance. In this way Gardiner would always know what the expert opinion on a subject was. Politics, or the adjustment of these recommendations to Metro Council's moods, was to be left to the chairman. Typically, the cabinet initiated a policy proposal, and the chairman then decided whether a majority in Council could be secured for that proposal, when the proposal should be brought forward, and whether any substantive changes would have to be made in the proposal to improve its chances of legislative approval. The administrative-politics literature often portrays administrators eager to embark on an independent political strategy. The Metro department heads, however, were not only satisfied with their less political role but apparently were attracted to the job in the first place by the promise that Gardiner would "take care of the politics."

At the same time Gardiner convinced the councilors that many areas of policy were technical in nature and that Council should defer to expert opinion on these matters. He encouraged Metro councilors to view themselves as a court of last appeal for municipalities and local groups dissatisfied with cabinet proposals.

Thus, under Gardiner's tutelage a clear-cut differentiation in roles emerged. For the most part the Metro councilors were concerned with preserving a regional parity in the distribution of Metro's capital expenditures and with transmitting grass-roots or neighborhood grievances to the Metro administration. Metro department heads were primarily oriented to the needs or problems of the metropolitan area, defining those problems in terms of professional values and programs. The administrators' reference groups were the other members of their profession and the administrative officials at other levels of government—that is, actors external to the Metro system. The administrators' contribution to the Metro system included identifying the demands of other social systems, maintaining Metro's external reputation, and securing the participation of external actors when it was required.

Having encouraged the emergence of this differentiation in roles, Gardiner then assumed the crucial task of reconciling adaptive and integrative demands. His key resource was that he alone participated in both the technical alnd political subsystems. Recognizing this fact, Gardiner insisted that all important communication between the legislative and administrative branches be channeled through him.

The two aspects of Gardiner's role, legislative floor leader and chief administrator, reinforced each other. Gardiner retained control of his cabinet because he was able to deliver majorities for cabinet proposals; his influence in Council was greatly enhanced by his ability to speak for the experts and his exclusive access to technical information. Success in one subsystem helped produce success in the other. Similarly, a loss of influence in one subsystem probably would have initiated a deflationary spiral.

Theoretical Implications

The emergence of an informal Metro structure, rather than revealing any new truths about political systems, confirms the validity of some old truths.

The Metro case again demonstrates that role differentiation is functional to a system's success, where the lines of differentiation correspond to the functional problems of the system.[8] In the Metro example, the administrators guaranteed that adaptive considerations were kept before the Council; and the Metro councilors saw to it that municipal commitments to the system were not strained in the process of problem solving. One may argue that, if the Metro councilors had been more eager to solve problems, differentiation would not have been necessary. But an elected official must inevitably be more responsive to his constituency than to the system's environment. It is unlikely that Metro councilors could have played both adaptive-oriented and integrative-oriented roles without sacrificing one orientation to the other. Differentiation ensured that both orientations were enthusiastically defended. Moreover, the Metro case suggests that adaptive considerations are most vigorously defended when the adaptive-oriented actors (the cabinet) are shielded to some extent from the integrative (political) demands of the system. The case of the Metro School Board, discussed in chapter 5, indicates what may occur when no differentiation emerges and when elected legislators play both roles.

Second, the Metro case testifies to the utility of having one role-occupant consciously and persistently attempt to reconcile the integrative and adaptive needs of the system. Metro would have been less successful than it was if it had left this reconciling task to chance or to an entire legislative body. To maximize success, mediation between adaptive and integrative needs should not only be undertaken by an individual but should become an institutionalized part of his role, so that successors naturally assume this task. The case of the Toronto Transit Commission (TTC), also discussed in chapter 5, suggests what may occur when differentiation develops without the institutionalization of a reconciling role.

Third, Metro, like many other political systems, seemed more likely to ignore its adaptive than its integrative needs. Students of administrative organizations have suggested that such organizations tend to emphasize internal over external needs—or to use Chester Barnard's phrases, to emphasize "efficiency" over "effectiveness."[9] The same law probably holds true for larger, democratically organized systems. As long as the final decisions rest with popularly elected legislators and the electoral channels remain free from serious obstruction, the integrative needs of the system will be better served than the adaptive. For this reason Gardiner, in reconciling the two functions, put slightly more emphasis on Metro's adaptive needs. The Metro system was more likely to ignore its environmental problems and grind to a halt than it was to shake municipal and neighborhood-group commitments to the system with an excessively ambitious rate of problem solving. It was far more difficult for Gardiner to convince the councilors of the need for problem solving than to convince the cabinet of the need for political adjustments in their proposals. A further indication of this tendency to favor internal over external demands is the evidence, presented in the final chapter, that adaptive actors were less satisfied than integrative actors with Metro's performance.

Fourth, although the emergence of a mediating role was central to Metro's success, its emergence cannot be seen as inevitable. The system developed in the direction it did because Gardiner personally supported the federal idea and intuitively understood the functional needs of the system. Without these two personal qualities—commitment and insight—being located in the individual occupant of a potentially important position, practices functional to the system's success would not have emerged. Thus, the story of Metro's initial development demonstrates that actor analysis must supplement system analysis. One must explain the emergent Metro structure not only in terms of the systems functional requisites but also in terms of Gardiner's personal preferences, backgrounds, and skills. If there is greater scope for personal choice and creativity in social systems than Parsons implies, individual decision making must be examined at some point in one's analysis.

The importance of personality and unique historical events in Metro's initial development also sets limits to explanations of the Metro system that rely on long-range social variables, like the political culture or social structure of an area. We return to this problem in later chapters, when such long-range variables are considered.

CHAPTER 3

THE SYSTEM'S
PERFORMANCE

Policy making in Metro Toronto can best be understood as the outcome of interactions between the Metro councilors, the Metro chairman, and the administrators. The chairman occupies the central position in this tripartite structure. The other two groups of actors interact with the chairman but not with each other. In the following pages I consider first the relations between chairman and cabinet and then the relations between chairman and Council, during Gardiner's eight and a half years in office. Chapter 4 develops the notion that each policy program may be viewed as a subsystem within the Metro system. That chapter also contains a discussion of Metro's policy output and of the systemic changes that occurred under Allen's leadership.

Performance of the Adaptive Function

An Executive-Centered System. Most issues considered by the Metro Council between 1953 and 1961 were initiated and defined by the heads of Metro's major departments. The 1962–1965 period saw no diminution in the cabinet's ability to identify environmental problems and set the agenda of Metro politics.

Table 6.1 lists 55 major decisions taken by the Metro Council from 1953 to 1965. Of these, 25 issues were initiated and defined by members of the Metro cabinet. In addition cabinet officials initiated six other issues in conjunction with the Metro chairman and six issues in conjunction with the Toronto Transit Commission (TTC). Singly or in cooperation with other actors, therefore, Metro administrators sparked consideration of more than two-thirds of the major questions considered by Metro Council. (If minor matters were included in this tally, the pattern of administrative initiative would be even more pronounced.) Most initiation was performed by six of the more policy-oriented department heads: the works commissioner, the roads commissioner, the planning commissioner, the housing and welfare commissioner, the traffic commissioner, and the finance commissioner. As already noted, proposals emerged not from formal meetings of all department heads but from interdepartmental committees.

The chairman alone initiated eight issues. Thus the administration, including Metro department heads, the chairman, and independent commissions, identified the problem and defined the solution in 47 of 55 issues. It is on the basis of these figures that I have labeled Metro Toronto an executive-centered system. Interest groups and members of the Metro Council played a very small part in the early stages of the policy-making process. Adaptation was the administration's responsibility.

Limits to Executive Initiative. The Metro department heads were unable to lead in policy areas that the Metro Council deemed to be political rather than technical. Appointments to independent commissions was a political question because, in Council's view, there could be no technical criteria on this subject. The structure of Metro Council was viewed as a political question because councilors thought that a legislature should have complete control over its internal organization. Councilors agreed that expert answers might be available on issues relating to the future of the federal system, but the legislators were too intensely committed to particular viewpoints on these questions to follow administrative leads. "Future of Metro" questions were political because of the intense feelings they aroused.

Since the line between technical and political issues was indistinct, Gardiner might have persuaded the councilors to expand their definition of technical issues. But Gardiner seemed to agree that the above issues, for one reason or another, were not technical in nature. Council, it might be added, was still prepared to have Gardiner initiate proposals in the political fields, but he could not claim that such proposals represented expert judgment. There was somewhat less legislative deference to Gardiner's leads in these nontechnical areas. Similarly there was less deference shown to the requests of independent boards when these requests were thought to reflect the wishes of the lay board rather than the board's technical staff.

Deference to technical leadership also required a prior agreement among the experts as to the desired policy. When the technicians could not agree among themselves—as in the case of subway route planning—the councilors concluded that there were no technical solutions to the problem and that decisions could be made on the basis of a political criterion, like municipal parity in the location of construction projects. Even though the Metro planners and the TTC staff reached agreement on route issues after 1959, the technicians could not recapture all of the initiative on subway matters.

Administrative unity and the administration's legislative effectiveness were mutually reinforcing. The cabinet remained unified mainly because of Gardiner's success in securing legislative support for administration proposals, and the large incidence of intra-administrative agreement provided the Council with clearly defined technical leads to which Council often deferred. Independent commissions presented a threat to both administrative unity and the administration's external effectiveness. In all cases but the TTC, however, Gardiner mediated between the Metro departments and the commissions and succeeded in minimizing intra-administrative friction. Conflict between the Metro planners and the TTC over subway routes was the only important intra-administrative clash that occurred during Metro's first thirteen years.

Gaps in Issue Initiation. Gaps in the adaptive performance of a system may be explained by the failure of a system to enact solutions urged by adaptive actors or by the failure of adaptive actors to propose solutions in all policy areas. This second type of adaptive failure is more relevant to the present discussion of issue initiation.

Identifying gaps in the issue-initiation process involves a search for "nonissues"—for issues that might have been initiated in the system but were not. In finding such nonissues, the author might simply state his personal views about what the unsolved problems were. A less value-laden means of identifying gaps in initiation is to ask: what issues are dealt with by similar systems but not by the system under study? and what issues not raised in the system are considered important by actors external to the system?

Using these two criteria, Metro's most significant nonissues were in the fields of public health, public assistance, libraries, fire protection, labor-management relations, intergroup relations and tensions, hospital construction, and the regulation of hydroelectric power companies. Not only has Metro's output in these policy areas been negligible, Metro has not even seriously debated the substantive questions in these areas.

The major reason for the relative neglect of the above issues was the chairman's and cabinet's weak interest in nonconstruction or "soft" programs.[1] Both Gardiner and the cabinet defined the problems of the area largely as physical problems and viewed public works as the top priority. In the chairman's view most "soft" programs were a provincial not a local responsibility. The cabinet's biases are partly attributable to the terms of Bill 80. With a few exceptions the "soft" programs were either left with the municipalities, delegated to independent commissions, or not mentioned at all in the Metro Toronto Act. Most of the important Metro departments had responsibility for some type of construction program. But the cabinet's strong interest in the "hard" programs cannot be explained entirely by the terms of Bill 80. The housing and welfare commissioner could have led the move for welfare amalgamation but instead confined his initiation to homes-for-the-aged issues. Although professional planners are sometimes interested in the social problems of the metropolis, the Metro planners confined their attention to physical planning.

In short, cabinet members might have taken steps to correct Bill 80's emphasis on public works programs but did not. In all likelihood Gardiner recruited department heads who agreed with his preference for construction programs.

Of course some of these nonissues were discussed at the municipal level. But the regional aspects of these problems were rarely articulated. Metro councilors and interest groups did *not* fill the gap left by the cabinet and the chairman. The regional aspects of library, public assistance, and public health problems were sometimes raised by the City administrators responsible for these programs. But there was no institutionalized means of regularly communicating these views to the chairman; and the chairman had no incentive, like the maintenance of cabinet morale, for heeding these suggestions.

Gardiner and the Cabinet

Sources of Agreement. Gardiner was much more than a skillful adjuster of integrative and adaptive demands. He had his own substantive program for the solution of the area's problems. He brought to his position as chairman his experiences as a former reeve of Forest Hill, a successful lawyer in Toronto's financial district, and a prominent member of the Progressive-Conservative Party. His general views on municipal and regional government were a mixture of business-oriented conservatism and good government, civic reform ideals.

The values and orientations that department heads brought to their positions were derived from the programs of their respective professions. To understand how these officials defined area problems, one need only examine the pages of the *Journal of Housing, Canadian Tax Journal, Habitat, Ontario Planning, Traffic Quarterly, Journal of the American Institute of Planners,* and the other professional journals published on both sides of the border.

These professional values and Gardiner's personal values did not always coincide. Sources of intra-administrative stress are examined below. But more important were the large areas of congruence between the chairman's good government values and the programs of the professional associations. The extent of agreement between chairman and cabinet apparently grew as the members of this administrative subsystem interacted frequently with each other. A process of mutual persuasion operated to some extent. Yet this harmony-producing factor would have worn thin had there not been considerable congruence in values at the outset. Interaction alone cannot account for solidarity in the administrative subsystem.[2]

Gardiner felt most strongly about the need for a sound fiscal policy. "Soundness," he thought, required the long-range planning of capital expenditures, a practice long advocated by professional planners and civic reformers though not accepted in any of the Toronto area municipalities. Gardiner's views on a prudent borrowing policy were initially in accord with, and also were later influenced by, the views of the Metro finance commissioner, G. Arthur Lascelles. The two men agreed that Metro's outstanding debt should not exceed 12 percent of area assessment and that only a tight rein on annual borrowing would guarantee Metro a good credit rating and low interest rates.

The cabinet's and Gardiner's strong interest in construction programs has already been noted. There was little administrative dissension in identifying the one program that should receive priority in the early capital budgets. The only crisis in the area, Gardiner and the cabinet agreed, was the absence of sewer and water-supply facilities in the outlying suburbs. A five-year program to build watermains, reservoirs, sewers, and water purification plants became the largest item in Metro's first five-year capital budget.

Gardiner and the cabinet supported the federal system but also favored the shifting of more powers from the municipal to the Metro level. Despite disagreements on strategy, Gardiner and the administrators could agree on an overall policy of Metro imperialism.

The administration's transportation policy was drafted by an interdepartmental transportation committee and then "sold" to Gardiner. Although not denying the importance of subway construction—long advocated by the TTC, City officials, and the Toronto press—cabinet officials assigned equal importance to expressways. Metro, the officials said, needed an arterial network of highways to take cars off the local streets and to permit through-traffic to bypass the downtown core. This balanced transportation plan, requiring both subways and expressways, agreed with Gardiner's personal views on the subject. The public, acting through the private market, had indicated its preference for automobiles, and Gardiner did not think that this preference could be ignored or reversed. He rejected the City's plea that highways be permitted to deteriorate and expressway funds be redirected to subways in order to force a return to public-transit riding. The cabinet not only convinced Gardiner of the need for an arterial network but also persuaded him that the five highway projects making up this network had to be approved by Metro Council *in toto*.

Gardiner took the lead in arguing for an immediate start on expressways and a delay in subway construction. With the province willing to pay about half the costs of expressway construction but unwilling to contribute to subways, proceeding with expressways would impose less of a strain on Metro's early capital budgets. Gardiner argued, and the cabinet agreed, that subways could be started only after the five-year water and sewer program had been completed. Perhaps if public transit had been represented in the cabinet and not delegated to an independent commission, there would have been more intra-cabinet conflict over this decision.

Sources of Stress. There were two sources of strain in the Gardiner's relations with the administrators: the chairman's insistence on making political adjustments in the cabinet's proposals before presenting them to the Council, and his inclination to follow his own personal views rather than the cabinet's leads in some areas of policy. Only the former was endemic or structural strain, that is, strain necessitated by the chairman's attempt to reconcile adaptive and integrative needs.

Gardiner sometimes altered the substance of cabinet proposals in order to make them more politically acceptable. He more often left their substance unaltered and dictated only the timing of their introduction into Council. Although the chairman's pace of problem solving was slower than the cabinet officials would have wished, they generally deferred to Gardiner's interpretation of Council politics. If his political adjustments had had less to do with timing and more to do with substance, Gardiner might have faced more significant cabinet discontent. As it was, he bridged the administrative-leader and legislative-leader roles without antagonizing the cabinet.

A more serious source of strain was Gardiner's occasional pursuit of his own policies and values, despite the recommendations of the cabinet. This nonstructural strain was most evident in Gardiner's relations with the Metro planning commissioner, Murray Jones, perhaps because the professional planners were among the more aggressive, ambitious, and policy-oriented members of the cabinet. While Gardiner accepted the planners' case for long-range capital budgets, he assigned to himself, and not to the professional planners, the central role in assembling this budget. Moreover, the chairman, though an advocate of long-range financial planning, remained a skeptic where long-range land-use planning was concerned. He would sooner trust his own intuition about the future patterns of development in the area than trust the planners' complicated surveys and studies. When the planners clashed with the TTC over the best route for an east–west subway, Gardiner decided in favor of the TTC's practical, experienced engineers. Although he respected Jones and followed his lead on many issues, Gardiner retained an image of the professional planners as pie-in-the-sky dreamers.

Another source of nonstructural stress was Gardiner's lack of enthusiasm for public housing. In 1954, a cabinet committee urged Gardiner to seek Council approval of a long-range housing program that would commit Metro to the construction of at least 1,000 new units each year. Gardiner, though not opposed to public housing in principle, thought that it was a matter of lesser importance, that the province eventually would assume full responsibility in this field, and that there was little point in Metro's outlining an ambitious program until the red tape involved in intergovernmental negotiations on such projects was reduced. His objections to public housing projects were not based on their expense, since Metro would only pay about 8 percent of the construction costs. Nor were his objections based on the difficulties involved in gaining legislative acceptance of housing projects. It is true that all the projects proposed by the cabinet committee were located in the suburbs and that suburban officials were opposed to the location of such projects within their municipalities, but Gardiner had sought and attained Council approval of other controversial cabinet proposals. If his personal commitment to public housing had been stronger, Gardiner would not have hesitated to press for an ambitious housing program.

Yet Gardiner seemed aware of the need to accommodate cabinet demands and maintain cabinet morale, even if it meant seeking legislative majorities for cabinet proposals that he did not enthusiastically support. From 1954 to 1957, the chairman refused to pursue a long-range program but *did* agree to seek Council approval of specific projects on the cabinet committee's list. In 1958, he reversed his earlier stand and sought Council approval of a long-range program. His purpose, it seems, was to prevent cabinet grievances from accumulating.

On the whole, however, Gardiner did not exert the full weight of his legislative leadership on behalf of public housing proposals. Housing proposals passed Council easily—for reasons indicated below. The real obstacle was the ability of a municipality to delay or kill a proposed project by refusing to grant zoning amendments and supportive public works. Gardiner took little action to break this deadlock. The cabinet prepared a proposal designed to weaken suburban obstructionism by providing public school grants to municipalities receiving public housing projects.

But Council was cool to the proposal; and Gardiner, though introducing the measure, did not apply his customary combination of persuasion, pressure, and compromise. Gardiner apparently could not play his legislative-leader role to the hilt when he did not personally believe in the proposals he was urging.

Both Gardiner and the cabinet agreed that the municipalities, particularly the suburbs, should not be pushed too hard in seeking transfers of municipal powers to the Metro level, but the chairman and the cabinet sometimes disagreed on which powers should be transferred first. On this issue Gardiner proved to be more committed to the "soft" programs than his cabinet. Gardiner, in 1953, thought that Bill 80 should not have left police, fire, and the licensing of occupations at the municipal level. The cabinet did not oppose the transfer of these powers to the Metro level but gave greater priority to the shifting of all public housing, urban renewal,[3] and traffic control responsibilities to Metro. In 1954–1956, Gardiner reached a tacit understanding with many of the suburbanites. If they supported the transfer of police and licensing, the chairman promised to call a halt to the further aggrandizement of Metro at the expense of the municipalities. From 1956 to 1961, Gardiner fought to maintain this understanding and to resist cabinet pressure for expanding Metro powers in the housing, renewal, and traffic areas. His only concession to the cabinet was to secure a slight expansion of Metro's traffic control powers in 1961.

The cabinet and Gardiner did not always see eye to eye on the continued independence of independent commissions. Members of the cabinet's transportation committee seemed particularly critical of the TTC's refusal to cooperate on transportation planning. Between 1959 and 1961, the Metro planning commissioner, Jones, apparently tried to convince the chairman that the TTC should be either abolished or stripped of its planning responsibilities and that a Metro department of transportation, to include both highways and public transit, should be created. Gardiner remained unconvinced. In response to Jones's arguments, the chairman could only suggest additional negotiations between the TTC and the departments as a means of resolving their differences.

Some signs of stress within the cabinet were more apparent than real. Gardiner at times encouraged cabinet members to state views that he personally supported but could not voice without jeopardizing his floor-leading role. At other times the chairman urged department heads to publicly advocate the "ideal" solution to some problem, even though it was a "radical" and politically unacceptable solution. This tactic was generally used to soften up the councilors—to convince them that some action on the problem would be required and to make them more agreeable to the less drastic proposal that Gardiner would later introduce. The chairman would then appear to be a moderate, and his proposal a compromise between the Council's views and the experts' ideal solution. In these cases, then, Gardiner deliberately exaggerated his differences with the cabinet in order to strengthen his hand in the legislature.

In summary, most of the strain in Gardiner's relations with the cabinet was personal rather than structural. If Gardiner had been less opinionated on certain policy questions, he might have agreed more often with his cabinet. On the other hand, Gardiner seemed most effective as a floor leader when he was strongly committed to certain policy solutions. Moreover, he probably would not have assumed a central position in the Metro system had he not held such strong views on substantive policy.

Cabinet Unity, Departmentalism, and Clientelism. Despite these sources of tension in Gardiner's relations with the administrators, no open break in cabinet unity occurred. There was a remarkable stability in the personnel of the cabinet from 1953 to 1961. Resignations of department heads were due to ill health or age; no one quit in disgust. Moreover, differences within the administrative branch were ironed out within the confines of the cabinet committees. No cabinet member publicly complained of his treatment at the hands of the chairman, and no cabinet member attempted to appeal a decision of the chairman to the Council.

In only 5 of the 55 issues listed in Table 6.1 did the department heads go beyond initiation and definition to perform more political activities, like persuasion, aggregation, or interest articulation. In each of the 5 cases, however, this venture into politics was sanctioned or encouraged by the chairman. So well was cabinet unity maintained and publicity avoided that it is difficult for the researcher to obtain extensive evidence on intra-administrative relations—hence my frequent use of "apparently" and other qualifying phrases in the preceding pages. Most intra-administrative tensions did not come to light until years after the fact, some perhaps not at all.

The policy-making role of public administrators has been one of the less explored areas of urban politics, perhaps because the early community political studies testified to the importance of interest groups, the business elite, and other nongovernmental actors.[4] What limited evidence there is on this subject suggests that the Metro pattern of administrative politics departs significantly from the pattern prevalent in large American cities. In the American pattern, most elaborately described in the Sayre—Kaufman study of New York City, the centrifugal forces within the administrative branch far outweigh the centripetal forces. The two terms most commonly employed to describe administrative politics in American cities (and at other levels of American government) are "clientelism" (the capture of a department by the interest groups who are served or regulated by the department) and "departmentalism" (the emergence of strong departmental loyalties that frustrate attempts at top-level, inter-departmental coordination). The contrast between the Metro and American patterns can be made more vivid by summarizing Sayre and Kaufman's conclusions on the political role of New York's department heads.[5]

In both Metro and New York City, "cabinet members" are appointed officials recruited by the chief administrative official. The paradox is that the New York mayor, officially the head of the administration, in fact presides over a feudal system, while the Metro chairman, lacking the formal powers of a chief administrator, in fact plays the dominant role in a united cabinet. In

New York each department head, or commissioner, fends for himself politically. Employee associations within each department press the commissioner to protect departmental jurisdiction and internal procedures from outside threats. The commissioner, willingly or reluctantly, soon becomes a spokesman for the institutional interests of the department. He strives to frustrate the mayor's interest in coordinating departments, rearranging the jurisdictions of departments, or urging policy innovations on these departments. Once appointed he ceases to be the mayor's man.

To provide support for the department when it takes its case to the city legislature, the department head must come to terms with those interest groups most directly concerned with the department's programs—with the department's "clientele." Friendly groups must be cultivated and mobilized; hostile groups must be tranquilized or isolated. The price of this search for political support is some loss in the department's ability to set its own goals. Regulatory agencies, for example, must often ease the stringency of their enforcement policies in order to appease the regulated groups.

The construction of separate, departmental bases of political support adds to the fragmentation of the administrative branch. The mayor must cope with autonomous administrative empires, whose prerogatives he may seldom challenge without incurring grave political risks. In all, the New York pattern is friendly to the preservation of routinized administrative procedures and hostile to innovation. Even the eager, reform-minded administrator soon makes his peace with the system. To quote Sayre and and Kaufman:

Faced by awesome combination of forces with vested interests in the existing situation, few commissioners are willing to invest the energy and take the risks required to make extensive changes in policy, organization, or procedure.[6]

In view of the centrifugal forces at work in New York City's administrative politics, the preservation of cabinet unity in Metro Toronto is all the more impressive. Metro administrators, far from becoming defenders of departmental routine or captives of interest group constituencies, were essentially generators of policy innovations. Rather than embark on independent political activities in support of departmental goals, Metro administrators relied on the political efforts of the chief administrator. Two basic factors, I have argued, account for Metro cabinet unity: the large degree of agreement between the chairman's and cabinet's views on policy, and the cabinet's satisfaction with Gardiner's ability to deliver legislative majorities for cabinet proposals.

Even if Metro administrators had been more inclined to bypass the chairman and seek support among the interest groups and Metro councilors, such a strategy probably would have yielded little results. As succeeding chapters will show, the commitment of councilors and interest groups to Metro issues was weak. Supportive coalitions made up of such groups or legislators would have been difficult to construct and, once constructed, would not have matched Gardiner's persuasive abilities in producing legislative majorities. But Metro administrators preferred concentrating on the technical side of their jobs. They would have ventured into politics reluctantly and only in response to strong dissatisfactions with the chairman's performance. In the intense and competitive politics of New York City, and in other broker leadership systems, the public administrators may be encouraged, even required, to become independent political entrepreneurs. The more "slack," low-pressure politics of Metro reinforced the administrators' inclination to rely on the chairman.

If the above factors help explain why clientelism did not appear in Metro, the newness of the Metro system may help explain why departmentalism did not appear. Perhaps the Metro department heads were innovators rather than protectors of departmental vested interests because the departments were in the process of being created and because procedural routines had not yet taken root. Indeed, the Metro cabinet may be more vulnerable to departmentalism than are cabinets at senior levels of government. The Metro department head, like his subordinates, is a technical staff man. The department head in Ontario or Canadian government is a political outsider who shares a loyalty to his department with a loyalty to his political party.

From the vantage point of 1965, it appeared that departmentalism, more than clientelism, posed a threat to the continuance of cabinet unity. Metro's employee associations were becoming better organized and more vocal. Successors to the initial group of department heads were being recruited from within the departments. Recruitment from within, of course, does not preclude a strong commitment to problem definition and policy innovation; but it may also produce, among the newer cabinet members, a strong commitment to the departments' institutional interests.

Another unifying factor, the Metro administration's common interest in "imperialism" at the expense of the municipal administrations, may help check the centrifugal impact of departmentalism. During Metro's first thirteen years, the expansive tendencies of Metro departments were directed not at other Metro departments but at the municipal departments responsible for related programs.

Finally, I would argue that one cannot fully explain cabinet unity in Metro without exploring aspects of the Canadian political culture and how it differs from the American. Although Canadian cities and provinces have borrowed many forms and ideas from American municipal government, Metro actors, in speaking of a Metro cabinet, appear to be operating with British–Canadian images of that institution. It is assumed by Metro participants—certainly by the Metro councilors and the press—that cabinet unity or collective responsibility will be maintained. In the Canadian tradition appointed officials do not try to appeal decisions taken by the chief political official in the administration, and appointed officials do not take their case directly to legislative committees. It is assumed that differences within the administrative branch will be worked out behind closed doors and that appointed officials will neither reveal the sources of intra-administrative disagreements nor rally outside political support for their side in a controversy. Of course, neither departmentalism nor clientelism is totally alien to the parliamentary–cabinet system; but the principle of collective responsibility of the cabinet serves to counteract these centrifugal forces within the administration. The fact that the Metro cabinet, unlike the provincial and federal cabinets, was composed of civil servants seemed to make little difference to Metro actors. The Metro system operated with the spirit and culture, though not the precise forms, of parliamentary–cabinet government.[7]

The Problem of Political Integration

Every political system must construct and maintain support among those individuals who are to play significant roles in that system. This support may stem from a feeling that the system is ideal and self-evident or from a grudging acceptance of the system's utility in certain limited realms. The first attitude is evidence of integration on a normative basis—the type of integration that sociologists generally speak of. The second type of integration, based on instrumental or calculative acceptance, will be called "nonnormative integration."

Metropolitan federations in North America have pursued differing integrative strategies. The political base of metropolitan government in the Winnipeg and Miami metropolitan areas has been the good government interest groups that had initially joined forces to urge metropolitan reform. Metro Nashville, although still in its early stages, seems to be following this pattern.[8] In all three cases the Metro legislators are directly elected, and the municipal officials have no institutionalized role to play at the metropolitan level. The excluded municipal officials have remained the systems' major critics. Only strong support from the reform groups and the Metro legislators has saved Metro Miami and Metro Winnipeg from political extinction.

This type of integrative strategy was not available to leaders of the Metro Toronto system. Metro Toronto was not the product of an indigenous reform movement that could have provided support for the system after its creation. Interest groups, moreover, were too weakly involved in Metro politics for anyone to contemplate basing the Metro system on their support. Nor could the municipal officials be excluded as they were in other federations. Without the support of municipal officials sitting on Metro Council, no items of policy could be approved. The major integrative virtue of recruiting Metro legislators from the municipal councils was the avoidance of conflict between directly elected Metro councilors and municipal officials—a form of conflict that has sometimes immobilized the Winnipeg metropolitan system. The weakness of the Metro Toronto plan was that support had to be secured from officials who remained committed to their municipalities and indifferent to the future of the Metro system.

The integrative problems of the Metro Toronto system resembled those of a new international federation. In both cases the key political actors at the federal level continued to represent pre-existing governmental units. The essence of the integrative problem was to secure some transfer of political loyalties from the constituent units to the new federal government.[9]

But Metro Toronto differed from international federations in one crucial respect. Federation in the Toronto case was imposed by a higher authority and was maintained through the constraint applied by that authority. Provincial compulsion, therefore, provided some of the necessary integration. The province's position guaranteed that the system would not collapse through the secession of one or more of its members.

Provincial constraint did not entirely remove the need for Metro to secure its political base. If municipal officials could not secede, they *could* obstruct Metro Council procedures or refuse to vote funds for the Metro administration. Having municipal officials sit on Metro Council made it more likely that the integrative battles of the Metro Toronto system would be fought out in the legislature, but there was nothing to prevent the losers from appealing Council decisions to the courts. Litigation has been a recurrent feature of the Metro Miami and Metro Winnipeg experiments. Finally, municipal officials could maintain their steady attacks on the Metro system and thus persuade the province to abandon or alter the plan.

To use terms developed by Karl Deutsch and others in their discussion of international federations, Metro Toronto represented an "amalgamated political structure" created in the absence of a metropolitan "political community."[10] Provincial officials were willing to create the formal structure first and gamble that a "community" would eventually follow. In the 1950s, a Metro government existed but "Metro mindedness" (to use Gardiner's term) did not. In comparison to federations like the "European community," Metro lacked—and never acquired—an emotional overlay. No one on Council, aside from the two Metro chairmen, advocated submerging municipal interests in order to promote regional unity and the Metro idea.

The imposition of a governmental structure on an area before there was widespread local support for these institutions helps explain why Metro lacked many of the features alleged to be requisites of all social systems. The Metro system, in 1953 and succeeding years, lacked norms, socialization and social control mechanisms, and a sense of solidarity. In Parsonian terms Metro was not a social system at all. Most of the system's important actors wished to see the system replaced with something else. More support for Metro came from without the system than from within.

Only Gardiner (and later Allen) was eager to see the system succeed and willing to try constructing a political base for the system. Gardiner's strategies, therefore, dominate the following discussion of Metro's integrative development.

Where a system has institutionalized adaptive roles, the occupants of those roles become important members, whose support for the system must be maintained. Securing their loyalty through problem solving may be viewed as part of the integrative, as well as adaptive, process. In the following pages, however, I focus on Gardiner's attempts to secure the support of nonadaptive actors—specifically the municipal officials serving on Metro Council. The support of these officials is obviously the *sine qua non* of Metro integration.

Gardiner and the Metro Council

Council Attitudes on the Metro System. From the outset Metro councilors saw themselves as municipal spokesmen attending an international conference. They were municipal officials first and Metro councilors second. (In fact the term "Metro councilor" was one that Gardiner and the newspapers coined, but one which the members of Council never used to describe themselves.) Basically, the municipal official sat on Council to protect his municipality from unwelcome intrusions by the "Metro giant" and to see that favoritism was not shown to other area municipalities.

Some reasons for this hostility to Metro and this continued defense of municipal interests have already been implied: the novelty of the Metro plan, the lack of indigenous support for the plan, and the recruitment of Metro councilors from the ranks of the municipal councils. In addition, Metro councilors thought the system would not last. Metro appeared to be a clever political compromise rather than a final solution to the area's problems. Provincial promises that the system would someday be reviewed and revised—promises made to soften initial municipal opposition to the federal plan—only strengthened local views about Metro's transient nature.

The strategy of municipal officials sitting on Council was to overstate their mistreatment at the hands of Metro in order to improve their bargaining position when the time came for provincial review. Statements of municipal opposition and provincial promises of review interacted in a cyclical fashion during Metro's first thirteen years. When the municipalities stepped up their criticisms of Metro in order to provoke a provincial review, the province would try to appease these municipal officials by indicating that a review was under consideration. Such a provincial statement would encourage municipalities to increase their level of attack on Metro. Impressed by these new criticisms, Ontario officials would then order a review. The 1957 review proposed, and the province agreed, that no changes be made in the Metro system. This provincial statement temporarily quelled municipal opposition to Metro; but, after 1960, the upward phase of the cycle reasserted itself. The result of the renewed criticisms was a royal commission in 1963.

Paradoxically, a strong statement of provincial support for the existing Metro system would have substantially reduced municipal opposition to Metro, but the existence of municipal opposition made the province unwilling to issue such a statement. Indications from the Ontario cabinet that Metro Toronto was just an "experiment" impeded political integration at the Metro level.

A transfer of loyalties from the municipalities to Metro did not occur, but neither did a municipal rebellion. Contrary to fears voiced in 1953, no officials tried to boycott Metro Council meetings or obstruct Council business. Only three decisions taken by the Council between 1953 and 1965 were appealed to the courts by the losing side.

A minimal degree of nonnormative integration emerged. Metro councilors would tolerate the system and cooperate in its proceedings as long as Metro provided tangible payoffs to the municipalities in the form of improved services and dramatic public works projects. More than this, the councilors thought that benefits, particularly construction projects, should be distributed in an equitable manner. Equity, or what I call "regional parity," required that each municipality receive benefits roughly in line with its tax contribution to Metro and that no one municipality benefit more from the Metro system than the other municipalities making a similar tax contribution. Members of the Council were particularly sensitive to the balance of capital expenditures between Toronto and the twelve suburbs, but the suburbanites also insisted on some balance among the northern, western, and eastern portions of the suburban area. Thus, Metro had to provide specific and tangible payoffs and had to do so in a manner that the municipal officials considered "fair."

This calculative attitude can be traced partly to the debate that preceded institution of the Metro system—particularly to the province's promises that Metro would yield immediate and tangible returns to the constituent municipalities. Gardiner, who thought that the provision of quick, observable results would be the best way of building municipal support for Metro, encouraged the emergence of these calculative attitudes. The emphasis on regional parity, moreover, added some flexibility to Council politics. As long as a councilor was satisfied with the overall distribution of capital expenditures, he would support particular projects in other municipalities and would give the chairman and cabinet large amounts of discretion in project planning. Thus, it is incorrect to see Council's attitudes as the stimulus and Gardiner's integrative strategies as the response. The two factors formed a circular chain of causation.

Gardiner's Integrative Strategy. In attempting to build support for the Metro system, Gardiner had no weapon at his command but the manipulation of Metro's policy output. Providing payoffs to the municipalities would only gain grudging acceptance for Metro in the short run; but Gardiner apparently hoped that in the long run this tolerance would evolve into diffuse support for the system itself. If integration were first achieved on a calculative basis, normative integration might follow. At some point in Metro's history, then, the system might become the object of emotional or affective loyalties. With the appearance of diffuse, noncalculative support for the system, policy decisions would be liberated, in part, from integrative considerations. Metro officials could then take for granted the overall stability of the system, thrust integrative considerations into the background, and focus more clearly on environmental problems.

Until that day arrived, the chairman's strategic choices were restricted. The core of Gardiner's integrative strategy was to emphasize his floor-leading role over the mustering of nonlegislative support, to base his legislative effectiveness on informal persuasion rather than on the authority of office, to build legislative majorities on an *ad hoc*, shifting basis, and to use substantive policies as a means of making payoffs to municipalities and building majorities. In its general terms, Gardiner's strategy seems to have been the most effective response to Metro's integrative problem. Whatever degree of integration Metro attained during its first thirteen years was largely attributable to the skillful floor leadership of Gardiner and Allen.

Gardiner's procedural strategy as legislative floor leader may be summed up in the following terms. Metro Council, he thought, could stand the strain of only one major, controversial issue per annual legislative session. Resolution of such an issue should be followed by a breathing spell, in which no issue of great import was brought forward. The breathing spell was an opportunity for tempers to cool and grudges to be partially forgotten. The tenuous unity of the Metro Council would be reasserted in preparation for the next divisive issue.[11]

This strategy also prevented controversial issues from accumulating. A divisive issue would not be brought forward until earlier controversies on other issues had been settled. Taking the big issues one at a time was designed to keep the temperature of Council politics below the boiling point.

The chairman would not press for Council approval of an emotionally charged issue unless he was certain of an overwhelming, as opposed to a bare, majority. If possible, Gardiner wanted a majority of both the suburban and City blocs behind the move. Excessive reliance on 13 to 11 or 14 to 10 majorities, he thought, would convince some municipalities that issues were being rammed down their throats. The chairman's insistence on consensual majorities is one reason that so few decisions of Council were appealed to the courts. Gardiner was not always able to obtain this large majority and sometimes proceeded to a final vote without it, but the bipartisan majority on controversial issues remained his ideal.

Some controversy-laden issues, particularly those relating to the organization of the Metro federal system itself, were kept out of Council. In a sense, the price of achievement on substantive issues was to take as unquestioned Metro's basic structure. When Gardiner did proceed with a highly contentious issue, he often sought Council approval by dividing the issue into smaller, less controversial segments. Council was sometimes backed into approving a proposal. In this piecemeal fashion Gardiner secured Council approval of most of the expressways network, apparently moving in a pragmatic, route-by-route manner but actually implementing the long-range plan prepared by his cabinet. A vote on the plan itself, however, was the last thing he wanted.

The chairman's decision about when to proceed with a controversial issue depended on his interpretation of Council's mood, particularly as it related to regional parity. If one bloc were dissatisfied, a proposal unfavorable to that bloc could not be pressed. In the water rates controversy, for example, Toronto sought a special consideration on wholesale rates because City residents had enjoyed low rates prior to 1953. The suburbanites favored a uniform wholesale rate. Gardiner thought that Toronto should not be pressed to accept uniform rates while initial capital budgets slightly favored the suburbs. Each year Gardiner tested the City's sentiment on water rates and, for six consecutive years, concluded that the issue should be put off. The chairman guessed—correctly, it now is clear—that the City's solid opposition to uniform rates would crack once the east–west subway were begun and Metro's capital budgets were more evenly balanced. Gardiner's view seemed to be that, given time, the correct moment to introduce almost any policy proposal could be found.

Gardiner's strong support for the continued independence of independent commissions partly reflected his personal view that businesslike programs (e.g., public transit) and regulatory programs (police or licensing) were best administered by such agencies. But he also favored these commissions because they helped keep controversial issues out of the Metro Council. The dispersion of power seemed to reduce the intensity of Metro politics.[12] Groups and individuals concerned with policy making to some extent operated in separate spheres, rather than confronting each other head-on. Certainly these commissions diverted pressures away from the Council and helped reduce the intensity of *legis-*

lative politics. Stated in functional terms, the independent commissions, by sharing in the performance of the Metro system's adaptive and integrative functions, made Council's problems more manageable.

Thus, much of Gardiner's legislative strategy involved regulating the *pace* of Council's problem solving. Gardiner's role was that of a gatekeeper.[13] He generally did not define the issues himself, but he did select those issues that would be brought to Council and did decide when they would be presented. Most problem-oriented actors in the Metro system found Gardiner's pace too slow. But, as the chairman realized, an increase in pace would have strained the already shaky municipal tolerance of Metro. Only if there had been diffuse support for the system could the rate of problem solving have been substantially accelerated.

Once an issue were brought before the Council, Gardiner generally assumed a tough line. To secure specific majorities he relied upon the persuasiveness of his arguments. He would not offer *quid pro quo*'s on specific issues or permit amendments on the floor. Cabinet proposals in particular were treated as packages, which Council had to accept or reject *in toto*. But it should be made clear that these tough tactics on the floor—so well publicized by the local press—were predicated on Gardiner's careful selection of issues and his correct interpretation of Council's moods. He proved so successful in ramming proposals through Council because he had already made the necessary accommodations prior to presenting proposals. He devoted as much attention to keeping issues out of Council as he did to demanding legislative action. Gardiner was impatient with *quid pro quo*'s on specific issues because such deals were not necessary to secure approval. A single deal had been struck in the annual capital budget. As long as parity were observed, the chairman could rely on persuasion in particular cases. Finally, Gardiner was shrewd enough not to employ these tough tactics in policy areas where the factional lines were clearly drawn or where deference to the chairman was weak.

When Gardiner pressed for approval of an issue that divided

the Council along factional lines, he generally relied upon the support of the bloc favoring the proposal and tried to split off enough rebels from the other bloc to muster a good-sized majority. However, Gardiner thought it essential that the chairman be seen as a middle man, affiliated with neither bloc. While he often based his majorities on one of the blocs, he was careful to alternate between reliance on the City and suburban blocs. His purpose was to prevent either bloc from becoming a permanent opposition and to prevent the chairman from becoming a factional leader. Thus, Gardiner's response to factional divisions in the Council was not to split the difference in the demands of the two blocs but to keep shifting the basis of his majorities.[14]

Alternative Legislative Strategies. Given the basic attitudes of the Metro councilors, it is difficult to see how any Metro chairman could have pursued substantially different legislative strategies.[15]

The chairman's only resource was his unofficial control over Council's agenda and floor proceedings. The formal prerogatives of the office were minimal, and Gardiner strongly believed that they should remain so. The effectiveness of his legislative performance rested on the very ambiguity and informality of his role. His leadership was tolerated mainly because it was not official—because it was based on persuasion rather than authority. Any attempt by Gardiner to increase the formal powers of his office would have jeopardized his effectiveness as floor leader. Gardiner measured his own effectiveness as chairman by how few times he had recourse to his only important formal power—the ability to cast tie-breaking votes in Council. The need to exercise this formal power, in Gardiner's view, indicated his failure to muster a sound majority and his miscalculation in proceeding to a final vote without a majority behind him. Such overt displays of authority only increased the councilors' resentment of the chairman.

The absence of stable factions in the Council made reliance on *ad hoc* majorities a necessity. There were no parties, factions, or alliances in the Metro area's municipal elections. Unstructured electoral politics produced unstructured legislatures. Since the City and suburban blocs often took differing stands on issues, Metro Council resembled a two-party legislature. In that respect Metro Council was more structured than municipal councils in the area. But Metro Council's blocs were far too loosely organized and incoherent to provide a chairman with stable majorities. Moreover, neither bloc controlled more than half the seats. Except on those rare occasions when absenteeism was a crucial factor, majorities had to include members of both blocs.

Even assuming that reliance upon one bloc had been a workable strategy, such a course of action would probably have produced a boycott or filibuster by the opposition bloc and subsequent intervention by the province. The integration of the system was not strong enough to permit a majority party and a loyal opposition. Regardless of feasibility, both Gardiner and the province thought that Metro integration *should* be based on the support of all the municipalities, not just one faction.

In a sense, Gardiner had a personal constituency within the Council. The chairman drew more consistent support from the councilors who were more moderate and slightly more "Metro minded" than their colleagues. But the chairman could not reward his most consistent supporters nor punish his enemies. Gardiner could propose and the Council would listen, but he could not resort to social control in order to bring deviants into line. Gardiner occasionally influenced appointments to the Executive Committee, but only in favor of men whom he considered more able and better equipped to carry the burden of committee business. "Loyalty to the chairman" was not seen by the councilors as an appropriate reason for promoting a colleague to the Executive Committee. It is true, however, that Gardiner sometimes urged the election of moderates to the committee, while couching his argument in terms of the candidates' ability to handle committee business.

The chairman could not build majorities on any basis other than the substance of public policies. He did not command any administrative patronage. Gardiner personally believed in the recruitment of middle- and lower-level administrative personnel through civil service procedures and insisted on technical experts for the top-level administrative positions. Moreover, the political culture of the area—heavily influenced by the values of the good government reform movement—was favorable to civil service procedures and businesslike efficiency in the administrative branch, fearful of bossism, and sharply critical of any official who would build a personal machine on the basis of administrative appointments. Council would have permitted political appointments only at the top administrative level and only if Council controlled the appointments.

An exception to these generalizations on patronage occurred in the appointment of Toronto transit commissioners. Since the initial policies of the Metro system gave somewhat greater attention to suburban problems, Gardiner attempted to forestall a City rebellion by letting the Toronto bloc name some of its own people to the TTC. Patronage of a sort was used, not to enhance Gardiner's influence but to increase City support for Metro.

Gardiner's attempts to build certain rituals and ceremonies into the Metro Council proceedings probably were designed to promote Metro integration on a noncalculative basis. It might be said that the chairman tried to construct a sense of solidarity in the Metro Council and facilitate his majority-building efforts through the elaboration of emotional symbolism—or what Charles Merriam called the "credenda and miranda of power."[16] Gardiner initiated the practice of making Metro Council's opening meeting, in January following each municipal election, a ritual-filled occasion. He also instituted the practice of having the chairman deliver a "speech from the throne," outlining his program for the coming legislative session. To some extent these opening meetings became characterized by the statements of good will and camaraderie that mark the opening days of federal and provincial parliamentary sessions.

But there were clear limits to how much diffuse support could be generated through the manipulation of "affect." These rituals had only a minimal impact on the councilors' view of Metro. Moreover, the press sometimes ridiculed this attempt to get solemn about Metro government. Symbolism and ritual were viewed as appropriate at the national level but somewhat ludicrous at the local level.

Extralegislative Strategies. Gardiner rarely went beyond a floor-leading role in his attempts to secure Metro integration. For the most part he took the status of public, press, and interest group opinion as given and did not attempt to build grass-roots support for the system or grass-roots pressure on the councilors to support the Metro idea.

Could Gardiner have secured greater Metro integration by taking his case outside the legislature and building stable relations with private groups and local newspapers? In Metro Winnipeg the first Metro chairman increasingly resorted to the mobilization of interest group support to counteract criticisms voiced by municipal officials. In the Metro Toronto area, however, such a strategy would have produced marginal gains. Interest groups were not intensely involved in Metro Toronto politics. Whether attempts at education and interest articulation would have activated these groups and provided a supportive coalition for the Metro system is debatable. An attempt to create widespread public support for Metro, in the hope that this support would lead to the election of more "Metro minded" municipal officials, also would have been a dubious strategy. More important, such strategies would not have been tolerated by the Metro councilors. Members of Council were willing to accept a leading role for the chairman, but they strongly opposed his becoming a popular figure. The councilors were prepared—indeed, pleased—to see Gardiner deal directly with private groups when the result was settlement of a particular controversial issue; but they opposed his going outside Council to stimulate grass-roots pressures on the councilors. Gardiner's influence in Council rested heavily on his ability to persuade; he could not maintain this source of effectiveness and at the same time resort to extralegislative pressures on the councilors. In the Winnipeg area, it might be noted, the directly elected Metro councilors generally shared the chairman's enthusiasm for the Metro system and joined in his public-relations efforts.

Gardiner, moreover, personally preferred the floor-leader role. As a former reeve of Forest Hill, Gardiner was no stranger to politics in its broader sense. Still, his temperament led him to emphasize intralegislative negotiations and to deemphasize appearances at ratepayer meetings, dinners, television programs, and ethnic holiday observances.

Integration and Conflict

Council Conflict and Consensus. From the foregoing account of Council's calculative attitudes, one might assume that councilors were constantly at loggerheads and that the chairman's majority-building job was a near-impossible one. In fact, Council rarely experienced intense conflict.

Approximately 80 percent of all Council votes recorded between 1953 and 1965 were unanimous. Admittedly most of these unanimous votes occurred on detailed matters, since Metro Council followed the practice of Canadian and American municipal councils in reviewing a host of specific administrative decisions. In the absence of comparable figures for other metropolitan or municipal councils, moreover, it is not possible to say whether Metro's degree of unanimity is unusual. Nevertheless, the chairman's virtually unchallenged control of the Council on detailed issues was impressive.

One may exclude the votes on "administrative decisions" and consider only votes on substantive issues in major policy areas. This is done in Table 3.1. When only votes on major policy programs are considered, the number of unanimous votes shrinks to one-third of the total.

Of course, not all the nonunanimous or split votes were closely contested votes. The factional vote—one in which a majority of the City bloc voted differently from a majority of the sub-

TABLE 3.1 Distribution of Unanimous, Split, and Factional Votes on Major Issues in Metro Council, July 1, 1953–June 30, 1965

Programs	Total Votes[a]	Percent Unanimous[a]	Percent Split[a]	Percent Factional[a]
All Construction Programs	172	45.9	54.1	11.6
Subways	60	35.0	65.0	20.0
Expressways	28	42.8	57.2	3.6
Public housing	14	57.1	42.9	7.1
Hospital construction grants	8	25.0	75.0	12.5
Other programs (roads, water, sewers, schools, homes for the aged)	62	58.1	41.9	8.1
All Service and Regulatory Programs	193	26.4	73.6	40.9
TTC service, fares, and subsidies	40	27.5	72.5	50.0
TTC appointments and reorganization	72	29.2	70.8	19.4
Water rates	57	14.1	85.9	57.9
Police	13	23.1	76.9	7.7
Licensing	8	62.5	37.5	1.3
Air-Pollution control	3	100.0	00.0	0.0
All Future-of-Metro Issues	72	19.4	80.6	38.9
Transferring powers to Metro level	39	33.3	66.7	25.6
Altering Metro's organization	33	3.1	96.9	54.6
All Issues	437	33.0	67.0	29.1

[a] Note that "unanimous" and "split" votes equal "total" votes. "Factional votes" is a subcategory of "split votes."

urban bloc—is a good index of intense controversy. When conflict in the Council was intense, the Council was almost always divided along City-suburban lines. (On the other hand, a factional division did not always indicate the presence of intense conflict; some issues were factional but not closely contested. Thus, use of factional voting as an index slightly overstates the degree of sharp conflict in the Council.)

Factional voting occurred on about one-quarter of the votes listed in Table 3.1. Fewer than 7 percent of all the votes in Council recorded between 1953 and 1965 were factional. Whatever test one chooses, the notion of a council divided into two disciplined, contesting blocs is clearly dispelled. Large, bipartisan majorities were the statistical norm in Council voting.[17]

Council Attitudes on Participation and Leadership. Council's hostile and calculative attitudes toward the Metro system created a potential for intense conflict, but Council's attitudes on participation and leadership depressed the incidence of conflict and gave the chairman additional room for maneuver.

Metro councilors were not aggressively interested in most Metro issues. These councilors remained far more committed to their roles at the municipal level and far more immersed in municipal business. The chairman often prevailed because he was the only Council member who had had the time and incentive to fully acquaint himself with the facts of the case and because he felt more strongly about the issue than did any of the councilors. The orientations of the Metro councilors were calculative but not intense. Weak commitment to the Metro system on the part of Council members meant not only weak support of the system but also weak interest and involvement in the resolution of Metro issues.

The areas of strong legislative interest centered on questions of regional parity and questions affecting the structure and continuance of the Metro federal system. In policy areas unrelated to regional parity or future-of-Metro questions, the legislative situation was fluid, slack, and amenable to the chairman's persuasive efforts.

Combined with this weak involvement in Metro issues was a belief in the need for firm leadership, as indicated by Council's willingness to delegate large amounts of discretion to the Metro chairman. The councilors were easily persuaded that one man had to be given responsibility for recruiting top-level administrators, preparing the operating and capital budgets, recruiting nominees for positions on independent commissions, preparing the Council's agenda, supervising the department heads, and providing a link between the legislative and administrative branches. Moreover, Gardiner was renamed chairman seven consecutive times, with minor challenges occurring on only two occasions. Lest these actions be interpreted solely as a tribute to Gardiner, it should be added that the same deference and automatic reappointment were accorded his successor.

Council deference to the chairman's political leadership was broader in scope than Council deference to the cabinet's technical leadership. Apparently no issue was outside the chairman's ken. On technical matters he was supposed to lead with advice of cabinet; on political issues he was supposed to provide leads on other than technical criteria. Gardiner was never criticized for meddling in matters outside of his jurisdiction. Yet Council deference to the chairman was greater when the issue was seen as a technical one and when Gardiner's leads were thought to embody proven, expert criteria.

Although Council support for Gardiner's initiation of issues did not necessarily mean Council enactment of all the chairman's proposals, most councilors were prepared to go along with the chairman on most issues. The councilors' first inclination was to support the chairman, since he was closest to the issue and had the facts at his command. That initial inclination might be reassessed, however, on questions directly affecting municipal prerogatives or benefits.

Deference was at its peak on financial matters. Capital and operating budgets sailed through Council generally without sharp debate and always without Council amendment. Councilors agreed that each budget embodied a carefully constructed political and financial equilibrium, which should not be disrupted by amendments from the floor. The operating budget—more specifically, "administrative duplication and waste"—was a favorite target of the councilors, but Council never cut an operating budget or rearranged funds among the various programs. The annual and five-year capital budgets were even more sacrosanct. The chairman was also given wide discretion on capital-borrowing proposals, since no one on Council was alleged to know more about the money market than Gardiner. Finally, Metro councilors were more willing to go along in policy areas that seemed to be within the chairman's domain as chief administrator: administrative appointments, personnel procedures, appointments to independent commissions, and the organization of administrative departments.

This legislative deference to the chairman's leadership was not consistent with the international conference image of Metro to which most councilors still adhered. The failure of the councilors to resolve this conflict in attitudes produced an ambiguous Council view of Gardiner's leadership. While continuing to follow his leads on most issues, the councilors frequently denounced "one-man rule" and referred to Metro as a "banana republic." Gardiner was a favorite target of attack during the municipal election campaigns. But, when he threatened to resign as chairman, the councilors urged him to stay on. This ambiguous legislative attitude also explains some of the limits on Gardiner's leadership. His leading role was supported by the councilors as long as it operated below the surface, rested on informal persuasion rather than formal authority, and depended on legislative rather than popular support. Councilors wanted Gardiner to provide the leads but also wanted complete freeeedom to accept or reject these leads.

The councilors' deference to leadership reduced the intensity of Council's politics and facilitated Gardiner's majority-building job. In chapter 6, I speculate on whether this deference reflected certain characteristics of the Canadian political culture. But it is also apparent that Gardiner's leadership performed useful tasks for the individual councilor. Gardiner's role as initiator structured the Metro political environment for the councilors, who generally were unable or unwilling to perform this task for themselves. By reducing the councilors' choices to manageable proportions, Gardiner's behavior made it easier for the councilors to cope with their Metro roles.

A Footnote on the Concept of Integration. In Parsonian analysis the normative integration of a system is viewed as a means of managing the tensions and conflicts that could tear the system apart. Thus, "integration" and "conflict" are often treated as reverse sides of the coin. Even the calculative types of integration defined above might make the system's members more willing to smother or settle their controversies in order to preserve the system.

It does not follow, however, that the alternative to integration, either normative or nonnormative, is intense conflict among the members of a system. Similarly, the absence of sharp conflict in a system cannot be taken as evidence of a system's integration.

Perhaps it is more accurate to see political integration as the center of a spectrum, with intense conflict at one pole and withdrawal and apathy at the other. Weak commitment to a system may mean that individuals press their particular demands without regard to the survival of the system and without recognizing any legitimate limits to their tactical behavior. But weak commitment may also lead to a reduction in involvement and a transfer of loyalties and interest to other systems. The Metro system, for example, developed in the direction of apathy rather than anarchy, in the direction of limited involvement rather than intense conflict. In such poorly integrated, low-involvement systems, an increase in membership commitment probably would expand the incidence of conflict over the short run, as members showed more interest in the system's policy output and raised the level of their demands. In the long run, increased commitment might produce elaborate normative controls on behavior and greater membership support for mechanisms that control conflict.[18]

CHAPTER 4

THE SYSTEM'S
PERFORMANCE (CONTINUED)

An Approach to the Study of Public Policy

In political systems responsible for a multiplicity of tasks or policy problems, the attitudes and behavior of the members may vary significantly from one policy area to another. To the extent that system members specialize in one or two problems, the personnel may also vary from one policy area to another. For these reasons it is possible, in dealing with national political systems, to speak of "a politics of agriculture," "a politics of national defense," or "a politics of housing," as well as "the politics" of the entire system. These variations in behavior must occur within the context of broader structural continuities; otherwise no generalizations on the system's structure would be possible. But the existence of such variations constitute qualifications to any across-the-board generalizations about a particular system. The behavior that surrounds each policy program may be viewed as a subsystem whose structure to some extent departs from the overall structure of the system.[1]

Each policy program apparently generates its own distinctive problems, attitudes, and conflicts. Thus, housing politics in widely divergent types of national systems contain many common features. The universal traits of a particular policy program combine with the distinctive style of a national system to determine the structure of a policy subsystem within that nation.[2]

At the urban level one would expect the autonomy of policy

subsystems to be greater in broker leadership cities and in cities with decentralized government bureaucracies. Such urban political systems have been described as holding companies for largely autonomous empires built around substantive programs.[3] In Metro the chairman and cabinet counteract these centrifugal forces. But behavioral variations from one policy area to another are still present. Even in the Metro case, a discussion of individual policy programs is necessary to qualify earlier generalizations about the structure of the system.

One way to characterize the politics of a particular policy area is by the pattern of legislative voting in that area. In Table 3.1, for example, the number of unanimous, split, and factional votes for each of Metro's major policy programs is listed. If one treats a high percentage of factional votes as an indicator of controversiality, construction programs were clearly less controversial than service, regulatory, or future-of-Metro issues. More specifically, TTC service, water rates, and Metro reorganization rank as the high-conflict programs; while expressways, licensing, and air pollution rank as the low-conflict issues. The extent of conflict in a policy area, as indicated in Table 3.1, will be treated as the dependent variable, which our following discussion seeks to explain.

The pattern of voting in the various policy areas can best be explained by reference to four attitudinal variables: the extent of generalized legislative support for the program or the extent of agreement on general principles; the degree of legislative interest and involvement in the program; the extent of legislative deference to leadership and expertise in a particular program; and the intensity of conflict over the detailed proposals that would implement the program's purposes. The degree of legislative conflict in particular programs may be seen as the net result of interaction among these four variables. Lack of generalized support for the program and disagreements over the implementation of the program are conflict-producing factors; deference to leadership and weak involvement in the program are conflict-depressing factors. If there is strong generalized support for the program, however, high involvement may help resolve conflict over implementation. Where overt conflict exists, it is important to know whether the source is a lack of generalized support for the program's goals or dissension over the arrangement of detailed implementing proposals. The absence of overt conflict in a policy area, however, need not indicate agreement on principle or implementation; such apparent harmony may be the product of disagreement on principle, weak interest in the program, and high deference to political and technical leadership.

The emergence of new policy programs in democratic systems appears to follow a discernible evolutionary pattern. The evolutionary model presented below accounts for the development of new programs in the Toronto area. In general terms this model also describes how new programs have emerged in Canadian and American cities and how new welfare programs have come to be accepted at the national level in these countries. Of course, not every program in every democratic system follows this model. We recognize that some programs may skip stages, that some may stagnate at particular levels of development, and that some may develop unique lines of development.[4]

In stage 1 of development no member of the system sees the problem or urges pursuit of the new program. At this point there is no generalized support for the program; but, since there is no involvement in the program, conflict is nonexistent. In stage 2 several adaptive-oriented actors urge approval of the program in principle, but as yet there is little political support for, or understanding of, the program's goals. Conflict remains minimal at this stage. The crucial problem for the reformers is to convince politicos that a problem really exists and that the proposed program is neither utopian, radical, nor inordinately expensive. At this stage education and propaganda are the reformers' most important political activities.

In stage 3 the program has broken through the threshold of the politician's understanding, and a great debate is held over the program's principles. The involvement but not the support of the politicians has been engaged. This is often the phase of maximum conflict. Education and propaganda continue to be important activities for the reformers, but the emphasis must shift from acquainting politicos with the problem to answering specific objections. If the program is to develop further, stage 3 must end with a political acceptance of the program's general goals.

In stage 4 the behavior of administrative and political officials is directed toward the preparation of specific proposals that would carry out the program's general goals. At this stage conflict continues, although it is more specific and sometimes less intense. Groups that object not to the program itself but to the terms of specific proposals are heard at this point. The ability of the officials to work out a detailed settlement and to proceed with the implementation of the program depends largely on how intense this specific conflict is and how firmly the agreement on principle was secured at the end of stage 3. At this implementation stage the specific tactics of aggregation becomes more important than education or interest articulation.

Stage 4 may extend indefinitely, with new proposals being presented by the administrators to expand or gradually modify the original purposes of the program. In some cases, however, one may identify a stage 5, in which the program undergoes some crisis that leads many political and administrative actors to reassess the original intention of the program. For example, public assistance and public housing programs in the United States seemed to be undergoing such a crisis and reappraisal during the 1950s. This crisis may lead to a decline or a new departure in the program.[5]

This evolutionary model permits one to develop a strategy for policy innovation and a critique of the tactics frequently employed by reformers. Reformers, for example, may press for agreement on a specific proposal before there is generalized support for the program's principles. As a result there is not sufficient agreement on principle to weather the specific controversies that arise over the terms of implementation.

To cite another example, reformers often resort to activities that are more appropriate to an earlier stage of a program's development. It is common for reformers to relive the great-debate phase of development, even though the program has entered the implementation stage. Thus, when specific objections are raised to the terms of implementing proposals, the program's supporters often interpret this as an attack on the program's general virtues. The reformers resort to education when interest-aggregation tactics are required.

Supporters of policy innovation, to cite another tactical mistake, sometimes lose interest in a program once the great debate has produced agreement in principle. They either assume that approval in principle is the end of the fight or they recoil from the detailed, day-to-day tactics necessary to produce agreement on detailed proposals. In this way reformers abandon the field to the program's enemies and fail to provide the continuing support that the program needs.

The purpose of this digression into the natural history of policy programs is to clarify Metro Council's attitudes on various programs. The status of the four variables outlined above reflects a program's current stage of development. The fact that different policy programs in the same political system may be in different developmental stages helps explain why the structures of policy subsystems vary.

Policy Programs As Metro Subsystems

Table 4.1 summarizes the status of Metro's major programs in terms of the four variables defined above. Thus, Table 4.1 is an explanation of the data in Table 3.1. In assessing the degree of involvement, deference, and conflict over implementation, I found that rough, qualitative estimates, like low, moderate, and high, were sufficient to my purpose. Whether there is agreement in principle on a program is indicated with a simple Yes or No. Where there is disagreement in principle or conflict over detailed implementation, I indicate whether the conflicts occur along City-versus-suburbs lines (factional) or cut across these lines (nonfactional). The following pages merely explain and develop that table.

TABLE 4.1 Metro Council's Views on Major Policy Programs, Analyzed in Terms of Four Attitudinal Variables

Programs	Council Attitudes			
	Agreement in Principle	Degree of Involvement	Deference to Chairman	Conflict over Implementation
Construction Programs				
Subways	Yes	Mod.–High	Mod.	Mod.–High (SF)
Expressways	No (NF)	Low–Mod.	High	Mod. (NF)
Public housing	Yes	Low–Mod.	High	Low (NF)
Hospital grants	No (NF)	Low	High	Low (NF)
Other programs (roads, schools, sewers, water, homes for aged)	Yes	Mod.	High	Low (NF)
Service and Regulatory Programs				
TTC service, fares, subsidies	No (F)	Mod.–High	Mod.	High (F)
TTC appointments and reorganization	No (SF)	Low–Mod.	High	Mod. (SF)
Water rates	No (F)	High	Low–Mod.	High (F)
Police	Yes	Mod.	Mod.–High	Mod. (SF)
Licensing	Yes	Low–Mod.	Mod.–High	Mod. (NF)
Air-Pollution control	Yes	Low	High	Low (NF)
Future–of–Metro Issues				
Transferring powers to Metro level	No (F)	High	Low	High (SF)
Altering Metro's organization	No (F)	High	Low	High (F)

Key to abbreviations: F= factional, NF = nonfactional, SF = sometimes factional, Low-Mod. = low to moderate, Mod. = moderate, Mod.-High = moderate to high.

Construction programs were the least controversial because there was strong generalized support for these programs, a varying degree of involvement, high deference to leadership, and generally low conflict over the terms of detailed proposals. At the other end of the spectrum were issues relating to the future of Metro. On these issues there was little general agreement on principle, high involvement, low deference, and a high degree of conflict over detailed proposals. Service and regulatory issues stood between these two extremes.

Public Works Politics. Strong generalized support for construction programs is not unique to the Metro system or even to urban political systems. The popularity and dramatic appeal of public works projects have been noted in different nations and at different levels of government.[6] Such projects are visible to, and are used by, most members of the general public. In comparison the benefits of service programs are often less tangible and less apparent. Moreover, some service programs, like public assistance, benefit a particular segment of the population rather than the public at large. Construction projects inconvenience few people beyond displaced site residents and residents of adjacent neighborhoods, and these interests are often the least organized and articulate in urban politics. Regulatory programs, on the other hand, generally arouse the ire of vocal business groups or labor unions.

At the local or regional level there are two additional reasons for the strong support given to construction programs. First, there is civic pride, the economic development ideology, and rivalry with other cities. A subway or new city hall add to a city's external reputation and, it is thought, attract investment dollars. A major factor in the approval of an east–west subway was Metro Toronto's desire to keep ahead of Montreal in subway construction. Second, local improvements have been the traditional responsibility of municipal governments in North America. Agreement in principle was reached on most construction programs in the nineteenth century. Not only are welfare and regulatory programs of more recent vintage, but there are local officials who see some of these programs as provincial rather than local responsibilities. In this view only local improvements are appropriate charges on the property tax.

There was relatively little Council conflict over some of the newer construction programs, like subways and public housing, because agreements in principle had been secured in City politics prior to 1953. During the 1930s and 1940s, the City of Toronto had held its great debates on these two programs. In 1946, the TTC began construction on the area's first subway. Toronto began its first public housing project a few years later. Since none of the suburban officials on Metro Council questioned the general purpose of either program, one may say that Metro inherited a settlement in principle on public housing and subways.

Table 4.1 presents an estimate of the councilors' overall involvement in various construction programs, but at this point another dimension must be added to the involvement variable. Councilors were highly involved in the regional-parity aspects of all construction programs but weakly involved in the pacing, financing, and planning of particular projects. This focusing of involvement on the parity question helped minimize conflict in the construction field. As long as balance in the geographic distribution of public works were maintained, few legislative objections were raised to specific proposals.

Because of this focus on parity, public works politics was rarely a sum-zero game, in which victories for one side necessarily meant losses for the other.[7] The suburbanites favored water, sewer, road, and school projects; the City urged top priority for subways and public housing. But there was agreement in principle on all these programs. If parity were observed, neither bloc objected to the other bloc's pet projects. Suburban opposition to the east–west subway developed only because that project threatened to unbalance the regional distribution of capital expenditures.

Even though the typical Metro councilor supported most construction programs in principle, he would still oppose the location of an obnoxious project within his municipality. Thus, there was somewhat greater controversy over implementation in the case of obnoxious projects, like public housing, expressways, and water purification plants, than in the case of desirable projects, like roads, schools, and subways. Because most undesirable projects were located in the three outlying suburbs—the only municipalities in the area with large vacant sites—Council opposition to particular sites rarely exceeded two or three votes. All construction projects except the Spadina Expressway were approved by overwhelming majorities.

The Politics of Particular Construction Programs. Smaller variations in legislative attitude and behavior occurred within the public works field. The difference between obnoxious and desirable projects gave rise to some variations. In addition, expressways and hospital construction were exceptions to the general rule of agreement-in-principle on public works programs.

Metro's program of capital grants to hospitals in the region attracted far less legislative support than the other construction programs. Some councilors saw hospital construction as a welfare program and a responsibility of the senior governments. Since Metro grants accounted for a small part of total construction costs, moreover, councilors could not claim new hospitals as Council's achievement. But neither were the councilors strongly opposed to such grants. Overt conflict did not occur in this program because the lack of agreement in principle was neutralized by the councilors' low involvement. Council instituted these grants mainly under pressure from the province, without having agreed or even held a great debate on the program's principles.

Metro did not inherit a consensus on the expressways question. The chairman-cabinet proposal for a network of highways provoked a great debate on whether the trend away from public transit and toward the automobile could and should be checked.[8] The debate, however, occurred largely between the chairman and City officials, not among the legislators. Suburbanites supported the program in principle but were weakly involved. Overt conflict over expressways would have been far greater if the general issues had divided Council along factional lines.

Because of Gardiner's determination to secure approval of the expressways plan even in the absence of agreement on principle, the specific controversies over implementation were difficult to resolve. There was no political credit, in the form of generalized support for the program, to draw upon. Metro's first two expressways disturbed no residential neighborhood. But the proposed Spadina expressway, which would bisect two suburbs and slice through high-income neighborhoods in the City, provoked strong grass-roots opposition. Thus, opposition in principle and opposition to a particular route were compounded. Some councilors opposed Spadina because they were defending their municipalities and some because they objected to all expressways. However, the Spadina route controversy, like the more general controversy over expressways, cut across factional lines in Council.

Subway politics also had its distinctive features. As subways became the most expensive program in the capital budget, Council involvement in subway issues grew accordingly. The source of initial controversy in this field was not general principles but the specific terms of a financing plan. Since an east–west line would be located within Toronto, suburbanites saw this as a City project. Proceeding with the subway might tilt Metro's capital budgets in the City's favor and might force cutbacks in suburban projects. The suburban answer to this problem was to delay subway construction and, when Metro did proceed, to build subways at a leisurely pace. Suburbanites also wanted Metro to pay a small share, and the TTC a large share, of total construction costs. The City's program was to build subways right away, to build at a rate of about six miles a year, to divert expressway funds for subway purposes, and to break Gardiner's ceiling on borrowing if necessary. Subway financing was the only construction issue that produced factional conflict in Council. It was, incidentally, the only factional issue that Gardiner settled by splitting the difference between the demands of the two blocs.

After Gardiner secured Metro Council approval of a financing plan in 1957, that aspect of subway politics remained largely settled. Succeeding councils pursued and slightly modified this plan in approving additional projects. But as the financial issues were being settled, the route questions were being reopened. Since the technical people could not agree on routes, Council deference to leadership was low. Since subways were assuming a commanding position in the capital budget, Council involvement was high. By the early 1960s, councilors were demanding not only parity in the overall budget but parity within the subway program as well. Conflict over whether to pursue east–west or north–south routes resulted.

Thus, high involvement and low deference combined to produce a high degree of Council conflict over specific subway proposals. But subway controveries in the early 1960s were less factional than they had been in the 1950s. As subway construction was extended into the suburbs, and subways ceased being viewed as City projects, generalized Council support for the program became even stronger. This stronger generalized support gave the councilors added incentive to resolve the specific conflicts over implementation. Moreover, the route conflicts did not pit City against suburbs. Toronto aldermen from the east end of the City, for example, joined with eastern suburbanites in urging more east–west lines.

The councilors exhibited generalized support for public housing but weak interest in seeing the program implemented. Public housing, like hospital grants, was seen as a welfare program, aiding a special clientele rather than the public at large. The result was what some public housing advocates call "lip service." Everyone on Council praised the idea of public housing but few councilors challenged Gardiner's decision to place lesser priority on the housing program. At the same time few councilors were prepared to challenge housing projects if the chairman and cabinet advocated them.

City officials were less satisfied with Gardiner's modest housing program, but even these officials were more committed to

THE SYSTEM'S PERFORMANCE (CONT.)

seeing results in the subway field than in the public housing field. The cabinet's view that public housing projects should be located on vacant, suburban sites and should be used to reduce population density in Toronto probably dampened the City's enthusiasm for such projects.

The Politics of Metro Services. In comparison to public works issues there was far less agreement in principle on Metro's service questions. Thus, Metro held great debates on whether Council subsidies should be provided to offset the TTC's operating deficits; whether such subsidies, if provided, should be made conditional on the pursuit of certain transit policies; whether the TTC, no longer financially self-sustaining, had outlived its usefulness as an independent agency; and whether uniform or varying wholesale water rates should be charged to the municipalities. Because the Council was uncertain about whether the TTC should continue to exist and whether its tasks were political or administrative, Council could not agree on whether businessmen and transit experts or politicians should be named to the TTC Board. Nor did the councilors ever reach general agreement on what the appropriate City-suburban balance on the TTC Board should be.

Disagreement in principle on service issues was accompanied by low deference to leadership. Service issues were not seen as technical matters to the extent that construction issues were. Deference to the chairman was somewhat greater on TTC appointments, because it was felt that only the chairman could privately and discreetly sound out candidates. Deference was somewhat greater on TTC reorganizations issues because the provincial premier followed Gardiner's advice in approving or disapproving Metro requests for reorganization.

Involvement and deference varied inversely. The more involved a councilor was in a particular issue, the less willing he was to go along. Involvement by councilors tended to be high where the issue would have some direct impact on the area's tax rates. For this reason there was more involvement and controversy over service programs, financed by tax levies, than over construction programs, financed in the short run by borrowing. For the same reason there was greater involvement in service questions affecting tax bills—water rates and TTC subsidies—than in service questions having no immediate effect on tax rates —TTC reorganization and TTC appointments.

Most service issues divided the Council along factional lines. The suburbs, angry over the inadequacy of suburban bus service, opposed any TTC subsidy and urged steps to increase Metro control over the commission. The City wanted regular, unconditional subsidies to the TTC and no diminution in the TTC's independence. To the City, expanded Metro control over the TTC meant subordinating the subway program to Gardiner's allegedly pro-expressways policy. It also meant increased suburban pressure on the TTC to undertake unprofitable suburban bus lines.

Policing, seen partly as a regulatory and partly as a service program, shared some of the characteristics of transit service issues. The suburbs wanted better police protection and, as a means to that end, sought increased suburban representation on the police commission. But, since the City usually did not object to increased suburban representation or challenge suburban complains about inadequate police protection, policing issues proved to be less factional and less controversial than transit issues.

The setting of wholesale water rates was the most clearly factional issue that Metro dealt with in its first thirteen years. There were several reasons why this issue stirred such strong emotions. If Metro were to charge uniform wholesale rates to all municipalities, the result would be a substantial increase in the pre-1953 rates paid by City dwellers and a substantial decrease in suburban rates. Toronto officials thought that they were entitled to special consideration on rates because the City had provided Metro with a waterworks system and had received no compensation. To add insult to injury, Metro's initial capital budgets emphasized water and sewer projects in the suburbs. Furthermore, water rates *was* a sum-zero game. The province required that the water system be financially self-sustaining; giving special consideration to one municipality meant increasing the rates for all other municipalities.

Finally, agreement on implementing proposals was difficult to reach in the service area, because most of the demands came from one bloc. The City was largely content with the *status quo* in the service field. Meeting the suburban grievances over transit and police could not be accompanied by any comparable service improvement for the older parts of the metropolitan area. Since the outlying suburban sectors were already receiving slightly more than a fair share of the early capital budgets, improving their services would further imbalance the distribution of benefits. Moreover, meeting suburban service demands would require the chairman and Council to assume command over most of Metro's independent commissions. This Gardiner flatly opposed.

Regulatory Politics. Regulatory programs in the United States seem to follow a common evolutionary pattern.[9] The groups and individuals that join forces to seek general approval of a particular regulatory program dissolve once agreement in principle is secured. Thus, most regulatory agencies can count on only vague, amorphous support. The political officials support the program in theory but remain weakly involved in its implementation. The groups to be regulated, however, are intensely involved and highly vocal. To guarantee its political survival, the regulatory agency must come to terms with its interest group clientele, often by weakening the original purposes of the program.

Many aspects of this American model apply to the Metro experience in regulation. No one in Council questioned the general goals of the licensing, policing, and air pollution control programs, but no councilor was intensely committed to maintaining the integrity of the enforcement process. In fact, the councilors—particularly the City bloc—became the major political spokesmen for those groups with grievances against the licensing commission. No councilor was prepared to defend the licensing agency. All councilors agreed that the commission was high handed and all councilors favored proposals increasing Metro control of the agency.

The police commission shared some of the political liabilities of the licensing commission and other independent agencies. Council spoke for groups protesting police brutality or police censorship of political demonstrations. All councilors favored increasing Council's representation on the police commission. On the whole, however, councilors showed more respect for policing than licensing. Dramatic incidents like a kidnapping or crime wave would periodically demonstrate the public's stake in tough enforcement and would revivify the Council's general support for the policing program. No such incidents occurred in the licensing field. Councilors also demonstrated greater support for policing because it was viewed partly as a service program.

Council had far less sympathy for the groups regulated by the air pollution control program (big business) than for the small businessmen and tradesmen regulated by the licensing commission. Pollution control, moreover, was a responsibility of the works department and was under Council's direct control. Thus, the pollution control program operated largely without legislative criticism. What the program lacked were funds for enforcement and sufficiently stiff penalties to deter violations. A surface calm characterized the pollution control program, but this harmony was largely predicated on the program's limited goals and limited budget. The lack of tough enforcement and stiff penalties may explain why the regulated industries did not protest more passionately. The councilors, though not inclined to press for stiffer enforcement, probably would have supported such a move if advanced by the works commissioner and the Metro chairman. But the works commissioner doubted whether Metro could achieve much in this field without substantial provincial intervention. (In 1966, the commissioner apparently altered his thinking. He presented to Council a new pollution control bylaw, increasing the penalties and providing for more elaborate enforcement.)

The Politics of Metro Reorganization. By far the most controversial issues were those that seemed to the councilors to bear on the future of the Metro federal system. On these matters deference to the chairman was low, agreement in principle was small or nonexistent, involvement was intense, and Council was divided along factional lines on both general principles and detailed proposals.

All proposals to alter the distribution of powers between Metro and the municipal governments fell into the above category. From the outset the City bloc decided to support any transfer of powers from the municipal to the Metro level, in the hope that municipal responsibilities would be gradually whittled away and that total amalgamation would be achieved in piecemeal fashion. The suburbs decided to oppose any such transfers and to fight "creeping amalgamationism." Thus, the City supported and the suburbs opposed transfer to the Metro level of: police, licensing, air pollution control, fire protection, and welfare responsibilities. Suburban opposition to transfer was more intense in areas (e.g., police and fire protection) where the suburbs already maintained active programs of their own and where transfer would have meant dissolving important suburban departments. The suburbs were slightly more amenable to the transfer of regulatory programs, since transfers in this field would not increase tax rates; the transfer of a service program, however, was usually followed by an upgrading of service standards in some municipalities and an overall increase in area spending for that service. The debate over welfare amalgamation was particularly bitter because suburbanites thought that Metro, by instituting assistance programs throughout the area, would make it possible for more welfare cases to move to the suburbs.

Factional conflict on transfer issues would have been greater had not the City later changed its strategy. In the late 1950s and early 1960s, the City opposed the transfer of traffic control, urban redevelopment and renewal, public housing, and off-street parking powers. Raising these powers to the Metro level would have had little effect on suburban governments and suburban employees, but it would have meant the dissolution of major City agencies. If these four powers were shifted to Metro, some City politicians said, the Toronto councilmen would be left with little to occupy their time and with small justification for their salaries. The details of traffic and parking policies, moreover, stood at the center of neighborhood politics and aldermanic elections; aldermen were loathe to lose control of these decisions. Finally, since the City had decided at that time to renew its bid to the province for total amalgamation, some City leaders thought that Metro should be denounced not strengthened. The suburbs were opposed to the transfer of traffic control, were cool to the transfer of urban renewal, and were open to persuasion on the transfer of public housing and off-street parking. In 1963, when fire and welfare amalgamation again came forward, the earlier City-versus-suburbs alignment reappeared.

Proposals to alter the structure of the Metro government produced strong controversy and stalemate. The City remained opposed to the federal idea; the suburbs would only concede that federalism was better than amalgamation. No single plan for redistributing the seats on Metro Council could gain more than a handful of votes. No agreement could be secured on proposals to rearrange municipal boundaries in the area. On some reform issues Metro Council's failure to act reflected a legislative consensus. Except for a brief period when City officials flirted with the notion of a popularly elected chairman, all councilors opposed changes in the status of that office. All councilors opposed the direct election of Council and favored continuing the system of *ex officio* membership.

Some substantive issues were made highly controversial by being redefined as structural issues. In the case of fluoridation, to cite the leading example, what began as a public health issue was redefined by several suburbanites as a Metro-versus-municipal issue. The suburbanites saw the move as a further accretion in Metro's powers and insisted that fluoridation was a prerogative of the municipalities as the retail distributors of water. City politicos, even though they had refused to institute fluoridation in Toronto prior to 1953, uniformly supported this move, for the same reasons that the suburbs opposed it. (Thus, in Tables 3.1 and 4.1, fluoridation votes are included in the transfer-of-powers category.) Fluoridation was carried without any major consideration being given by Council to the public health aspects of the question.

Policy Outputs

Policy Outputs and Gardiner's Leadership. The most succinct way of characterizing policy outputs during 1953–1961 is to say that Gardiner's version of policy invariably prevailed. Gardiner suffered only two major reversals on the floor, and on both these issues his viewpoint eventually won out.

If one were to examine only action on the floor, Gardiner would appear invincible, and his intentions would accord perfectly with Metro's policy outputs. But the more important part of Gardiner's strategy involved decisions about which issues to bring forward and which to keep out of Council. The way in which these decisions were made provide the key to an understanding of Metro's policy output between 1953 and 1961.

A variety of factors—the demands of the cabinet, Council's attitudes on policy, Gardiner's personal policy preferences, and his interpretation of effective integrative strategy—impelled Gardiner to give first priority to construction programs. Within the Council there was minimum controversy over these programs. No other type of program could provide such tangible and dramatic demonstrations of Metro's utility to the municipalities. No other program would win municipal support or tolerance for the Metro system so quickly. In the public works field the problem was simple: a lack of roads, schools, and similar facilities. The solution was just as simple: build the necessary structures. By comparison problems in the nonconstruction programs seemed more subtle, and the solutions more elusive. In addition, such "soft" programs provided intangible benefits, aided a special clientele within the general public, and generated more controversy in Council. Quick returns were ruled out in some welfare programs, like public housing, by the laborious nature of intergovernmental negotiations.

Thus, Gardiner's personal preferences dovetailed with tactical considerations. To both Gardiner and the councilors, achieving results meant building projects. The type of issues that Gardiner saw as more divisive—reform, service, and regulatory questions —were also the issues that Gardiner personally considered less important.

There was a minimum amount of conflict between the adaptive and integrative needs of the Metro system in the area of public works. The technical and political personnel agreed that the metropolitan area needed extensive public construction. As long as parity considerations were met, the politicians on Council left the detailed planning of projects to the cabinet. As a result there was little conflict between the long-range planning of projects and the operation of democratic politics.[10] Political demands, mainly relating to the geographic distribution of capital budgets, could be met without damaging the integrity of the long-range plan.

Proceeding with construction projects, therefore, meant strengthening both the integration and the problem-solving achievements of the system. In that sense the common commitment of the councilors, the chairman, and the cabinet to construction programs was functional to the system. But this common commitment also explains why gaps in issue initiation, left by the cabinet, were not filled by the councilors or the chairman. If the cabinet had neglected public works issues, these other actors probably would have stepped in to fill the gap. But it was precisely in this construction field that the cabinet needed little assistance. The chairman and councilors were too weakly committed to the "soft" programs to provide the initiative where it was needed.

Adaptive and integrative considerations came into sharpest

conflict over the question of increasing Metro's powers. The cabinet saw additional transfers of power as essential to the solution of regional problems. Gardiner, although personally agreeing with the cabinet on most transfers, insisted on deferring to Council opinion. In this policy area Gardiner subordinated his personal views to tactical considerations. Structural reform was the area of Gardiner's smallest achievements.

The chairman's personal policy preferences and integrative tactics coincided in the service and regulatory fields. Gardiner personally believed in the need for independent commissions in some policy areas, but also thought that keeping most service and regulatory issues out of Council would promote Council unity. These views often brought him into conflict with one or both blocs in Council. Gardiner proved successful in these policy areas because he was fighting defensive actions. Majorities could very seldom be mustered over his opposition, and Gardiner could always use his informal veto at the provincial level as a last resort.

While Gardiner's views on service and regulatory questions brought him into conflict with various elements in Council, these views did not weaken his ability to maintain a middle position between the two blocs. He disagreed with the suburbanites on transit and police questions and on the continued independence of these two agencies; he disagreed with the City on continued independence for the licensing commission and on the need for TTC subsidies.

Council and cabinet did not agree on the independent commission question. No single proposal could have increased the satisfaction of both integrative and adaptive actors. The councilors were most eager to see increased Metro control of licensing and police; the cabinet wanted increased Metro control of public transit.

The Evolution of Policy Programs. Another way of characterizing policy output is to describe the extent of program development measured in terms of my evolutionary model.

Gardiner preferred securing specific majorities for specific proposals and avoiding debates on general principles. On matters dividing Council along factional lines, Gardiner did not think that he could advocate general principles and still maintain his position as flexible middle man. On most issues Gardiner believed that the more specific the proposal, and the more circumscribed the debate, the greater chance of that proposal being approved. Debates on general principle, he thought, were too emotional and too damaging to Council unity. Even when he sought to implement a long-range cabinet plan, Gardiner took the projects one at a time and refused to have Council consider the general purposes of the plan. On the whole Gardiner did not attempt to alter the councilors' general attitudes on policy programs.

This pragmatic style made the chairman particularly adept at working out detailed settlements in areas where agreement in principle already existed. Under Gardiner's leadership most construction programs moved from the agreement in principle stage to the implementation stage. But this strategy was poorly designed to secure agreement in principle where it did not exist. Where agreement in principle was lacking, Gardiner either kept the issue out of Council (as in the case of most service, regulatory, and reform issues) or pressed ahead with implementation in the absence of general agreement (as in the case of expressways).

With two exceptions those programs that lacked general agreement in 1953 still lacked that agreement in 1961—and in 1965, it might be added. The water rates issue was settled in principle by the adoption of uniform rates in 1959. Air pollution is discussed below. On the other unsettled issues Metro Council either did not hold or did not resolve its great debates.

The case of air pollution control suggests that attempts to skip stages or telescope development may produce weaknesses in a program. The pollution control program emerged from obscurity to quick recognition, agreement in principle, and implementation, all within two years. But approval in principle was too quickly and too lightly given; and the program was then relegated to the background. A prolonged and searching debate might have cemented stronger loyalties to the program and might have encouraged some councilors to press for stiffer enforcement in succeeding years.

It has been argued by one astute observer, Albert Rose, that Metro under Gardiner tackled and solved only the "easy problems."[11] In several senses this is true. Gardiner emphasized the least controversial programs—public works. He confined his floor-leading efforts to securing the implementation of generally agreed-on programs. Where general agreement was lacking, he did not try to secure it. He left to his successor a host of unsettled issues in the more difficult areas of regulation, services, and structural reform. Gardiner's success as chairman must be seen in this context.

"Spillover" and the Autonomy of Policy Subsystems. Gardiner's integrative strategy and his image of Metro's future development were analogous to the position taken by gradualists on questions of international organization.[12] Gardiner, like the gradualists, believed that an international organization could be strengthened by degrees, if the noncontroversial issues were dealt with first and the divisive issues put off. The satisfactory resolution of the easy issues and the obvious achievements of the system in these fields would increase member loyalties and would subsequently make the controversial issues easier to resolve. In time all the issues that Gardiner deferred could be settled by Metro Council, but it was first necessary to build up a reservoir of good will. The effect that Gardiner hoped to produce is often referred to as "spillover."[13]

Spillover did not occur in the Metro system. The ease with which construction programs were implemented did not make the nonconstruction issues any more tractable. Metro's achievements in public works helped produce municipal tolerance for the Metro system, and this tolerance helped create a spillover effect within the construction field. Satisfaction with one's share of the capital budget made one inclined to go along with construction projects located in other municipalities. But because

Council attitudes on "soft" programs differed significantly from Council attitudes on works programs, there was no spillover of good will from the construction field to the nonconstruction field. The fact that policy areas constituted partially self-contained subsystems limited the extent of spillover from one policy area to another. Negative spillover was more likely to occur. The bitterness engendered by an emotional debate might impede issue resolution for the remainder of Council's annual session.

In general terms, and despite some specific successes on the floor, Gardiner's gradualist strategy was a failure.

Gardiner and Allen: The Interaction of Role, Personality, and Situation

Role. In general terms the behavior of William Allen as Metro chairman followed the pattern set by Gardiner. The large areas of similarity in the behavior of these two men suggest that Gardiner's style as chairman had become institutionalized. Gardiner had created certain expectations among the other Metro actors and had demonstrated the utility of certain tactics; successors to that office would inherit both the expectations and the proven strategies.

All the major participants in the Metro system expected Allen to set the agenda of Metro politics and to pilot measures through Council. The councilors, the press, and the interest groups continued to assume that the administration would lead and that the chairman was the head of the administration. Allen would have been strongly criticized for retreating to the role of a presiding officer.

But Allen clearly was committed to playing a leadership role. He needed no convincing on this point. Furthermore, Allen was committed to playing this leadership role largely through the tactics that Gardiner had employed: the emphasis on legislative rather than extralegislative support, the reliance on *ad hoc* majorities in Council, the use of an issue-by-issue approach, the preference for construction programs, and the maintenance of a middle position between the City and suburban blocs. This strategy commended itself to Allen because it had worked for Gardiner and because there seemed little reason to abandon it. For the same reasons Allen continued the essential features of Gardiner's administrative strategy. Allen interacted regularly with the cabinet, assumed the responsibilities of a chief administrator, stressed the need for professionals in the top administrative positions, and deferred to the experts' policy proposals. The change in chairmen occurred without any disturbance in administrative operations or changes in administrative personnel. Allen worked with Gardiner's cabinet.

Personality. Much of the continuity in the behavior of these two chairmen is attributable not to an institutionalized role but to similarities in the personal styles and viewpoints of the two men. Gardiner, though not taking a public stand, apparently had a major part in naming his successor. He preferred Allen because Allen agreed with most of Gardiner's views on substantive policy and the Metro system and because Allen was both willing and able to execute the tactics that Gardiner thought necessary.

On some substantive policies Allen's views differed from those of his predecessor. These distinctive Allen viewpoints brought the chairman closer to the cabinet's views on policy and eliminated some nonstructural tension that had existed between Gardiner and his cabinet. Allen, for example, was far more sympathetic than Gardiner had been to the cause of public housing and to the transfer of public housing, urban renewal, public assistance, and off-street parking powers to the Metro level. On the matter of TTC reorganization, the new chairman was willing to see Metro Council expand its control over the commission but would not consider abolishing the agency as the Metro planning commissioner urged.

Allen's distinctive viewpoints on public policy did not increase or decrease the overall level of tensions that had existed between Council and chairman during Gardiner's years. Allen's willingness to breach Gardiner's debt ceiling made him more popular with both blocs in the Council. In conceding that the suburban complaints about inadequate police and transit service were legitimate grievances and appropriate matters for Council to deal with, Allen won suburban support without greatly antagonizing City officials. But his advocacy of increased powers for Metro stirred up controversies that Gardiner had carefully avoided. Allen, moreover, made a significant effort to fill Metro's problem-solving gap by directing attention to nonconstruction programs. His attempts to secure some general accord in the transit service field and to make public assistance a Metro responsibility generated some of the sharpest controversies that Council had experienced. It is important to add that Allen's viewpoints, though somewhat different from Gardiner's, did not coincide with the views of any one bloc. Despite his background in City politics, Allen retained the tradition of the chairman as middle man.

The most significant difference between Allen and Gardiner related to procedural strategy in Council. Allen gave first priority to the administrative aspects of his role. He performed the floor leader aspects less carefully, less consciously, and less consistently than Gardiner. Debate in Council after 1961 was less controlled and the final Council action less predictable than had been the case in earlier years. Allen still set the agenda and presented issues to Council. In comparison to Gardiner, however, Allen less often adjusted his decisions on timing and pace to the moods of Council, less often anticipated specific objections to proposals in order to forestall amendments on the floor, less often canvassed votes in advance to avoid surprises on the floor, and less often made use of persuasion and negotiation to consciously construct large majorities. Allen was more aggressive in Council when defending the administration against criticism. In addition, his legislative style departed less from Gardiner's in those policy areas, like public housing and public transit, where Allen was personally committed to achieving results.

Within the administrative branch Allen's powers, though still informal or nonstatutory, rivaled those of a strong mayor. In the Council, however, Allen behaved more like a city manager, whose main responsibilities were protecting the administration

[123]

from political interference or attack and proposing issues so that Council might dispose of them.

Allen apparently enjoyed the administrative aspects of his role more than the legislative. Furthermore, he believed that Council should not and could not be as closely controlled as it had been under Gardiner. The councilors, Allen thought, were becoming less and less inclined to tolerate the tough tactics that had prevailed in Metro's early years.[14]

On many issues Allen permitted, and even encouraged, department heads to fend for themselves in legislative politics. The new chairman did not insist on being the sole link between the legislature and administration, although he apparently did insist that department heads clear it with him before proceeding on their own. In 1965, it appeared that some department heads had begun to build stable relations with the chairmen of the Council committees overseeing their departments and with members of the Executive Committee.

Effectiveness. There were no significant differences in the behavior of Gardiner and Allen as chief administrator. If we define a successful head of administration as one who builds and maintains the morale, commitment, and efficiency of his administrative personnel, both men were equally successful in this chief administrator role.[15] The professional planners, it seems, were more dissatisfied than other actors in the administrative branch, but the planners were no more dissatisfied with one chairman than the other. Neither Gardiner nor Allen gave to the planners the central role in administrative coordination they thought they deserved.

By any criterion of success Allen was less effective than Gardiner as floor leader. Allen, more often surprised by the extent of floor opposition to his proposals, undertook more strategic retreats. In four years Allen suffered more than twice the number of floor defeats on important proposals than Gardiner had suffered in over eight years. Even many of Allen's victories were carried by the type of close vote that Gardiner eschewed. Allen used the tie-breaking vote twice as often as Gardiner in less than half the number of years. Close votes often proved to be pyrrhic victories. Votes of this kind always left a residue of bitterness that spilled over into other issues. Moreover, the province would not agree to a Metro request unless a good-sized Council majority had supported the request.

Allen proved less than successful in his attempt to draw Metro Council into a greater emphasis on "soft" programs. The City sabotaged the moves to transfer off-street parking, urban renewal, and public housing powers. Welfare amalgamation passed Council; but, because the vote was 13 to 11, provincial officials refused to add their assent. Allen also tried but failed to settle general questions in the public transit field. His plan to provide annual operating subsidies to the TTC, if the commission agreed to expand suburban bus service, died in Executive Committee. Shifting his emphasis, Allen then urged that Council become responsible mainly for the capital (i.e., subway) costs and that the TTC be left to meet operating deficits by its own devices. But Allen could not convince the suburbs that Metro should assume a large part of the TTC's outstanding capital debt and could not convince City officials that TTC deficits should be met by fare increases.

Allen also was less successful than Gardiner had been in fighting dilatory or defensive actions. Allen could not prevent the City bloc and a handful of suburbanites from approving a 1963 subsidy to the TTC. Nor could he prevent passage—and provincial approval—of a resolution giving Metro Council the power to name members of the licensing commission. Compared to his predecessor, Allen, a Liberal, had far less influence over the Ontario cabinet and hence far less influence over the Council on reorganization issues.

By 1965, Metro seemed to have reached an impasse on policy outputs. Councilors could agree to continue and expand the constructions programs initiated during Metro's first five years, but would not explore new policy areas. Allen proved largely un-successful in his attempt to assert the importance of welfare, service, and reform questions.

Situation. Local newspapermen and other informed observers were inclined to attribute all the differences in Gardiner's and Allen's legislative achievements to differences in the personalities and tactical skills of these two men. This heavy stress on personal factors is inaccurate—not to mention unfair to Allen. There also are situational factors that help explain why the accomplishments of 1961–1965 were not as dramatic as those of the earlier period.

First, Allen was trying to achieve breakthroughs in the most controversial areas of policy. Contrary to Gardiner's hopes, initial solution of the easy problems did not make the service, regulatory, and reform problems any more amenable to settle-ment. Second, the impressive degree of personal influence that Gardiner had commanded at the provincial level, based partly on his activism in the Conservative Party and partly on his long-time friendship with Premier Leslie Frost, was unlikely to be dupli-cated by any succeeding Metro chairman. Third, Allen had to face more aggressive City leadership, particularly during 1963, than Gardiner had had to contend with in any of his years as chairman. Because the chairman's persuasive tactics were most effective when bloc lines were fluid, the presence of forceful bloc leaders detracted from the chairman's success as floor leader.[16] Gardiner was fortunate in this respect; Allen was not.

The most important situational factor limiting Allen's legis-lative effectiveness was the reopening of the Metro organization issue in 1962. City officials, having decided to renew their cam-paign for total amalgamation, refused to cooperate with the Metro system, opposed any enhancement in its powers, and sought to disparage its achievements. After the province indi-cated that it was considering a review commission on Metro's future, Council politics virtually came to a halt. This hiatus was to last over three years. Councilors were unwilling to make any major policy decisions until they knew what Metro's new structure would look like. Moreover, each municipality inflated its grievances against the Metro system in order to extract more concessions from the province at the final, decision-making stage of reorganization.

The Future of the Metro Chairman's Role. If my earlier analysis of the chairman's role is correct, the legislative and administrative aspects of the role are interdependent. No occupant of that office could choose to ignore one aspect of the role without destroying the other aspect. A chairman who lost the support of the administrative personnel would find it increasingly difficult to build legislative majorities for his proposals. More relevant to the present problem, a chairman who ceased building legislative majorities for the cabinet's proposals would soon see his control of the administration crumble.

Allen, partly for personal and partly for situational reasons, came dangerously close to ignoring the legislative aspects of his role. In the short run, and viewed from the outside, Allen's legislative style seemed to have no effect on administrative morale. It is likely, however, that cabinet discontent with Metro Council's policy impasse was accumulating. If Allen were to continue that style, administrators probably would be further encouraged to seek out their own alliances, cabinet unity would be shaken apart, Metro would lose the benefits of role differentiation, and the chairman's legislative influence would be further diminished by his inability to speak for the experts. As the centrifugal forces in the bureaucracy were let loose, the chairman's *de facto* control of the administrative branch would dwindle. Within the Council the standing committees, particularly the Executive Committee, probably would become more important, all at the expense of the chairman's legislative influence. Closer ties would develop between the chairmen of committees and the department heads.

One crucial question, in assessing the future development of the Metro system, is what direction Allen's style will take after the reorganization issue is settled. If Allen's behavior between 1961 and 1965 reflected personal factors more than situational factors, there should be no change in his style. If uncertainty over Metro's future were the more important determinant, Allen may move to break the policy impasse and to reassert the importance of the chairman's floor-leading activities.

Over the longer run the informal and largely noninstitutionalized nature of the chairman's role may be a basic weakness of the Metro system, particularly in view of how important the chairman has been in making the system operate successfully. Of course, the effectiveness of any political role depends partly on the personality and skills of individual occupants. But in the case of weakly institutionalized roles, where very little is required of occupants, the reliance on personality and skills is far greater. Individual chairmen have wide latitude to define the role as they see fit. Future chairmen, like Allen, might prefer the administrative (or "command") side of the role to the legislative (or "negotiation and persuasion") side.[17] If this preference persisted, the role of chairman would lose its central importance in the Metro system.

CHAPTER 5

INDEPENDENT
POLICY–MAKING
SUBSYSTEMS

The functional approach to the study of bureaucratic or administrative organizations is basically concerned with the problems of organizational survival and success.[1] Administrative organizations are seen as having two functions: the maintenance of internal solidarity, which Parsons calls the "managerial" problem and which I call the "integrative" problem; and the linking of organization to environment, which Parsons sometimes calls the "external" or "political" problem and which I call the "adaptive" problem. Thus, the terms "integrative" and "adaptive" acquire different connotations when applied to administrative subsystems. For example, in the Metro system adaptation could be equated with problem solving; in administrative subsystems adaptation involved the political survival of the organization. In Metro as a whole integrative considerations were generally synonymous with political or representative considerations; in administrative subsystems an integrative orientation often was a commitment to the values of the technical staff and to problem solving.

The survival and growth of an administrative organization depend on how successfully it performs its assigned tasks, whether it seeks out new tasks, and whether the organization makes any unrecognized but important contributions to other systems. The maintenance of a benign environment and the securing of continued inputs from other systems are seen as preconditions to the attainment of internal integration. The functional approach also suggests that there will be a persistent—and not permanently soluble—tension between the internal and external needs of an organization. Analysis is centered on the organization's leadership stratum, for it is at this level that the internal and external needs of the organization converge. The functional problems of the organization, then, may be viewed as problems in administrative leadership and strategy.

I have added to Parsons' analysis, the notion of policy equilibrium. A policy equilibrium exists when the administrative leaders have found a set of organizational goals and strategies that largely satisfy both internal and external demands. Searches for new policies tend to occur when there is a perceived strain between internal and environmental demands, that is, when a policy equilibrium has been destroyed.[2]

The following pages attempt to demonstrate the utility of this approach and at the same time describe policy-making subsystems that stand more or less outside the chairman-cabinet-Council network. Preceding chapters equated the chairman, cabinet, and Council with the Metro system; an account of independent subsystems will qualify that generalization. Particular attention is devoted to the TTC for two reasons, one theoretical and one substantive. The TTC provides an interesting case study of how policy equilibriums break down and how new ones are sought. Furthermore, the pattern of transit politics departed significantly from the low-pressure pattern that characterized the Metro system as a whole.

The Toronto Transit Commission

McBrien's System. The Toronto Transportation Commission was created in 1921 to operate public transit in the City of Toronto. It was to be a financially self-sustaining and politically independent public corporation. The Toronto Transportation Commission's governing body was a board of three commissioners, appointed for overlapping, three-year terms by the Toronto City

Council. During the pre-Metro years, the commission operated bus services in many of the suburbs under contractual agreements with these municipalities. In 1953, when it became responsible for all public transit in the Metro area, its name was changed to the Toronto Transit Commission, its governing board was enlarged to five, and power to appoint commissioners was vested in the Metro Council.

For almost thirty years, until his death in 1954, William C. McBrien served as the chairman of the board and as undisputed leader of the transportation system. During the McBrien years transit politics was remarkably free of controversy. McBrien found a set of policies that met his own personal preferences and that reconciled the internal and external needs of the commission.

McBrien's long-range external strategy was to build up support among the press and interest groups for public transit in general and subway construction in particular. Owing largely to McBrien's persistent, proselytizing efforts and his ability to enlist the aid of all three Toronto newspapers, the need for subway construction and the evils of expressway construction became unquestioned gospel in the Toronto area. The chairman's tactics also explain why local interest groups became more involved in transit than in other policy areas and why public transit politics represented an exception to the low-pressure politics that characterized Metro as a whole. Thus, the transportation commission was the only City administrative agency, and later the only Metro agency, that had its own independent sources of political support.

The price of this support might have been interest group intervention in transportation policy making and a resulting loss of organizational autonomy. But McBrien sought and attained a united front within his commission, so that external groups would not have the opportunity to intervene. The other commissioners, respecting McBrien's long tenure on the commission and his skill in external affairs, deferred to his leads on transportation policy. "Maintaining TTC unity" really meant closing ranks behind McBrien's interpretation of the situation.

McBrien also gained interest group support for the notion that the transportation commission, in order to prosecute a bold, expansionist policy, had to remain independent of the timid and perhaps pro-expressway City councilors. McBrien's emphasis on an independent and expansionist organization met the demands of all the internal groups: the other commissioners, the technical staff, and the unionized labor force. The genius of McBrien's policy program was that it united the organization's desire to survive and expand with the local groups' interest in seeing dramatic subway projects built.

At the same time McBrien gave the technical staff wide discretion to set transit policies on all but the most general level. Tension between board and staff—the problem of discerning where policy ended and administration began—was usually settled in the staff's favor.

The City Council respected McBrien's demand for independence and made its appointments to the commission's board without conditions or warnings. Incumbents were returned to the board with little debate. When the commission made requests of Council, they were usually granted. Of course this political independence rested largely on the commission's fiscal independence. In addition, so little controversy surrounded transit issues, and so few threats to independence were made, because transit service generally met the demands of neighborhood groups. The commission added to its popularity, both in Council and in the community at large, by financing the first subway entirely out of its own accumulated surpluses.

The Challenge to McBrien's System, 1953–1954. Bill 80 presented several threats to the policies and strategies that McBrien had pursued. The TTC was to become responsible for all suburban bus lines, most of which yielded operating deficits. Though expected to maintain its financial self-sufficiency, the TTC was not provided with subsidies or compensation for these new unprofitable suburban routes. If McBrien wanted a subsidy, moreover, he would have to deal not with the friendly City Council but with a council containing twelve new suburban faces. The suburbs would expect better transit service and, with half the seats in Metro Council, would be in a position to enforce that expectation. This conflict might even reach within the TTC. The Board of Commissioners was to be expanded from three to five, and it was tacitly understood by all members of Metro Council that the two new appointees would be suburbanites.

There also were problems unrelated to Bill 80. As transit riding declined sharply after 1945, the TTC's operating surpluses and its financial self-sufficiency disappeared. By the early 1950s, the TTC could not balance its operating budget, let alone continue subway construction.

Before his death in 1954, McBrien indicated in what directions the TTC's future strategy should move. This new formula was consistent with his earlier emphasis on an expansive organization and dramatic subway projects. The decline in transit riding and the appearance of operating deficits should be met not with higher fares or retrenchment in services but with an ambitious subway construction program. The Metro Council should agree to an immediate start on an east–west subway and should pay for a substantial part of the construction costs. Metro's substantial involvement in subway financing, however, was not to be accompanied by any diminution in TTC independence. The commission would plan the subways, and Metro would help pay the bills.

Preservation of the TTC's policy-making autonomy was one reason why McBrien sought Metro assistance in the capital rather than operating field. Annual operating subsidies, he thought, would lead to Metro interference in TTC policy making and eventually to the abolition of the independent transit commission. Subsidies would be accepted only if Metro Council offered them and placed no conditions on their acceptance.

This refusal to meet the decline in patronage with cuts in wages or in the size of the TTC labor force won praise from the transport workers' union and the Toronto and District Labour Council. The TTC technical staff and the interest group constituency were pleased with the emphasis on subways as the solution to the public transit crisis and the emphasis on TTC control of subway planning.

Suburban bus service was McBrien's most difficult problem. If the TTC insisted on a fiscally sound basis of decision making and refused to undertake any route that did not pay its own way, suburban opposition to the TTC might reach a danger point and spill over into Metro Council. But meeting most suburban requests would mean running up large deficits, going to Council for subsidies, and inviting Metro interference in TTC policy making.

McBrien's bus service policy was designed to quiet suburban demands without actually meeting them. There would be no retrenchment in the pre-1953 level of suburban service, even though many of the suburban lines were not self-sustaining. But neither would there be any dramatic improvement in suburban service. Suburban bus routes would be extended slowly, as the density of the suburban population increased. A fare-zone system would be immediately instituted so that short-trip riders, mainly City dwellers, did not indirectly subsidize long-trip riders, mainly suburbanites.

As a support-securing strategy this compromise failed. Announcement of this policy was followed by a barrage of motions in Metro Council aimed at abolishing the TTC, stripping it of its power to plan bus routes, or compelling it to expand suburban service. McBrien was inclined to dismiss these suburban complaints, perhaps because he was used to dealing with a friendly City Council and because he remained pro-City in his personal orientations. What saved the TTC in 1954 was Gardiner's ability to delay or defeat the suburban motions. Informally, Gardiner told the TTC that it should at least receive briefs from the suburban municipalities and appear to be considering them.

Suburban officials remained the TTC's permanent opposition in Council. Since the smaller, inlying suburbs were content with their bus service and were located wholly or partly within the first fare zone, they usually voted with the City in support of the TTC. Thus, McBrien's strategies produced a friendly majority of about fifteen councilors and the militant opposition of about nine.

Role Differentiation within the TTC Board. During most of its history as a Metro agency, the TTC was internally divided over the question of whether McBrien's aggressive strategy should be continued. Behind this question was a growing conflict in the demands of the TTC board's internal and external constituencies. The technical staff apparently favored some moderation in McBrien's tactics, since the author was not available to carry them out. The supportive interest groups urged a continuation and perhaps intensification of the aggressive strategy.

In response to this conflict two distinct roles emerged among the TTC commissioners. (A list of the commissioners is pre-

TABLE 5.1   Members of the Board of the Toronto Transit
Commission, 1953–1965

Member	Tenure	Chairman	Major Career Prior to TTC Appointment[a]
William McBrien[b]	1953–54	1953–54	Business
William Russell[b]	1953–63	1954–55	Labor
Charles Walton[b]	1953–	1959–60	Politics (and business)
J. A. Scythes	1953–60		Business
Clive Sinclair	1953–60		Business (and politics)
Allan Lamport	1954–60	1955–59	Politics (and business)
Ford Brand	1960–		Politics (and labor)
Clarence Downey	1960–	1960–63	Business (and politics)
Gordon Secord	1960–63		Business
Ralph Day	1963–	1963–	Business and public administration (and politics)
Douglas Hamilton	1963–		Labor

[a] Since some businessmen dabble in politics and since most local politicians maintain their private businesses, law practices, or trade union positions after winning elective office, it is necessary to distinguish the major or more recent career (stated first) and the subsidiary career (stated in parenthesis) of each commissioner.

[b] The three members of the old Toronto Transportation Commission who were reappointed to the new Metro TTC.

sented in Table 5.1.) The politico, like Allan Lamport or Ford Brand, came to the TTC from an elective office or from the labor movement, maintained his close association with interest groups and politicians after joining the board, and emphasized the importance of harmonious relations between the TTC and the political community. Because the politico held more pronounced opinions on transit policy at the time of his appointment to the board, he was less likely to defer to the leads of the technical staff. In fact, politicos were inclined to see the technical staff "usurping the powers of the board" and to favor curbs on the staff's discretion. Although at odds with the technical staff, the politico was still responsive to the demands of the TTC's unionized labor force and was often the subject of praise from the Toronto Labour Council.

The administrator, like Clarence Downey, Ralph Day, or J. A. Scythes, had spent most of his career in business or public administration, emphasized the importance of the TTC's internal solidarity and morale, spoke more about an efficient organization than an expanding one, and usually deferred to the leads of the technical staff. As a result, the technical staff informally backed administrators as candidates for TTC chairman. In electing a chairman, the board's choice was often between a candidate who could better secure staff support and a candidate who would be more effective in dealing with the political environment.

The politico, who held stronger views on transit policy, was more likely to initiate issues within the board. Although all commissioners were loyal to the organization, the politicos were also loyal to substantive policies. The administrators' loyalties were more to the organization *per se*. If a majority of the commissioners pursued policies the politico opposed, he would not hesitate to denounce the leadership, even if this factionalism damaged the organization's external reputation. The two types of commissioners also differed on whether overt conflict within the board was proper. The politicos viewed the board as a small municipal council; the administrators viewed it as the board of directors of a business corporation. In their attempt to preserve the organization's united front, the administrators often acceded to the politicos' demands. Thus, the politicos exerted an influence over TTC policy far out of proportion to their numbers on the board.

The politico was more likely to be a City spokesman. He either initiated his own candidacy or had his candidacy urged upon the Metro chairman by City officials. The administrator was more likely to be a suburbanite, recruited by the chairman in order to provide the board with more business—administrative experience and more suburban representation. This pattern of appointments explains why there were no militant suburban spokesmen on the board and why the board was not divided by City-suburban conflict. The suburbanites on the board were administrators, who favored decision making on a fiscally sound basis and thus opposed expansion of unprofitable suburban bus routes. (Even the administrators, however, did not favor eliminating any existing, unprofitable route.) The politicos were more attuned to the political advantages that might be gained from softening up the suburban opposition. Paradoxically, the case for expanding suburban bus service in dramatic fashion—and then putting pressure on the Metro Council to pay the resulting deficits—came from the City politicos on the TTC board.

The pattern of appointments also explains why politicos were more militant than administrators on the question of TTC independence. Because they lacked any basis of support in the political community, administrators relied on the Metro chairman's backing and his skill as floor leader for their reappointment to the commission. As a result, the administrators were sometimes responsive to suggestions made by the chairman. The politicos, who equated Gardiner and Allen with the expressways program, resented these intrusions.

The Lamport Years: McBrien's Strategy Without McBrien. From 1955 to 1959, the former mayor of Toronto, Allan Lamport, served as TTC chairman and attempted to apply McBrien's expansionist strategies. The core of Lamport's program was to maintain pressure on the Metro Council for an immediate start on the east–west subway, substantial Metro involvement in the financing of that project, and the approval of the TTC's proposed Bloor Street route. In the interim all operating deficits were to be met not by drawing on TTC reserve funds or increasing fares but by demanding unconditional subsidies from the Metro Council. By threatening to raise fares if Metro Council did not provide the subsidies, Lamport hoped to increase pressure on the councilors and to put the onus for any subsequent fare increases on their shoulders.

One way of securing favorable Council action would have been to win over the Metro chairman and to rely on his floor-leading skills. Such a tactic, however, ran counter to Lamport's flamboyant, individualistic style. Lamport was convinced that bringing the TTC into the chairman–cabinet orbit would mean a subordination of public transit to expressways. Only intense and persistent pressure, he thought, would persuade the chairman to approve the TTC's program. Thus, Lamport's strategy in dealing with the Council was to denounce the chairman's transit policies and to rely on support from the City bloc and the TTC's interest group constituency.

To Lamport, independence also meant resisting the Metro planners' intrusions on TTC policy making. Gardiner urged that the TTC and the planners cooperate on the selection of a route for the east–west subway, but the TTC ignored the planners and proceeded with plans for a Bloor Street route. When the planners subsequently rejected Bloor Street and proposed an alternative route, Lamport was certain that Gardiner had instigated this move in order to delay or kill the subway proposal. Lamport's cool relations with the planners, it might be added, extended to other Metro department heads. All were seen as "Gardiner's men."

Lamport was prepared to go one step further than McBrien had in appeasing the suburban opposition. Under Lamport the TTC decided not to alter the gradual rate of service extensions but to give the suburban councils a major voice in deciding exactly which routes would be extended first. After 1954, TTC decisions on extensions were based largely on the specific route proposals and the priorities contained in municipal briefs.

It is easier to describe Lamport's tactics than to gauge their precise effectiveness. His suburban service policy probably accounted for a slight reduction in suburban attacks on the TTC after 1954. His pressure on the Metro chairman for a 1955 subsidy probably helped convince Gardiner that some form of operating assistance should be made available to the TTC. Yet Lamport could not duplicate this subsidy in succeeding years. The TTC chairman's major victory was securing Metro approval of the Bloor Street subway route in 1958. By preserving TTC unity on this question and by refusing to compromise, Lamport convinced Gardiner that approval of the planners proposed route would destroy the TTC's morale and efficiency.

After 1958, however, a reaction to Lamport's style set in. The TTC chairman had outmaneuvered the planners on the route issue, but had alienated much of the Metro cabinet and many good government interest groups in the process. Lamport's tactics in this route controversy sparked the debate over whether comprehensive transportation planning could be attained while public transit was in the hands of a militantly independent agency. The groups and individuals favorable to central planning values also claimed that the TTC's suburban service decisions relied too much on politics and improvisation and too little on a long-range plan for service extension. Lamport's persistent pressure and personal lobbying also stirred some reaction among Metro councilors. Council tired of being threatened with fare increases and resented the TTC's large expenditures on public relations.

This apparent decline in external effectiveness was causally related to Lamport's loss of the TTC chairmanship in 1959. The four administrators on the board had reluctantly voted for Lamport as chairman because he was the most accomplished politician on the board and because no one could solidify City support for the east–west subway better than a former mayor of Toronto.

With the Bloor subway approved, however, the other board members saw less need for Lamport's style of leadership. More than this, the administrators believed that Lamport's tactics had provoked the 1959 Council debate over the reorganization or abolition of the TTC. The organization was in danger, they thought, because it had been too aggressive and visible, because the Lamport–McBrien strategy stirred more resentment than its achievements were worth. The administrators' answer to this crisis was a hiatus in TTC pressure on Council and a retreat from the political limelight.

The administrators were also concerned about the loss of morale and personnel within the ranks of the technical staff. Lamport had been at constant loggerheads with the technical staff, partly because he viewed them as a threat to his control of the TTC and partly because his policies were more expansive than the staff would support. The administrators on the TTC board thought it was time to reassert the internal solidarity of the organization, even if this meant selecting chairmen who were less skilled in external affairs.

During 1959–1960, Lamport tried to recapture his leadership within the TTC. In 1960, he resigned from the commission to run—unsuccessfully—for mayor of Toronto. Although the Lamport–McBrien point of view was stated in succeeding years by commissioners Ford Brand and Douglas Hamilton, the politicos were never again in control.

Did Lamport's downfall indicate that the McBrien strategy could no longer provide the basis for a policy equilibrium within the TTC? To what extent were the strains produced by Lamport's policies structural—that is, inherent in the McBrien strategy—or nonstructural—a product of the way in which Lamport applied this strategy?

The McBrien strategy could not have been as effective in a divided Metro Council, with a permanent suburban opposition, as it had been in a united, friendly City Council. There also were inherent difficulties involved in the pursuit of an aggressive strategy when the TTC was no longer financially self-sustaining.

A TTC leader had to demonstrate that the commission was destitute and badly in need of operating subsidies, but he also had to demonstrate that the TTC held sufficient financial reserves to pay for its share of subway costs. A TTC leader had to seek Metro operating assistance and then spend part of that aid for public relations and indirect pressure on the Council. Metro Council had to be convinced that it should expand all forms of aid to the commission without in any way diminishing the TTC's control of transit policies. Whether McBrien could have made this strategy work is a moot point. Obviously it was less successful in the hands of anyone but McBrien. No one person in the TTC had all of McBrien's personal resources: long tenure on the Commission, a reputation for expertise on transit matters, and considerable finesse in dealing with politicians.

Much of the 1959 reaction must be attributed to Lamport's style rather than the strategy itself. As a former mayor of Toronto and an advocate of total amalgamation, Lamport was too closely affiliated with one faction to apply the strategy with maximum effectiveness. He could rally the City bloc behind TTC proposals, but his mere presence at a Council meeting would exacerbate suburban antagonisms to the TTC. Many suburban officials saw operating subsidies as grants to Lamport, not to the TTC. Furthermore, Lamport's frequent threats to run for mayor, if the Council did not give him what he wanted, weakened City support for TTC proposals. If some City politicians were going to face Lamport in a future election campaign, they were not eager to help build a strong record for him as TTC chairman. Finally, Lamport employed the aggressive strategy unceasingly. McBrien's strategy probably would have been more successful if used with moderation and with frequent breathing spells. Lamport followed too closely the tactics that McBrien had used in the City Council and learned too little from the tactics that Gardiner used in Metro Council.

Lamport's conflict with the technical staff was partly structural and partly personal. Since the politicos and the staff disagreed on external strategy and on some substantive policies, it was difficult for any TTC leader to secure, as McBrien had, an expansionist foreign policy *and* harmonious relations between board and staff. But much of the conflict between Lamport and the staff stemmed from Lamport's apparent interest in becoming general manager as well as chairman, a goal in no way dictated by the expansionist strategy.

The Search for a New Equilibrium, 1960–1965. The Lamport years accentuated the differences between administrators and politicos and made each type of commissioner more insistent on his own viewpoint. The administrator, who thought that the expansionist strategy had been tried with disastrous results, was less willing to defer to the politicos. The politicos felt that Lamport had been betrayed. Growing conflict within the board also reflected a growing disparity in the demands of the TTC's staff and its external constituency. The technical staff, like the administrators, thought that the TTC needed a period of internal consolidation and political obscurity. The interest group constituency demanded a return to the Lamport policies. It became increasingly difficult to find one set of policies that would satisfy both the integrative and adaptive needs of the organization.

The staff and the external constituency also began disagreeing on substantive policies. The politicos, City officials, and interest groups supported, while the administrators and staff opposed, a dramatic expansion in suburban bus service. The staff and the administrators were more willing to accept Metro subsidies with some strings attached, but they also insisted that subsidy proposals be initiated by Council not by the TTC. By 1959, the staff, reversing some of its earlier views, had come to support the Metro planners' program for future subway routes. The politicos and interest groups insisted that the program favored the suburbs over the City and put too much emphasis on combined expressway-rapid transit projects rather than subways. In addition, the technical staff's support for the planners' scheme was seen as a surrender of TTC autonomy in the planning field and as an attempt by the staff to usurp the board's policy-making powers.

In theory the administrators should have had little difficulty in implementing their viewpoint, since they always controlled at least three votes on the board. But the board's majority bloc was fearful of pursuing policies that would antagonize the external constituency. On several occasions the administrators would edge toward a decision only to retreat in the face of pressure from the politicos, City officials, and interest groups. The administrators sometimes resolved these deadlocks, much to the staff's annoyance, by giving the politicos half or most of what they wanted. On a few important subway planning questions, however, the TTC board could reach no decision. Eventually the Metro chairman and Council had to settle these questions.

Conflict within the TTC board would have been less intense had not the supportive interest groups intervened in each internal dispute. As long as it had maintained a united front, the TTC could protect itself from the close scrutiny of its friends. But once the organization revealed its lines of internal division, group pressures increased and the organization's autonomy decreased. The interest groups were all the more eager to intervene because they opposed the policies of the board's majority. Although the supportive groups publicly deplored the TTC's indecision and delays, these groups clearly preferred deadlock to implementation of the administrators' policies. In all, interest groups played a far more important role in the TTC subsystem than in the Metro system as a whole.

When the administrators *did* pursue their strategy, they were not able to remove the TTC from politics. The administrators hoped to protect the commission from excessive pressures and scrutiny. However, their decision to bar everyone but the press from board meetings generated new criticisms of the agency. In addition, Metro cabinet officials complained that the commission was even more sparing in its release of information and its indication of future TTC plans. Since the TTC was less insistent on its legislative program, there was less Metro Council hostility toward the agency. But City officials and interest groups, who believed that an independent agency was necessary to provide vigorous leadership on behalf of transit proposals, were disappointed with the TTC's new-found reticence. The administrators' policies, rather than make the TTC noncontroversial, merely shifted the bases of criticism.

Conclusions on the TTC As a Subsystem. According to functional theory, the survival of a subsystem depends on its making contributions or fulfilling tasks of importance to the larger system. The development or decline of that subsystem would depend on whether its contributions and tasks were growing or diminishing in importance. The problem with this theoretical formulation is that it assumes a consensus in the larger system about the purposes or tasks of the subsystem. Metro Council's attitudes toward the TTC were uncertain, ambiguous, and inconsistent. Whether the TTC should be abolished, whether it should be retained with increased Metro control over its policies, whether transit should be treated as a public service or a self-sufficient business enterprise were all unsettled questions in Metro Council. Indeed there would not have been a mixture of administrators and politicos on the board but for Metro Council's uncertainty about the purpose of the TTC.

Everyone on Council viewed the TTC as a businesslike corporation, responsible for operating a large transit system in an efficient manner. The City bloc and the Metro chairman also saw the TTC as a political or policy-making agency; but no member of Council would concede the legitimacy of overt conflict within the TTC board. As a businesslike or administrating agency, the TTC was expected to maintain a united front. Its failure to maintain that unity discredited the agency in the eyes of the councilors. As one TTC commissioner said: "The Metro Council 'debates,' the TTC commissioners 'squabble.'"

The City bloc was also inconsistent on the transit leadership question. City officials expected the TTC to press vigorously for transit proposals, but these same officials were horrified at the evidence of TTC expenditures on advertising, receptions, and other public relations activities.

The TTC's own functional problems would have been less complicated if the larger system had resolved its thinking about the agency. For example, if Council had stripped the TTC of its policy-making tasks and had left it to administer the existing transit system, most interest group pressures would have shifted to the Council, and the TTC board could have given first priority to internal considerations. (From Gardiner's point of view, however, the TTC's major unstated task was to help draw group pressures away from the Council.) On the other hand, if the Council had more consciously recognized the policy-making tasks of the TTC, the board might have been able to pursue the lobbying tactics urged by its external constituency without incurring legislative hostility.

Consistent Council attitudes, however, would not have eliminated all the tensions between the TTC's internal and external needs. Disagreements between the staff and the interest groups over substantive policy would have persisted. As long as there were tension between the integrative and adaptive needs of the TTC, role differentiation and conflict within the board was functional to the system's survival. The presence of both politicos and administrators on the board guaranteed that both internal and external demands were considered. Everyone outside the TTC urged more unity within the board, but the question was around whose viewpoint this unity would be built. The consistent pursuit of either the politicos' or the administrators' program would have weakened the TTC's functional performance.

Despite this representation of both viewpoints on the board, the TTC clearly was losing much of its importance. Its formal tasks and its contributions to the Metro system were less significant in 1965 than they had been in 1954. Some of this decline can be traced to the prevalence of the administrators' viewpoint after 1960. The emphasis on efficient administration and internal integration often led the board to avoid major policy questions. Where the questions concerned subway planning, the Metro chairman and Council stepped in to fill the policy-making vacuum. The drift of power from the TTC to Metro Council can also be attributed to stalemates within the board. In this sense, role differentiation and conflict on the board were dysfunctional to the TTC.

The basic flaw in the TTC board's internal structure was not the presence of role differentiation and conflict but the absence of a mediating role. No one commissioner consciously attempted to resolve the integrative and adaptive needs of the organization. No one TTC commissioner combined the broad perspective and persuasive skills of a Gardiner or McBrien. Role differentiation was carried to the point of bipolarization; newcomers were soon thrust into one or the other faction. Each commissioner's sources of support and reference groups were outside the board. No commissioner tried to build a personal constituency based on the support of other commissioners.

Without a mediator the TTC board veered sharply first in the direction of assertive leadership and then in the direction of administrative efficiency. In each case the particular strategy was pushed too far. One damaged the integration of the organization and provoked hostile legislative responses; the other damaged the agency's relations with its external constituency. No fusion of the two strategies occurred. The TTC case suggests that, while a certain degree of role differentiation is functional to a system, differentiation without mediation can be dysfunctional.

By 1965, there was generally less criticism of the TTC but also less praise. The commission was somewhat less controversial than it had been in 1954, but it also was making a more modest contribution to the Metro system.

The Independent Regulatory Agencies

The Metro Police Commission and the Metro Licensing Commission were created in 1957, after the province had approved a Metro Council request to transfer these powers to the Metro level. The police commission (MPC) consisted of the Metro chairman serving *ex officio*, one member of the Metro Council appointed by the Council, and three judicial officials named by the province. The Licensing Commission (MLC) contained the Metro chairman and two judicial officials named by the province.

In both cases, it might be added, laymen could be given judicial appointments at the same time that they were named to the commissions. Thus, the statutes did not prohibit the appointment of politicians to either board.

Table 5.2 summarizes the major differences between the TTC and the two regulatory commissions in terms of legislative attitudes, interest group clientele, internal staff demands, the nature of role differentiation within the governing boards, and the overall functional performance of the commissions. In the present discussion, lesser differences between MLC and MPC may be ignored.

In the case of both regulatory agencies, the most vocal interest groups were the ones being regulated. These groups were generally hostile to the agency and usually demanded greater flexibility or greater concern with individual rights in the enforcement process. No groups intervened in Metro politics to support the general purposes of the police or licensing programs, as the pro-transit groups did in the TTC case. Legislators supported the general goals of the regulatory programs, as they supported the goals of the transit program, but legislative support for regulation was less intense or focused. In the short run Metro Council was highly responsive to the groups that criticized regulation. Councilors also were more critical of the regulatory commissions than the TTC because Council had less control over MLC and MPC appointments. In contrast to the ambiguity that surrounded the TTC's purposes, the Metro legislators clearly saw MLC and MPC as policy-making bodies and would have tolerated a certain degree of dissension within the boards of these two agencies. But the Council was sharply critical of the regulatory agencies for holding most of their proceedings in secret. No member of Council favored abolishing MLC or MPC, as some councilors favored abolishing the TTC, but the Council was almost unanimous in supporting increased Metro control over the regulatory agencies.

A crucial difference between the TTC and the regulatory agencies was the presence of the Metro chairman on the latter. This presence gave the chairman an opportunity to influence commission decisions and made the chairman more willing to

TABLE 5.2 A Functional Analysis of Independent Policy-Making Subsystems in Metro Toronto

	Toronto Transit Commission	*Police and Licensing Commissions*	*Metro School Board*
Interest group attitudes	Suburban neighborhood groups hostile; strong support from Labor and City press	Groups being regulated hostile; no countervailing generalized support	Most groups channel demands through local boards; problem-oriented groups critical of board's performance
Legislative attitudes	Strong support for program, but more specific support from City bloc; suburban officials respond to neighborhood group criticisms	General but weak and unfocused support for programs; Council responsive to groups criticizing agencies; agencies rely on Metro chairman	Support for program, but frequent criticism of extravagant spending; Council would increase its control over school board budgets
Internal, staff demands	Moderate expansion; continued independence	Tough enforcement standards; protection from hostile groups	Minimal staff oriented to general policy problems in education
Board structure	Role differentiation along integrative-adaptive lines; no mediating role	Some differentiation, but integrative or problem-solving orientations prevail	No differentiation; integrative or "representative" orientations prevail
Assessment of functional performance	Neither function ignored; but internal stalemate often results	Adaptive performance (articulation with Metro system) is weak	Adaptive or problem-solving performance weak

defend commission policies before the Council. Gardiner fully exploited these opportunities. He became largely responsible for defining the foreign policies of regulatory commissions and for relating these agencies to the broader political system. The basic adaptive strategy of MLC and MPC was reliance on the chairman's influence in Council, and Gardiner's basic goal was to protect these agencies from their hostile political environment. Thus, while independent in name, the two commissions actually were integrated into Gardiner's administrative subsystem.

MPC and MLC probably had little choice but to rely on the chairman. These agencies could not have pursued the TTC's strategy of bypassing the chairman and relying on an interest group constituency. Local interest groups were not heavily committed to participation in politics. McBrien's coalition had taken decades to construct. Moreover, regulatory programs could not have secured group support to the extent that service and construction programs could.

Gardiner, it seems, was able to translate this control over the commissions' adaptive strategies into influence over the commissions' policy-making processes. It is significant that all of Gardiner's views on these two regulatory programs coincided with the policies of these agencies and that most of Gardiner's suggestions for new directions in regulatory policies later became commission policy. The commissions' departure from some of Gardiner's views after 1961 also attests to his influence over the policies of these commissions during his tenure as chairman.

Much of Gardiner's influence within the commissions was attributable to the fact that the Metro chairman, like the other members of the commissions, believed in the need for tough or adequate enforcement. External pressures for flexible enforcement had to be resisted. There was little role differentiation or conflict within these two commissions, because most of the commissioners had internalized the values of rigorous enforcement and resistance to political pressure before their appointment to the commissions.

The absence of role differentiation on these commissions was part of Gardiner's original design. In 1956, he convinced the province that dedicated commissioners had to be recruited if the regulatory process were to retain its integrity and that Council control of commission appointments would be inconsistent with the recruitment of dedicated commissioners. Thereafter, the province generally followed Gardiner's suggestions on commission appointments. Thus, provincial control of appointments really meant that Gardiner could recruit commissioners committed to tough enforcement without having to secure the assent of Metro Council. Independence, or minimal Council control of appointments, protected the regulatory process from constituency pressures and maximized Gardiner's influence within these agencies.

The commissioners' strong support for regulatory goals and strict enforcement were consistent with the integrative needs of the two organizations. The staffs of these organizations demanded protection from unwarranted or unjust complaints leveled at the staff by those persons being regulated. Staff and commissioners agreed on the need to protect the integrity of the enforcement process.

In Gardiner's view, adaptation to the political environment would have to be secured without relaxing the stringency of enforcement. Wherever possible, Gardiner sought to make concessions to Council on grounds other than substantive policy. He tried to increase Council support of the regulatory commissions by nominating two Metro councilors as the first chairmen of these commissions. Yet Gardiner was careful to name two men who would support the regulatory purposes of the agencies as strongly as the other commissioners did. Thus, Reeve Bick (chairman of MPC) and Reeve Hall (chairman of MLC) did not assume distinctive roles within their respective commissions. These politicos did not become advocates of adaptation through relaxation in enforcement procedures.

But adaptation remained the regulatory agencies' major problem. The basic flaw in Gardiner's solution was that it depended too heavily on his personal abilities as floor leader and on his

influence at the provincial level. Grievances in the political environment were permitted to build up, but punitive action against
the commissions was blocked by the chairman's ability to veto
many Council actions at the provincial level. Gardiner, in other
words, provided a personal but not a structural solution to the
adaptive problems of these two agencies. It is not surprising that
all the environmental discontents flared up once Gardiner departed.

With less influence in Council and at the provincial level, Allen
proved less successful in protecting these agencies from their
hostile environment. Moreover, Allen played the adaptive role
less consistently and less consciously than did Gardiner. Allen
did not leap into the center of the legislature controversies relating to these agencies. As a result these commissions had to fend
for themselves. In order to forestall threatened legislative rebellions, these commissions made some concessions on substantive
policy. On matters like the secrecy of commission meetings or
the ban on transferring licenses from one holder to another, Allen
supported substantive concessions.

There also were signs, after 1961, of increasing role differentiation in each of the two boards. Within the MPC, for example,
both the chairman of the commission and the mayor of Toronto
—Metro Council's one appointment to the commission—played
a more significant role in the setting of external strategies.

As a qualification one should add that all the above trends were
just beginning to emerge. If the more recent patterns continue,
one might expect growing role differentiation within the boards,
more concessions on substantive policy, some reduction in the
staffs' satisfaction with board policies, a search by each commission for sources of support other than the Metro chairman, and
a strengthening of the tendency for the Metro system to become
more decentralized than it had been under Gardiner.

Form of Organization and Functional Success

The performances of Metro departments and Metro's major independent commissions have been discussed at separate points

in the study; here, I intend to draw this data together and to consider which form of organization is more conducive to subsystem success. The following discussion, though relevant to reform questions, should not be construed as a case either for or against independent commissions. Functional analysis can only suggest the conditions contributing to a subsystem's survival and growth; it cannot take into account other possible values, like central administrative coordination, or administrative responsibility to elected officials.

Since the Metro department head was a technical man, attuned to the values of the technical staff, the staffs of some independent commissions probably would have been happier within departments. Uniformed policemen, for example, indicated that they would rather be responsible to a commissioner of police, recruited from the ranks, than to a lay board. Similarly, the TTC technical staff might have preferred an expert commissioner of transit to the TTC board, although the transport workers clearly preferred the independent board.

Some technical-staff members seemed more willing to take their chances with an independent board than with the Metro Council, perhaps on the assumption that a board dedicated to one program would be easier to capture. Where staff proposals eventually had to be approved by the legislators, and where the independent commissioners were submissive or at least highly friendly to the staff, the prior approval of staff proposals by the commission could be an important advantage for the staff when it took these proposals to the legislature. On the whole, however, changing the form of organization from independent commission to department probably would have produced a net gain in the internal integration of most Metro subsystems.

During the Gardiner years, administrative agencies were most effective in the political environment operating as part of the chairman's administrative subsystem. No administrative agency could match Gardiner's influence by pursuing an independent course. If the chairman's influence were to erode and if each administrative agency were to seek out its own sources of support, the construction agencies would probably expand more rapidly as independent commissions than as departments. Agencies administering popular programs would have little difficulty in finding sources of political support; and, as McBrien often noted, independent commissions were less inhibited than departments in their politicking. Regulatory programs, and to some extent service programs, were more in need of a strong chairman. Aside from variations in the popularity of policy programs, Metro councilors accorded more deference to the proposals of expert department heads than to the proposals of lay boards. This attitude was one adaptive advantage of the department as an organizational form. On the other hand, in the absence of a strong chairman oriented to political considerations, the expert department head could become overly responsive to the internal needs of his department. The presence of politicos on an independent board often guaranteed that adaptive requirements were kept in the forefront of subsystem policy making.

The Metro School Board

The factors that distinguish the Metro School Board from the agencies I have been describing are the board's complete independence of Metro Council, the recruitment of board members from the thirteen municipalities, and the board's lack of major administrative responsibilities or an elaborate administrative staff. The Metro School Board, like the Metro Planning Board and the Metro and Region Conservation Authority, was seen by Metro councilors not as an administrative agency but as a little legislature. In the school board system, integrative considerations were generally political, and adaptive considerations generally "technical" or problem oriented (see Table 5.2).

The task of the Metro School Board, as clearly stated in Bill 80, was to help equalize the capital and operating costs of education among the thirteen municipalities, while leaving a maximum amount of policy making at the local school board level. The Metro board consisted of twenty-two members, ten named

by and from the Toronto Board of Education, ten from the suburban boards, and two from the Separate (i.e., Catholic) School
Board. There were only ten suburban representatives because
the three Lakeshore municipalities maintained a single board.
The local boards were popularly elected.

The Metro School Board's internal structure adhered closely
to the original, international conference image of Metro. The
board was a good indicator of what the Metro Council might
have looked like if Gardiner had never served as chairman. The
school board members, like the Metro councilors, spoke for their
respective municipalities and initiated solutions or issues only in
response to a municipal grievance. The crucial difference between the board and the Council was the absence in the former
case of any adaptive or mediating roles. The school board's
chairman was one of the municipal representatives. The board
had neither an extensive staff nor a tradition of deferring to
technical leadership. Most professional educators remained attached to the local boards and raised problems at the local level.
Problems were perceived and solutions offered by the Metro
school superintendent, but there was no political official who
regularly urged these solutions on the board, encouraged board
deference to expertise, and protected the superintendent from
hostile political reactions. Without this political support there
were limits to how vigorously an appointed official could press
proposals on the board.

As a result, harmony within the board took precedence over
problem solving. Board action depended on enough municipalities having a similar grievance on the same issue. The coalitions
shifted from one issue to the next, as the nature of municipal
grievances shifted. Little conscious effort was made to construct
majorities. Either majorities emerged from the various municipal
viewpoints, or no action was taken.

The major characteristic of the board's policy output was a
sluggishness in revising the basis of its capital and operating grants
to municipal boards. Consequently, these grants lagged behind
the rapid increases in educational costs. Differences in educational

expenditures and school tax rates from one municipality to the next, far from being equalized, were growing. Problem-oriented actors—in academic circles, at the provincial level, among Toronto newspapermen, and within some segments of the educational profession—argued that the board was not fulfilling its stipulated task.

The outlying, growing suburbs supported increases in capital or school construction grants, but the City of Toronto and the smaller suburbs, who were more the donors than the recipients of these grants, were reluctant to see the formula revised upward. The City was angry that the costs of rehabilitating old buildings were not included in the board's capital grants, but the suburbs lined up solidly in opposition to their inclusion. The City's attempts at logrolling, offering support for increased capital grants if the outlying suburbs supported inclusion of rehabilitation costs, failed.

(In the field of operating grants a deadlock developed between the board and the province. All the board members were uncertain about increasing the extent of operating assistance while the local boards continued to compete for teachers. The board agreed that a uniform teachers' salary schedule for the entire area should be adopted; but the province, under pressure from the teachers' federation and from local boards throughout Ontario, vetoed this proposal.)

The board also was close to stalemate on the question of its own future. The City members wanted educational amalgamation, the small suburbs wanted no change in the *status quo,* and the larger suburbs wanted a reduction in the number of local boards to five or six and an increase in the basis of the Metro board's capital grants. The City and the outlying suburbs could agree on the need for a common school tax rate in the Metro area, and the entire board agreed on a uniform salary schedule. This common denominator became the basis of the board's brief to the 1963 Royal Commission on Metro Toronto.

CHAPTER 6

THE SOCIAL CONTEXT
OF METRO POLITICS

The political scientists who first directed their attention to urban phenomena were interested primarily in the formal institutions of local government. Over the last three decades, however, the sociologists' community studies, and the political scientists' own growing interest in noninstitutional or informal aspects of the political process, produced a shift in orientation. Not the organization of local government but the distribution of power in the local community became the focus of analysis. This growing concern with the social basis of politics was reinforced by the substantitve conclusions of early studies, particularly the indications that nongovernment actors, like a business elite, sometimes dominated local politics.[1]

The more recent approach to local political systems consciously seeks generalizations linking politics and social structure, with social structure as the independent variable.[2] This approach sees issues being generated in the social sphere and then transmitted to the political. To paraphrase David Truman, groups resort to politics to correct disturbances in an earlier pattern of intragroup or intergroup relations.[3] The style and content of local politics will reflect the number and type of groups in the community, their expectations and demands, and the degree and nature of intergroup conflict. Thus, the extent of social homogeneity in a community helps determine whether political power is concentrated or scattered; a socially homogeneous environment may be more conducive to elitist than pluralist politics. The emergence of an integrated metropolitan political community may depend on the presence of an integrated metropolitan social community, with factors like social homogeneity, intraregional mobility, and intraregional telephone calls serving as indices of social integration.[4] Although this more recent approach may sometimes degenerate into a crude form of social determinism, in which politics always reflects nonpolitical variables, few students of political systems would deny the need to see politics in a broader, social context.

This chapter and the next explore the social context of Metro politics. I argue, for example, that the beliefs and values of the area—or what will be called "the political culture" of the area —help explain many features of the Metro political system. But my major conclusion on the social determinants of the Metro system is a negative one. The demands, expectations, and tensions present in the larger community do *not* set the agenda of Metro politics. In this sense, social structure is important for the effect it does not have on Metro politics. The Metro case is relevant to theories of politics and social structure mainly because it demonstrates how a political system can become largely autonomous of social forces in the community at large.

The most politically influential people in Metro were the appointed and elected officials—in contrast to both the business elite and broker leadership systems. These public officials, moreover, made their decisions in a low-pressure environment. The creation, agitation, and resolution of issues occurred within the formal institutions of government. Interaction among public officials was far more significant for the outcome of issues than interaction between officials and private actors. The Metro councilor, far from viewing himself as an interest group spokesman or as a mediator of group demands, often seemed unaware of what the groups wanted in particular cases. The councilor was largely free to set his own style in Council. He had to decide on the basis of his own predispositions—or internalized values—what the public wanted or needed. At times the councilor seemed disappointed that local groups did not communicate their views more clearly and help structure the issue for him.

This low-pressure environment is a partial explanation of the executive-centered system. If councilors had been subjected to more pressure, they would have been less willing to go along.

In addition, the ability of the political officials to generate their own issues helps account for the heavy Council emphasis on regional-parity and structural-reform questions. This interest in governmental organization and the defense of the municipalities' corporate interests did not appear to extend outside of Metro Council. No interest group in the area was half as interested in these questions as the councilors were. In the 1962 area-wide referendum on fluoridation, moreover, the voters apparently did not see this question as a Metro-versus-municipal matter, even though Metro Council had discussed it in these terms. Support for fluoridation was strongest in areas with large numbers of school-age children. The City officials supported fluoridation in Metro Council because it would hasten total amalgamation, but the City voters rejected fluoridation. The suburban officials in Council were divided on this question, but the suburban voters overwhelmingly backed fluoridation. Although no evidence on public opinion in Metro was assembled, it seems reasonable to conclude that the low-pressure environment was a prerequisite for Council's preoccupation with Metro-municipal relations. If more social demands and conflicts had been translated into political issues, Council would have shifted some of its attention from structural to substantive issues.

There is an obvious irony in my line of argument. Having accepted the need to see politics in its social context, I must now explain why social factors were not important in the Metro case —why the links between social structure and Metro politics were not stronger. The following pages offer two explanations.

First, Metro lacked many of the social tensions present in other large metropolitan areas. The low temperature of Metro politics reflected a large degree of social consensus. Second, the actors who regularly convert social demands and tensions into political issues did not perform these activities in the Metro system. Even if there had been more social tensions in the area, they would not necessarily have been transmitted to the political arena. In Metro the interest-articulation activity was poorly performed. Broker leadership systems may suffer from a lack of interest aggregation and a resulting tendency towards stalemate and inaction. The Metro system, though able to move ahead more easily with important decisions, suffered from the weak interrelation of politics and the larger community.

The focus of the following discussion is on the actors and mechanisms that generally transmit social messages to the political system. In examining any political system, it is important to know not only what the social messages are but also whether they are being transmitted to, and received by, the political system, whether selective screening of messages occurs, and whether messages change in the process of being transmitted. The actors responsible for translating social message in most democratic systems are the interest group and party leaders. The major mechanisms of translation are elections and group involvement in policy-making politics. My purpose is to describe how and why these mechanisms and actors did not consistently perform the interest-articulation activity in Metro. The remainder of this chapter examines group involvement in policy making; chapter 7 discusses Metro elections as interest-articulating mechanisms and then considers the impact of political culture on Metro politics.

The Interest Groups: Involvement and Goals

Much of the following discussion is based on Table 6.1, which summarizes the extent and direction of group involvement in fifty-five major issues coming before the Metro Council between 1953 and 1965.[5] The table includes all the major private interest groups in the Metro area. The Real Estate Board and the political parties are excluded since they did not voice an opinion on any of the issues. The various ratepayer and neighborhood merchant associations are lumped into the "neighborhood groups"

TABLE 6.1 Interest Group Involvement and Goals in 55 Major Decisions Made by Metro Council, 1953–1965

Issues	Official Decision Makers				Good Government Bloc					Liberal-Welfare Bloc			
	Chair-man	Cabi-net	City Bloc	Sub-urban Bloc	Globe & Mail	BMR	BofT	AWE	SPC	Star	Tele-gram	LC	Neigh-borhood Groups
Low-Conflict, Low Involvement Issues													
1. Approve 5-year water and sewage program, 1954	A	A	A	A	A					A	A		
2. Stop hospital construction grants, 1958	A		A	A									
3. Approve Don Valley expressway, 1955	A	A	A	A	A					A	A		
4. Give Bloor subway extensions priority, 1962	A	A	A	A	A					A	A		
5. Partially amalgamate traffic control, 1961	A	A	A	A	A					A	A		
6. Appoint Lamport to TTC, 1954	A		A	A									
7. Pass Allen's TTC reorganization plan, 1962	A		A	A	A					A	A		
8. Pass air pollution control law, 1958	A	A	A	A	A					A	A		

Low-Conflict,
High Involvement Issues

Issue											
9. Resume hospital construction grants, 1963	A		A	A	A	A		A	A	A	A
10. Establish long-range housing program, 1958	A	A	A	A	A	A	A	A	A	A	A
11. Assume 70% Bloor subway extension costs, 1962	A	A	A	A	A				A	A	A
12. Approve subway construction speedup, 1961	A	A	A	A	A			A	A	A	A
13. Approve subway construction speedup, 1963	A	A	A	A	A			A	A	A	A
14. Approve revised Lakeshore expressway route, 1954	A	A	A	A	A	A		A	A	A	A
15. Amalgamate police, 1956	A	A	A	A	A	A		A	A	A	
16. Approve Warden Woods public housing project, 1959	A		A	A	A	A	A				
17. Grant operating subsidy to TTC, 1955	A	A	A	A				A	A	A	A
18. Compromise, naming Day and Hamilton to TTC, 1963	A	A	A	A				A	A	A	A
19. Defer decision on Spadina expressway, 1957	A	A	A					A	A	A	A

TABLE 6.1 (continued)

	Official Decision Makers				Good Government Bloc					Liberal-Welfare Bloc			
Issues	Chairman	Cabinet	City Bloc	Suburban Bloc	Globe & Mail	BMR	BofT	AWE	SPC	Star	Telegram	LC	Neighborhood Groups
Moderate Conflict, High Involvement Issues (Conflict among decision makers but consensus among interest groups)													
20. Reject long-range housing program, 1954	A	D	D	A	D			D	D	D	D	D	D
21. Reject education grants to suburbs getting public housing, 1961	A	D	A	A	D				D	D	D		
22. Approve Bloor subway financing plan, 1958	A	A	A	D	A	A	A			A	A		
23. Reject fire amalgamation, 1963	A	A	D	A	D					D	D		
24. Reject parking amalgamation, 1962	A	D	A	D	D	D				D	D		
25. Approve welfare amalgamation, 1962	A	D	A	D	A	A		A	A	A	A	A	
26. Reject traffic amalgamation, 1961	A	D	A	A	D					D	D		

Issue							
27. Reject redevelopment	A	D	A	D	A	D	D
28. Approve public housing amalgamation, 1961	A	A	D	A	A	A	A
agencies amalgamation, 1962							
29. Approve TTC subsidy, 1963	D	D	A	D	A		A
30. Approve wholesale water	D	D	A	D		A	
rates compromise, 1955							
31. Approve uniform water	A	A	D	A	A	A	
rates, 1958							
32. Reject per-rider	D	D	A	A	D	D	
TTC subsidy, 1962							
33. Appoint Brand to TTC, 1959–60	A	A	D	A		A	A
34. Appoint Hamilton rather than	D		D	D		A	A
Day to TTC, 1963							
35. Give Metro power to name	D	A	A	A		A	A
1 member of MLC, 1962							
36. Assume 70% TTC debt, 1963	A	A	D	A	A	A	A
37. Defer subway speedup, 1959	A	A	D	A	D	D	D
38. Choose Bloor route over	A	D	A	A	A	A	A
U route for subway, 1958							
39. Construct Y subway	A	D	A	A	D	A	A
facility, 1960							
40. Approve original Lakeshore	A	A	A	A	D	D	D
expressway route, 1954							

TABLE 6.1 (continued)

Issues	Official Decision Makers				Good Government Bloc					Liberal-Welfare Bloc			
	Chairman	Cabinet	City Bloc	Suburban Bloc	Globe & Mail	BMR	BofT	AWE	SPC	Star	Telegram	LC	Neighborhood Groups
Moderate Conflict— High Involvement Issues (Conflict between general purpose groups and grass roots groups)													
41. Approve Lawrence Heights public housing project, 1954	A	A	A	A	A				A	A	A	A	D
42. Approve Thistletown public housing project, 1959	A	A	A	A	A			A		A	A	A	D
43. Choose location of water and sewer projects	A	A	A	A	A					A	A		D
44. Choose sites for homes for aged	A	A	A	A	A					A	A		D
45. Keep mayor of Toronto on MPC, 1964	A	A	A	A	A					A	A		D
46. Reject expansion of police commission, 1964	A		A	D	A					A	A		D
47. Reject reorganization of TTC, 1954	A	A	A	D	A					A	A		D

Moderate Conflict—
High Involvement Issues
(Conflict among official decision makers and among general purpose interest groups)

	BMR	BofT	AWE	SPC	LC
48. Postpone start on Bloor subway, 1954	A	A	D		D
49. Refuse to halt expressways program, 1954–63	A	A	D		D
50. Begin move to approve Spadina expressway, 1957	A	A	D		D
51. Approve Spadina expressway, 1961	A	A	A		D
52. Retain Metro federal system, 1964	A	A	D	A	D
53. Approve Gardiner's TTC reorganization plan, 1960	A	A	D	A	D
54. Decide not to abolish TTC, 1962	A	A	D	A	A
55. Approve fluoridation, 1955–63	A	A	D	A	A

Key to abbreviations:
BMR = Bureau of Municipal Research
BofT = Board of Trade
AWE = Association of Women Electors
SPC = Social Planning Council
LC = Labour Council (Toronto and District)

Symbols:
A = Group's public stand on issue prior to decision *agreed* with outcome
D = Group's public stand on issue prior to decision *disagreed* with outcome
blank = Group took no public stand on issue

Note: Expressions of approval or disapproval with a decision already made are not included, since my purpose is to summarize participation in policy making. The table does not try to measure the intensity of a group's feelings, i.e., between pressuring for a viewpoint and merely announcing it.

SUMMARY OF TABLE 6.1

	Index of Partici- pation	Index of Agreement with Policy Outcome	Index of Agreement with the Chairman	Index of Agreement with the City Bloc
Chairman	100.0	90.9	—	72.7
Cabinet	67.3	72.9	81.1	59.5
City	100.0	81.8	72.7	—
Suburbs	100.0	81.8	83.6	63.6
Globe	87.3	76.6	78.3	68.1
BMR	20.0	72.7	72.7	45.5
B. of Trade	10.9	83.3	83.3	50.0
AWE	14.7	87.5	88.9	87.5
Soc. Plann.	10.9	66.7	66.7	83.3
Star	96.4	70.0	69.6	84.9
Telegram	92.7	70.6	68.6	84.3
Labour	50.9	71.4	60.7	92.9
Neighborhood Groups	20.0	18.2	18.2	27.3

category. It was decided to include the Social Planning Council (SPC), an organization supported by both private and public funds, in the list of private interest groups.

I have attempted to summarize the role of each interest group in Metro policy making through four indices:

1. An index of participation: the number of issues in which the group took a stand divided by the total number of issues considered (fifty-five).
2. An index of agreement with policy: the number of times a group agreed with the policy outcome divided by the number of times the group took a stand.
3. An index of agreement with the chairman: the number of times a group agreed with the stand of the Metro chairman divided by the total number of times the group took a stand.
4. An index of agreement with the City bloc: the number of times a group agreed with the stand of a majority of the City

bloc divided by the total number of times the group took a stand.

Group Involvement and Conflict. Table 6.1 belies any notion of extensive group involvement in Metro policy making. Only the three Toronto newspapers were regular participants, taking a stand on over 90 percent of the fifty-five issues. The Labour Council (LC) was involved in over half of the issues. But all the other groups intervened in less than one-quarter of the issues listed. Although no similar chart is available for American cities, one may conclude from this chart and from the descriptive accounts of interest group politics in American cities that Metro groups are much less active than their American counterparts.

Table 6.1 also belies any notion of extensive conflict among Metro interest groups. On forty issues, or almost three-fourths of the total, all the groups taking any stand were in agreement. In only fifteen cases were there any differences of opinion among the active groups.

One factor reducing the incidence of group conflict was the tendency of most Metro groups to specialize in differing areas of policy. The Bureau of Municipal Research (BMR) specialized in questions of finance and governmental structure, the Board of Trade (BofT) in questions of finance and urban planning, the Association of Women Electors (AWE) in questions of housing and welfare, the neighborhood groups in matters relating to the location of capital projects, and the Social Planning Council in questions affecting welfare. The areas of specialization of these groups only partially overlapped; only occasionally did these groups find themselves making demands in the same area of policy.

The Bases of Group Conflict. One source of conflict among interest groups in Metro was the differing perspectives and tactics of neighborhood groups (primarily ratepayers' associations and neighborhood merchants' associations) and region-wide or general-purpose groups (BMR, BofT, AWE, LC, the Toronto press). Most of the groups listed in Table 6.1 were organized on a region-wide basis and were interested in influencing general policy rather than detailed decisions. Such groups were motivated largely by a commitment to abstract or ideological goals, even though these goals bore some relation to the more immediate interests of the members. The neighborhood groups, on the other hand, usually acted in response to specific decisions they did not like, sought to divert the impact of that decision, conceded that they were acting in their self-interest, and made no claim to speak for the public interest. The most important neighborhood groups, the ratepayers' associations, were designed to protect the homeowner from skyrocketing municipal taxes, to defend the neighborhood from re-zoning and unwelcome intrusions, and to secure more services and improvement projects for the neighborhood. These groups intervened in Metro policy making sporadically but intensely. While the general purpose group was often content to present a brief on an issue, the neighborhood groups resorted to the traditional tactics of pressure groups: the noisy demonstration, the petition, the letter-writing campaign, and the threat of reprisals at the polls. The general purpose groups often dismissed the neighborhood groups as narrow-minded obstructionists who lacked any overall program or concept of the area's needs.

Of the fifteen cases of interest group conflict listed in Table 6.1, seven involved conflict between the general purpose and the neighborhood groups. When neighborhood groups opposed the location of "obnoxious" projects in their areas, the general purpose groups supported the project and urged Metro Council to ignore neighborhood complaints. The attitude of the general purpose groups on neighborhood complaints about inadequate Metro service was more ambiguous. The Toronto press, for example, usually denounced suburban pressures on the police commission and the TTC, but also urged the commissions to do something about these grievances. When suburban members of Council tried to reduce the independence of these agencies to make them more responsive to grass-roots pressures, the general purpose groups opposed this move.

The general purpose groups agreed on most of the issues coming before Metro Council. Of the fifty-five issues contained in Table 6.1, only eight involved conflict among the general purpose groups. When conflict among these groups did occur, two distinct blocs emerged. The *Star*, the *Telegram* and the Labour Council had a perfect record of agreement. Also in perfect agreement with each other, though not with the Star bloc, were the *Globe and Mail*, the Board of Trade, and the Bureau of Municipal Research. The two blocs disagreed mainly on subways versus expressways, TTC reorganization, capital financing, and the future of Metro. The *Globe* bloc more regularly supported the chairman and the cabinet. The *Star*, *Telegram*, and Labor bloc almost always supported the City's point of view on Metro issues, while the *Globe*, BMR, and BofT bloc occupied a more central position in City-suburban controversies.

Banfield and Wilson, in *City Politics*, describe the conflict in most large, American cities between the good government, middle-class, reform groups and the working-class and ethnic groups.[6] The reform groups advocate businesslike efficiency and economy in municipal government, long-range capital budgeting, central planning, a high degree of professionalization in the city's administration, widespread use of independent commissions, and the election of civic officials with managerial or business backgrounds. The working-class and ethnic groups more readily accept political appointments in the city's administration, put more emphasis on government spending than on economy and low taxes, and often prefer to see a colorful, ethnic representative rather than an administrative expert in the mayor's office. The good government groups generally oppose party intervention in municipal government and often exert their influence over local elections through nonpartisan, ticket-endorsing associations, with names like the "League for Better Government" or the "Civic Reform Association." Working-class and ethnic groups more often condone party activity at the local level and generally exert their influence over local affairs through the labor unions or the Democratic Party.

This conflict was present in Metro Toronto—although in

highly muted form. The *Globe* bloc represented the good government values applied to Metro government: respect for the expert opinion of the cabinet, strong support for comprehensive planning and Metro's professional planning staff, and praise for the caution and soundess of Gardiner's capital-financing policies. The *Star*, *Telegram*, and Labor bloc was more concerned with public assistance, public housing, urban renewal, and public transit. These latter groups saw themselves as a liberal or left-of-center bloc in Metro and municipal politics. Metro issues were sometimes defined by this liberal bloc in class terms—as cases of conflict between the working-class City and the wealthy suburbs. The liberals supported subways over expressways partly because they considered subways to be of major benefit to the working man and expressways of major benefit to the higher-income suburbanite. Gardiner's debt ceiling was denounced by the liberals as too restrictive on vital capital programs and was interpreted by this bloc as proof of Gardiner's subservience to the money lenders. The liberal bloc also interpreted Gardiner's opposition to TTC subsidies as evidence of his hostility to public enterprise.

This cleavage among Metro interest groups resembled liberal–conservative differences in federal and provincial politics. The position taken by these Metro groups was roughly consistent with the position they took in politics at the senior levels of government. The *Globe*'s support for the conservative–reform position in Metro politics was consistent with that newspaper's support of conservative policies and the Conservative Party at senior levels. The tendency of the *Globe* and business-supported groups to agree on Metro issues was not surprising. Similarly, the *Star*'s espousal of liberal–welfare policies at the local level, and its agreement with Labor on Metro issues, was consistent with that newspaper's left-of-center orientation in federal and provincial politics. Far more surprising was the *Telegram*'s support for the *Star*–Labor position on Metro issues, in view of the *Telegram*'s support for conservatism at senior levels and in view of the traditional animosity between the *Star* and *Telegram*. As rival evening papers, the *Star* and the *Telegram* once invariably took opposing stands on important local issues. After 1945, however, the *Telegram* began to move leftward on local issues, apparently in a bid to capture new readers among Toronto's immigrant population and to stem the decline in *Telegram* circulation. As a result the positions of these two newspapers on local issues became indistinguishable, even though the two papers continued to differ radically on provincial and federal questions.[7]

The Social Planning Council and the Association of Women Electors stood between these two blocs. In membership and general orientation, these groups were more akin to the middle-class reformers. AWE drew its membership primarily from the middle- and upper-income parts of the metropolitan area; and the SPC's views largely reflected those of the social work profession. But because these groups focused their interest on housing and welfare issues, rather than on planning or finance, the two groups generally found themselves in agreement with the City and the *Star*, *Telegram*, and Labor bloc.

There was, then, an ideological conflict, and to some extent a class conflict, among interest groups in Metro Toronto. This conflict, moreover, resembled the conflicts that prevail in large American cities and in Canadian federal and provincial politics. But group conflict in Metro was overshadowed by the large areas of consensus that existed among these groups. The liberal working-class groups, for example, agreed that political parties should be kept out of local politics, that tax rates should be held in check, and that administrative positions should be filled through civil service procedures rather than political appointment. All three Toronto newspapers agreed that persons with managerial experience make the best mayors and Metro chairmen. Similarly all the middle-class reform groups endorsed public housing, subways, and urban renewal. Metro lacked a radical left or radical right; the groups clustered at the center of the ideological spectrum, with only shades of difference among them.

The working-class liberal values and the middle-class reform values were incompatible only at a few specific points. Group conflict occurred in Metro when that incompatibility became apparent and choices had to be made. The reform bloc believed in public housing but insisted that a cautious capital-borrowing policy came first. The liberals believed in central planning, but not if it involved delays in subway construction.

Only in one sense was ideological conflict more intense in Metro than in American cities. The Metro versus amalgamation controversy was unique to the Toronto area, and served to heighten disagreement between the liberal and reform blocs. The *Star, Telegram,* and Labor bloc supported the City's viewpoint that Metro should be replaced with one metropolitan city; the *Globe* bloc urged that Metro be strengthened not abolished. Even on this issue, however, there were significant areas of consensus. All general purpose groups, although ostensibly organized on a region-wide basis, were more interested in the problems of the central city than in suburban problems. All groups agreed that Metro had failed to give enough attention to problems of urban renewal and public welfare. Group conflict concerning Metro's future centered on the question of whether City needs could be met and these neglected problems solved through the framework of metropolitan federation.

Factors Depressing Group Involvement. One way of explaining this low-pressure environment is to explore the attitudes of interest group leaders on participation in policy making. Except for item one, the following list presents attitudinal explanations of why general purpose groups did not play a more significant political role. My description of these attitudes is based on personal interviews and conversations with many of the interest group leaders, the public statements of these leaders, and my own inferences about the attitudes of these leaders based on their behavior in policy-making situations. At the conclusion of chapter 7, I speculate on whether these attitudes reflect the area's political culture.[8]

1. Grass-roots groups were aggressively involved in the protection of neighborhood interests, but most issues directly affect-

ing these interests were dealt with by municipal councils. Federal forms of government tend to reduce the temperature of politics by dispersing the centers of decision making and thus dispersing the pressures on decision makers.[9] In addition, the Metro federal system, by allocating the emotional neighborhood issues to the municipal councils and leaving Metro Council to deal with more general policies, diverted much of the group activity away from Metro Council.

2. One reason for the weak involvement of general purpose groups was their satisfaction with Metro policies. Group leaders expressed this satisfaction to the author. It also is worth noting that the index of agreement with policies for all groups except the neighborhood groups exceeded 66.6 (see Table 6.1). In other words, all general purpose groups agreed with more than two-thirds of the policy outcomes. It may be that the lesser involvement of good government groups, like BMR and the BofT, was due to their greater satisfaction with Metro policies. The index of agreement for these groups was slightly higher than the index for the liberal–welfare bloc.

3. The large areas of consensus among Metro groups helped depress group involvement. Group leaders indicated that they would be prepared to intervene if some other group holding radically different views acted first. But with all the groups clustering around the center of the spectrum, there was no group that sufficiently irritated the others to provoke increased involvement.

4. The group leaders did not see their organizations as pressure groups. Most group leaders viewed pressure on government officials as slightly unethical, denied ever resorting to it, and criticized the ratepayers for being mere pressure groups. The group leaders intervened when they thought that they could add something to the debate—when they thought that a certain point of view was not being considered. Thus, the general purpose groups sometimes communicated their views to Metro Council but rarely urged, demanded, threatened, or cajoled. If a group had any influence, it was because the substantive arguments or documen-

tation presented by that group succeeded in changing some official minds. When one of the newspaper's editorials effectively stated a group's viewpoint, the group did not feel compelled to intervene at all. That group's viewpoint had been heard.

5. Not only the morality but the effectiveness of pressure was questioned. Many leaders were convinced that more serious attempts at pressure by general purpose groups would be resented by officials and the public at large. Leaders of business groups stated this point with particular vehemence, noting what they considered to be an antibusiness mentality in the Toronto area.

6. All group leaders emphasized how disruptive to an organization consistent political activity could be. General purpose groups existed for primarily nonpolitical purposes, e.g., servicing and coordinating member-organizations or member-firms, collecting information, and publicizing certain nonpolitical causes. Political action could divide the members and jeopardize the major purposes of the organization. In the absence of any strong dissatisfaction with policies or any major disagreement among groups, the risks of political action outweighed the group's incentive to intervene.

7. Group leaders, like Metro councilors, respected and deferred to the cabinet and chairman. Group leaders precluded involvement on issues alleged to be technical. Such issues, it was thought, should be determined by the experts. Of course, this deference might have diminished if the groups had been less satisfied with resulting policies.

8. During the early years group deference to official leadership was reinforced by the group leaders' image of a Metro system completely dominated by Gardiner. This popular image, largely fostered by the Toronto newspapers, convinced group leaders that intervention by their groups would have little effect on the outcome of issues. At the same time, there was no increase in group involvement after 1961, even though Allen's control of Council proceedings was less complete and even though group leaders recognized this fact.

9. Metro groups were more likely to intervene when there was

some disagreement within the official center of decision making, when the outcome was uncertain, or when the political officials were genuinely searching for solutions. Metro groups saw themselves as service agencies, willing to break a deadlock or add something to the official debate by offering new evidence or arguments. Greater conflict within the formal government would have encouraged greater group involvement. But these same groups remained passive when intragovernmental conflict became too rigid or intense. When an issue became a source of City–suburban conflict, that issue, in the words of the interest group leaders, had "hardened" or become "mixed up with politics." In such cases the groups concluded that the attitudes of the legislators were closed to suggestions, that group intervention would have little effect, and that only the Metro chairman could find some workable solution. For the same reasons, group leaders stayed clear of issues, like TTC appointments, that were enmeshed with strong personal antagonisms or personal rivalries within the official circle.

10. Groups were more likely to intervene when their intervention was solicited by administrators or Metro councilors. The TTC encouraged this participation but other Metro agencies did not. Group inactivity and the officials' disinclination to stimulate interest group support fortified each other.

Group Influence

Within the limits set by weak involvement, what influence did interest groups have on Metro policy making? This section argues that the influence of Metro groups lay more in their ability to help structure Council's general attitudes than in their ability to affect the course of decision making in specific instances.[10]

Group Influence on Issue Outcome. One may demonstrate the ineffectiveness of groups in particular policy-making situations by referring to the issues listed in Table 6.1. In the first two categories of the table (eighteen issues or almost one-third of the total) both the interest groups and the Metro Council supported the proposal of the chairman. These were low-conflict issues, whose outcome was never in doubt. Council was predisposed to accept the chairman's proposal. In a few of these issues group support may have strengthened Council's inclination by adding an aura of consensus to the measure. The groups were important in these eighteen cases only for the opposition they might have raised but did not.

The same conclusions about group influence may be reached for the seven issues included in the fourth category (items 41 to 47). These issues involved conflict between the general purpose and the grass-roots groups. In all these cases, however, the chairman and a majority of the Council were resolved from the outset to override grass-roots opposition and pass the proposal.

In the third category (twenty-one issues or about 38 percent of the total; items 20–40) the official decision makers were divided on the appropriate course of action, but all the groups taking a public stand were in agreement. This type of issue provided the conditions for maximum group influence over specific Metro decisions. With the officials either disunited or undecided about their next step, a united interest group sector could tip the balance in favor of a particular policy alternative. But the interest groups could not tip the balance in their favor—that is, they disagreed with the outcome—in nine of the twenty-one issues contained in the category. Most of these nine issues, in which the interest groups failed to win out, involved conflict between the City and suburban blocs. The outcome of these issues was determined by the chairman's skill in overcoming factional division and building a majority. Because the alignment in Council had hardened, and because most general purpose groups denounced the emphasis on parity and municipal rights as parochial, group influence in these issues was minimal. Of the twelve remaining issues, in which the groups agreed with the outcome, group influence was clearly important in two cases, possibly important in five cases, and clearly not important in the other five cases.[11]

In the last category (eight issues; items 48 to 55) there was conflict both within the official decision-making circle and among general purpose groups. Most of these issues—six to be exact—involved opposition by the *Star*, the *Telegram*, Labor, and the City bloc to Gardiner's public transit and expressway policies. In all of these six cases, however, the chairman's views prevailed. Moreover, the decisive factor in his victories was not the mild support he received from some good government groups but his own skills as floor leader.

In none of the cases in which there was conflict among interest groups (items 41 to 55) did the final policy outcome represent a compromise or adjustment of group demands. Nor did any Metro decisions represent the victory of one interest group coalition over another. Metro's approval of the Spadina expressway, over the opposition of many ratepayer associations, has been portrayed by local journalists as a case of successful pressure politics.[12] The retail firms who would be located in the new suburban Yorkdale Plaza and who needed the expressway to provide easy access to the Plaza presumably secured Metro approval of this project over the opposition of less forceful groups. But the crucial event in the passage of that expressway was the ability of the cabinet, in 1953–54, to convince Gardiner of the need for an expressway system and of the importance of the Spadina project to that system. Any pressure exerted by groups in favor of the project in later years was superfluous. The opponents of the Spadina expressway were outmaneuvered by a skillful floor leader but not outpressured by a superior coalition of interest groups.

Similarly, the decision to proceed with the Bloor Street subway route rather than the Metro planners' proposed route has been attributed to the larger number and better organization of interest groups supporting the Bloor route. But in this issue as in the Spadina case the pivotal decision was Gardiner's, and his decision was made without reference to the alignment of private interests on the question. Gardiner selected the TTC's Bloor route rather than the planners' proposal because he would not consider imposing an unwelcome route on the agency responsible for building and operating the subway.

In summary, interest groups clearly altered the outcome of Metro issues in two cases and possibly affected the outcome of another five. There were also a handful of cases in which groups may have reinforced the predispositions of official decision makers and made a probable outcome more certain. In many cases the groups were ineffective because the outcome was a foregone conclusion. In other cases the groups had a minimal impact because conflict in Council was intense and factional. Maximum group influence occurred when the officials were divided (but flexible) and the interest groups were in agreement. No Metro decision was a compromise between conflicting group demands, although one decision, the final Lakeshore expressway route, was a compromise between the demands of private groups and public agencies. In almost 90 percent of the issues considered in Table 6.1, the outcome would have been the same if no groups had intervened.

Pervasive Influence. The three Toronto newspapers helped set the overall ideological and intellectual climate of Metro politics. Influence over the politician's frame of reference, unstated assumptions, and picture of the world may be called "pervasive influence," as distinguished from the type of influence that alters specific outcomes.

Newspapermen, through written accounts and informal conversations, provided Metro councilors with information on what various officials and interest group leaders were thinking, but this communicating task had little consistent effect on the system's structure or policy outputs. The newspapers contributed significantly to the councilors' image of events but did not consciously attempt to create any particular images. This potential source of influence was not regularly used to promote the press's policy viewpoints.

The substantive views of the three dailies centered on the recentralization ideology.[13] Beginning in the 1940s, newspaper editorials had hammered away at the need to combat haphazard suburban sprawl, revive public transit, place tight controls on

the use of automobiles, minimize expressway expenditures, renew the central core, and draw the middle class back to central-
city living. Within this overall framework, all the newspapers
gave particular emphasis to subway construction. All papers
agreed that the City's problems were not being solved by Metro.
The *Star* and the *Telegram* proceeded to the conclusion that the
City's problems would not be met until total amalgamation replaced the federal system.

Because of this substantive viewpoint, the press's pervasive influence was largely confined to the City bloc. In the cases of public housing and subways, the newspapers' long-range crusades
apparently helped produce an area-wide agreement in principle.
Thus, newspaper influence could cross bloc lines. More often,
however, the suburbanites would dismiss the press's viewpoint
as pro-City.

Rather than change any minds, the press provided City officials with an ideological rationale for views they already accepted. Newspaper influence, moreover, seemed to strengthen the
intensity with which City views were held. The net effect of
press influence was to stiffen the City's militancy on structural
and regional-parity issues. Toronto's emphasis on subways over
other City projects was also attributable in part to the newspapers' indirect influence. Aside from the public housing and subways issues, where the newspapers helped move these programs
to the agreement-in-principle stage, the press's influence over final
policies occurred through its ability to raise the level and intensity of City expectations and thus indirectly affect the chairman's
behavior.

Pervasive influence, then, operated mainly at the issue-initiating phase of policy making and often even prior to that phase.
Newspapers would indicate what the general problems were and
would urge that "something be done." But they generally would
leave the preparation of detailed proposals to the cabinet and
the mustering of support for specific proposals to the chairman.

In view of their common interest in problem finding, a certain
amount of tension between the press and the administration was

inevitable. In the case of the *Star* and the *Telegram*, this tension was aggravated by substantive disagreements. As defenders of the Metro system, the chairman and cabinet informally criticized the press's "hysteria" over amalgamation. The administration also felt that newspaper overemphasis on subways made the councilors irrational on that subject and less willing to follow technical leadership. Conflict was muted by the newspapers' willingness to let the experts provide specific solutions and by overall press support for the cabinet's emphasis on construction programs. Rather than fill the problem-defining gap, the newspapers added to the political support behind public works programs.

The pervasive influence of the press made the chairman's floor-leading problem a bit more difficult. In the Gardiner years, newspaper descriptions of Metro as a one-man system annoyed councilors and sometimes provoked mild floor rebellions. By increasing the militancy and unity of the City bloc on some issues, the press helped harden the lines in Council and encouraged the chairman to accommodate City demands more than he otherwise might have. But since Gardiner's initial policies slightly favored the suburbs, newspaper influence helped produce a better balance in Metro's initial policy output. Not every behavioral pattern that diminished the chairman's legislative success was dysfunctional to the system.

CHAPTER 7

THE SOCIAL CONTEXT
OF METRO POLITICS (CONTINUED)

Electoral Politics in the Metro Area

Elections translate social issues into political issues in several ways. Candidates may seek out social issues as part of their campaign strategy. Elections may provide groups with an opportunity to support particular candidates, make group views known, extract concessions, and establish good working relations with particular officials. The electoral process often determines whether some groups will have better access to the political elite than other groups. By recruiting officials from particular segments of the social system, the elections may decide whose values will be over-represented in the political elite.

This section examines Metro elections as potential channels for the transmission of social demands and conflicts. My central argument is that the unstructured, issueless, and placid character of Metro area elections helps explain the weak linkage between Metro politics and social structure.

Classifying Urban Electoral Politics. The most useful way to classify local elections in North America is to place these elections along a structured–unstructured continuum.[1] Where parties or *ad hoc* electoral alliances prepare slates or tickets to guide the voter in his selection, that election may be classified as relatively structured. Unstructured elections exist where no bracketing or

[181]

grouping of candidates occurs, where party or factional labels are missing, and where each candidate runs his own separate campaign.

Table 7.1 tries to make this distinction more precise by dividing the electoral process into component activities, just as Table 1.1 reduced policy making to component activities. Three ideal types of electoral politics—partisan, factional, and nonfactional—are constructed and compared to the Toronto area pattern. Each type of election is described in terms of whether the component activities are performed at all and, if so, by whom they are performed.

The most highly structured form of electoral politics exists in partisan cities, even though there are almost endless varieties within this category. The common feature of all partisan elections is that stable, enduring organizations try to win control of city government and to maintain some degree of party unity in the policy-making process. The city may be overtly partisan, like New York, or may be ostensibly nonpartisan yet actually dominated by one party, like Chicago. The parties may correspond to the national, state, or provincial parties; on the other hand the parties may operate under labels like "the City Charter Committee" or "the Citizens' Association" and may have no organizational ties to the regular parties in the area.

By and large Canadian political parties do not overtly contest local elections.[2] No Canadian city government is controlled by one of the provincial and federal parties. Only Montreal approaches the degree of structured politics evident in U.S. partisan cities. In Montreal a purely local organization, called the Civic Party, controls a large majority of the seats in city council and maintains voting discipline in council proceedings.

A "faction" will be defined as an electoral alliance that dissolves once the election is over. Factional cities have slates of candidates in local elections but do not have disciplined, party voting in the council. The purpose of the faction is to elect certain individuals to office, not to carry out any policy program or to influence the behavior of the elected officials on policy matters.

TABLE 7.1   The Performance of Electoral Activities in the Metro Area and in Three "Ideal" Cities

Electoral Activities	Actors Performing the Activities			
	Partisan City	Factional City	Nonfactional City	Metro Area
Initiating candidacies	Parties, interest groups and individual candidate	Individual candidate, sometimes factions and interest groups	Individual candidate; sometimes interest groups	Individual candidate
Endorsing candidates	Parties; sometimes interest groups	Factions; sometimes interest groups	Interest groups	Interest groups
Campaign activities: canvassing, getting out vote, etc.	Parties	Factions or individual candidate	Individual candidate	Individual candidate and parties (not all activities performed)
Raising campaign funds	Parties and individual candidate	Factions and individual candidate; sometimes interest groups	Individual candidate; sometimes interest groups	Individual candidate
Preparing slate of candidates	Parties	Factions	Not performed	Not performed
Preparing policy program for slate	Parties (not always performed)	Factions (rarely performed)	Not performed	Not performed
Disciplining legislative voting	Parties (not always performed)	Not performed	Not performed	Not performed

This type of election may produce a majority bloc in the legislature but it does not produce a cohesive bloc, capable of governing. The elections are structured, through the use of labels and the grouping of candidates' names on the ballot, but the politics of the municipal council in the period between elections is not structured. Often these factions will dissolve and reappear under different names from one election to another. The voter is presented with a list of factions, but the names may be substantially different than the names of the factions contesting the last city election.

Factional elections occur in several large Canadian cities. The Civic Election Committee in Winnipeg and the Nonpartisan League in Vancouver are excellent illustrations of stable but loosely organized alliances, seeking to elect certain types of candidates (non-Socialist, non-Labor candidates) but not seeking to become governing parties. In Edmonton, on the other hand, the names of the factions change from one election to the next.

The least structured variety of electoral politics exists in those cities that have neither parties nor factions. Each candidate runs his own campaign, refuses to attach any labels to his name, and refuses to link his name with any other candidates running for different offices. The voter is presented with a ballot consisting of a long list of individual names, in no way formally classified or identified. Nonfactional politics prevails in many American cities, like Minneapolis, Detroit, and Los Angeles, and in Canadian cities, like Calgary, Hamilton, Ottawa, and Windsor. Canada apparently contains a larger percentage of nonfactional cities than does the United States.

Metro's Unstructured Electoral Politics. Electoral politics in Metro's thirteen municipalities was highly unstructured. Each candidate for local office ran and financed his own campaign, recruited his own organization of campaign workers, ran on his own record, refused to use any labels in the space provided on the ballot, denied affiliation with any of the established parties, and refused to comment on any contests for local office other than his own. Candidates for mayor or reeve studiously avoided involvement in aldermanic contests, and candidates for council seats remained neutral on mayoral contests. There was no mayor's ticket as is the case in some American factional cities.

Factional lines appeared in York Township after a judicial inquiry found irregularities in the town's land dealings. A "reform" faction and an "old guard" faction contested the 1958 and 1960 elections. By 1962, however, York had returned to its traditional nonfactional pattern.

Metro area elections also were characterized by an emphasis on personalities rather than issues; an emphasis on detailed, neighborhood grievances rather than city-wide or town-wide issues; low-keyed, sedate campaigns; and a great likelihood that incumbents seeking reelection would be returned. Such features seem more likely to occur in unstructured than structured elections, but Metro area elections were even more issueless and placid than elections in most nonfactional cities. It can be seen in Table 7.1, for example, that some campaign activities performed in my typical factionless city were sometimes not performed at all in Metro. Other differences between Metro and most factionless cities arose from the failure of Metro groups to provide some structuring of the electoral process.

Rivals for municipal office in the Metro area usually agreed that there were no issues in the contest other than the personalities, honesty, and administrative abilities of the candidates and the question of which candidate has deeper roots in the community. All candidates for a suburban office would denounce total amalgamation, promise to hold the line on taxes and to service neighborhood requests, criticize inadequate police and transit service, and advocate the attraction of more nonresidential assessment to the municipality. Candidates in the City would agree on the shortcomings of the Metro federal system and on the need for more parks, subways, public housing, and downtown redevelopment. Higher levels of government were usually blamed for Toronto's "runaway" tax rate. The major issue in aldermanic contests, in both the City and suburbs, was which candidate had done more or could do more for the neighborhood. In those suburbs where one person had served as reeve for ten or fifteen years, the challenger would try to make bossism the issue. In larger suburbs an important issue was whether the reeve would come from the northern or southern part of the town.

The most obvious characteristic of voting in Toronto area elections was the tendency to vote for friends and neighbors.[3] A candidate usually polled his strongest vote in the areas where he had been born and raised, where his wife had been born and raised, where he presently lived, and where his office or business was located. Even candidates for a city-wide or town-wide office had their neighborhood strongholds. This voting pattern suggests that, in the absence of issues or factions, the extent of a candidate's personal, business, and neighborhood affiliations were crucial factors in electoral success. The candidate with deep social roots in the community, the long-time resident of a neighborhood with an extensive network of personal relations, was difficult to beat.

Incumbents were also difficult to beat. Voters in Metro apparently responded to the most familiar names, and incumbents usually were better known than challengers. One measurement of the ease with which incumbent officials are returned to office is the incumbency ratio. Of the 180 incumbent Metro councilors who sought reelection to municipal office between 1953 and 1965, only 26 were not returned to Metro Council. Thus, the incumbency ratio in the Metro area was approximately .86— that is, about 86 percent of the incumbent Metro councilors seeking reelection were returned to the Council. Of the 26 defeated councilors, 13 were Toronto aldermen who dropped to second place in the ward vote and thus lost their Metro seat but not their municipal seat. If these 13 aldermen are treated as incumbents returned to office, Metro's incumbency ratio rises to .93.[4]

Another indication of the security of incumbent officials was the large number of uncontested elections in the suburban municipalities. In a typical election year three or four of the twelve suburban reeves and mayors were returned to office by acclamation. Reeve Dorothy Hague of Swansea was returned to office without a contest in nine consecutive elections. During Forest Hill's first forty-four years as a municipality, less than one-quarter of its elections for reeve were contested. Suburban contests were more likely to occur when an incumbent retired. In addition, offices were contested a bit more vigorously in the larger suburbs.

The Toronto area's campaigns were also more nonchalant than campaigns appear to be in most large American cities. Even in the City of Toronto, where political competition was keener than in the suburbs, campaigning was largely confined to a three-week period. A candidate making his first campaign for electoral office, or an alderman making his first campaign for controller or mayor, might have to spend generous amounts of money to make his name known; but incumbents seeking reelection were able to obtain reelection with minimal campaign expenditures. Candidates, particularly incumbents, often dispensed with certain campaign activities, like door-to-door canvassing, mailing campaign literature, and getting out the vote on election day. This lack of excitement and intensity was probably transmitted to the voters. Voter turnout was as low as 20 percent in some municipalities and rarely exceeded 35 percent in any municipality.

Group Involvement in Metro Elections. One reason Metro's electoral politics remained more sedate and issueless than electoral politics in other nonfactional cities was the failure of interest groups to become involved in Metro elections. In American factionless cities where private groups make endorsements of candidates for local office, the electoral process becomes more structured or meaningful. Issues are thrust into the foreground, and the importance of personalities and personal acquaintances recedes. In these cities the groups step in and fill the vacuum left by the absence of factions or parties. In some cases interest groups defend the exclusion of parties from local elections precisely because these groups are better able to dominate nonpartisan elections.[5]

In Metro some groups sought influence over policy making but not over elections. Included in this category were the BMR, the Board of Trade, the Social Planning Council, AWE, and most neighborhood groups. Other groups, mainly the political parties, sought influence in the electoral arena but not in the policy-making arena. There was, therefore, a gap between the policy-making sphere and the electoral sphere. Most Metro interest groups did not try to maximize their influence over elections as a means of enhancing their control over policy decisions. Even the Toronto newspapers and the Labour Council, which *did* make endorsements of local candidates, did not consistently use these endorsements to promote particular viewpoints on policy. This gap between the electoral and policy-making spheres helps explain why Metro groups generally did not try to pressure Metro councilors, why groups in Metro relied more on the persuasiveness of their case than on threats of reprisals at the polls.

But the participation of the parties, the Toronto press, and the Labour Council in local elections did give some structure to the electoral process. The description of Toronto area elections as disorganized and personal must be qualified with an account of the electoral roles these groups played. It is also important to know why these groups participated at all and why they did not participate more.

The Parties. Except for an occasional CCF-NDP candidate (the Cooperative Commonwealth Federation became the New Democratic Party in 1961), the political parties did not openly endorse candidates.[6] The parties, however, did play a covert and sometimes important role in municipal campaigns, particularly in the City and in the larger suburbs. Larger constituencies apparently encouraged candidates to seek out party assistance and to rely less on personal organizations. A political party usually helped candidates who had been members of that party with organizational assistance but not party funds. In addition, party supporters were privately encouraged to vote for local candidates unofficially identified with the party. The CCF-NDP supported not only persons affiliated with that party but also candidates recruited for the Labor movement.

Of course party assistance was not automatically given. The major parties appeared more likely to intervene in a contest if an unofficial Liberal were opposing an unofficial Conservative. The parties usually did not intervene when two members of the same party were contesting the same office, although there *were* a few instances of a party taking sides in a contest between two members of that party. The factor governing the party's choice in such cases, and the factor determining the party's degree of enthusiasm for a local candidate affiliated with that party, was whether the local candidate had been an active or merely a nominal member of the party. The CCF-NDP, which rarely had a mayoral candidate to support, devoted major attention to selected aldermanic contests.

It was customary for both candidates and parties to deny that any party assistance was being provided. The candidate hoped to benefit both from the assistance of one party and from the support of voters affiliated with other parties. The parties felt that the public was hostile to partisan intervention in local elections and would react against the first party that overtly intervened. For this reason the two major parties considered but rejected an open invasion of Metro area elections. Both the Liberals and Conservatives seemed willing to offer an official slate of local candidates, but each party wished the other to take the first step so that intervention could be justified as a defensive move. In the meantime, each of these two parties understated its own involvement in municipal politics and deplored the involvement of the other. The CCF-NDP was more willing to acknowledge its covert role and, in the early 1960s, seemed to be on the brink of open involvement.

The parties' fears about a popular reaction applied even more strongly to the question of partisan involvement in local legislative politics. The parties did not take stands on issues coming before Metro Council or the municipal councils and did not attempt to organize voting in the councils along party lines. The

Liberals in Metro Council did not have a program and did not vote together on Metro issues. CCF-NDP officials were no more left-wing than their colleagues, nor were local Conservative officials more right-wing. Only once did party considerations intrude into Metro Council proceedings. When the Council was considering a successor to Gardiner, several Conservative councilors suggested that a Conservative Metro chairman might have better relations with the Ontario government. The Council proceeded to name a Liberal despite the predominance of Conservatives on the Council at that time.

The involvement of parties in local elections, therefore, had no relevance for policy making at the Metro and municipal levels. Like factions, the Metro area parties helped structure local elections but did not structure legislative politics in the intervals between elections.

The lack of party involvement in policy making was one reason for the narrow range of ideological differences in Metro politics and the clustering of groups and viewpoints at the center of the spectrum. The ideological differences that prevailed at the provincial and federal levels were not carried over into municipal and Metro governments. Left-of-center and right-of-center attitudes were not translated by the parties into terms relevant to municipal politics. To some extent the Toronto press performed this translating activity, although the *Star* more vigorously applied liberal–welfare values to Metro affairs than the two Conservative newspapers applied right-of-center values.

Labor. Throughout the 1950s, Labor's political spokesmen put primary emphasis on bread-and-butter issues, like whether municipal and Metro contracts would be awarded only to firms hiring union labor. Labor's electoral goal, during those years, was to expand the number of Labor officials serving on municipal councils. The Labour Council confined its endorsements to union officials entering politics. In the 1960s, there was a noticeable expansion of Labor's involvement in local politics and an increase in Labor's commitment to general, liberal–welfare values.

In 1962, the Labour Council broke with tradition and endorsed Donald Summerville, a Conservative, for mayor of Toronto. Two years later Labor endorsed another nonunion man, Philip Givens, for the same office. Labor leaders conceded that their earlier insistence on endorsing only union officials had unduly restricted Labor's influence in local elections.

But the scope of Labor's electoral involvement, though expanding, was still small. Labor did not make any endorsements in suburban elections or in City aldermanic races, unless a union official were contesting one of the seats. Labor's willingness to endorse friendly non-Labor candidates extended only to the contest for mayor of Toronto. Moreover, Labor endorsed Summerville in 1962 not because of his stand on local issues but because his opponent, Mayor Nathan Phillips, would not respect a picket line surrounding the Royal York Hotel. In 1965, Labor had not yet demonstrated a willingness to enforce broad policy viewpoints through the use of electoral endorsements.

Toronto Labor's caution stood in sharp contrast to the pattern in some other large Canadian cities. Metro politics was more sedate because Toronto never had an aggressive, politically conscious, or radical Labor movement and never had a strong socialist movement. In Vancouver, the labor unions, in alliance with the CCF-NDP and with independent socialist groups, have been active in city politics for over three decades. In the 1930s, this socialist bloc came close to winning control of City Hall. As a result, the businessmen and the traditional political parties rallied to "save the city from socialism," and Vancouver city politics became bipolarized along ideological and class lines. A similar bipolarization occurred in Winnipeg, another city with a radical left-wing tradition. But Toronto Labor was more in the tradition of bread-and-butter, nonpolitical unionism, and Metro's CCF-NDP proved more reticent about open involvement in local politics than did sections of that party in other cities. Correspondingly, neither Toronto businessmen nor the traditional parties felt threatened, and neither had an incentive for more intensive involvement. Signs of Labor's growing inter-

est in civic politics may rouse Metro's business groups to intensify their own efforts, but the degree of business-Labor conflict
prevalent in Vancouver or Winnipeg appeared unlikely to
emerge.

The Press. Only the three Toronto newspapers regularly attempted to influence the outcome of both elections and policy
decisions. The three dailies presented full slates of endorsed City
candidates prior to each municipal election. In 1962, the newspapers began issuing full slates for suburban elections as well.
But the press, in making its endorsements, failed to consistently
reward officials who agreed with its policy views and punish officials who disagreed. For this reason the press only partially exploited its potential influence over policy making.

One important criterion of press endorsements was the unofficial party affiliation of the municipal candidates. The *Globe*
and the *Telegram* endorsed slates largely composed of Conservatives; the *Star* generally endorsed Liberals. But since partisan
affiliation did not correspond to viewpoints on Metro policies,
a newspaper, in approving candidates from the same political
party, was rewarding individuals with a variety of attitudes on
local policy questions. The *Telegram*, for example, rewarded
many Conservatives who opposed *Telegram* policies on local
questions and punished many Liberals and New Democrats who
supported that newspaper's local views. The gap between policy-
making and electoral politics in Metro was often demonstrated
in the editorial pages of the Toronto press. A newspaper could
repeatedly condemn an official for his views on Metro or local
policies and then, just prior to the local election, endorse that
official with fulsome praise.

Thus, partisan considerations not only failed to structure policy making in Metro, they served to distract both the voters and
the interest groups from a consideration of local issues and of
the possible differences among candidates on local questions. A
party supported local candidates not because it wished certain
policies to be carried out, but because it wanted to see more Lib-

erals, Conservatives, or New Democrats sitting on municipal councils. In making endorsements on the basis of party affiliation, the press further removed the campaign from a consideration of the issues facing Metro or broader social issues. The press also sacrificed much of its influence over policy making to enhance the status and fortunes of particular political parties.

A second criterion governing press endorsements of local candidates was the personal abilities of the individuals. The three newspapers agreed that persons with managerial backgrounds or skills made the best mayors and controllers. The press also preferred activists who raised problems and agitated issues. At times the press endorsed aggressive politicians with strong viewpoints, regardless of whether the press agreed with those viewpoints. William Archer, to cite one outstanding example, received the unanimous support of the three newspapers in his 1964 bid for reelection as City controller, even though he had disagreed with most newspaper policies during the preceding two years. In endorsing Archer, all the newspapers emphasized personality and personal skills.

The Functional Significance of Metro Elections. To summarize, Metro's fluid issueless brand of electoral politics was a poor mechanism for the political articulation of demands and conflicts present in the larger community. Metro's unstructured elections produced unstructured legislatures and had a minimal impact on policy making.[7] These elections did not produce governing majorities or legislative factions of any kind. By no stretch of the imagination could it be said that any election in Metro produced a mandate for particular policies or produced a legislature inclined in one direction or another on policy questions. With respect to attitudes on Metro policies, one Metro Council was very much like another.

The major structuring factor in Council voting was the councilors' defense of municipal interests. Metro area elections did not provide any issues to challenge this concern with federal questions and did not provide any alternative basis of division or structuring in Council. Perhaps the transmission of more substantive or social issues to Council would have weakened the almost exclusive concern with municipal rights and thus facilitated the political integration of the Metro system.

Voting in an unstructured legislature is fluid, the alignments shifting from one issue to the next. Anyone assuming a leadership role in this type of legislature must rely on *ad hoc*, unstable majorities. The absence of a stable majority may have hindered the Metro chairman's floor-leading efforts. At the same time, because Metro elections did not produce a legislature with clearly defined policy attitudes, the legislators were highly susceptible to the chairman's persuasive efforts. A fluid legislature, though somewhat unpredictable, provided the chairman with room for maneuver. Both Gardiner and Allen were committed to preserving this fluid style of legislative politics.

In structured legislatures a partisan or factional caucus may seize the initiative on policy questions, but legislatures with minimal internal organization, like the Metro Council, are more likely to respond to the leads of extralegislative actors than to provide their own leads. Metro Council's fluid internal structure strengthened its deference to administrative leadership.

Metro politicians interpreted the security of incumbent officials, the relative absence of group involvement in elections, and the issueless character of local campaigns to mean that councilors had a good deal of discretion in defining their own policy positions. Although Metro politicians were not innovators, they did not hesitate to support innovations because of possible repercussions at the next election.

But Metro's departure from the broker leadership model cannot be ascribed wholly to unstructured electoral politics. Many nonfactional cities in the United States are also broker leadership cities.[8] Because he cannot rely on a party or faction for electoral support, because he must respond to the full range of local interest groups, the politician in the factionless city often seeks to alienate as few groups as possible by taking as little action as possible. Even though the incumbent politician in a factionless city may be relatively secure, he still may attribute his success at the polls to his caution. In short, the Metro councilor's image of himself as a relatively free agent emerged from a constellation of factors: the weak involvement of groups in policy-making politics, the unity and aggressiveness of the Metro administration, the local political culture, as well as the unstructured nature of local elections.

The impact of unstructured legislative politics on the overall performance of the Metro system might be further demonstrated by speculating on the probable impact of partisan legislative politics.[9] These speculations are more than a purely heuristic exercise. In 1965, it seemed only a matter of time before the three political parties in the area began openly contesting municipal elections. Increased partisan intervention, rather than any change in interest group involvement, appeared to be the most likely source of change in Metro's electoral pattern. In the short run, however, the parties will probably behave as factions, preparing electoral slates but not attempting to create a disciplined party bloc in the Council. The NDP appeared more committed than the other parties to executing policy programs at the local level; if the New Democrats were to hold a significant number of seats on Metro Council, the shift from factional to partisan politics would be hastened.

In a Council with a partisan majority the chairman's role would probably change into that of a majority party leader. If the majority were committed to problem solving and were willing to defer to technical expertise, the cabinet and chairman might find their legislative support more consistent and predictable. At the same time, whatever the views of the majority party, a better organized legislature would be more insistent on providing its own initiative in some cases and would be less willing to play a passive role. If the chairman were reliant on a party caucus for his appointment and reappointment, he might be less able to defer to cabinet leads. The chairman would be more a man of the legislature and less a man of the administration.

If no party held a majority, the chairman might either be

the spokesman for the largest party or a nonpartisan mediator. In either case the alignments in Council probably would be more rigid than they were in 1965 and the conflicts might be more difficult to resolve.

Of course, concern over municipal rights would not simply disappear. If party lines cut across existing bloc lines, so that each party held both City and suburban seats, disciplined party voting on many issues would be difficult to maintain. If a ma-jority party were to be composed largely of City delegates or largely of suburban delegates, the political integration of the system would be threatened.

Thus, party intervention in legislative politics would most likely reduce the Council's deference to the cabinet and the coun-cilors' willingness to go along. Intervention might intensify con-flict in the Council and preclude the kind of easygoing, accom-modative style that prevailed during Metro Council's first thir-teen years. The chairman would lose much of his flexibility and discretion. On the other hand, partisan legislative politics would probably reduce the reliance of the Metro system on the per-sonal, floor-leading skills of individual chairmen. The 1961–1965 impasse over policy output might be broken, and gaps in the system's adaptive performance—the relative neglect of noncon-struction programs—might be filled.

In the short run Metro's pattern of electoral politics facili-tated the chairman's legislative tasks and made it relatively easy to get things done. The pattern of endless delays and accommo-dations, so evident in many American cities, was generally absent in Metro. Over the long run, however, the Metro system ran the risk of alienating large segments of the community. In the ab-sence of survey data, no definitive statements about Metro pub-lic opinion can be made. But there were frequent complaints about the blandness and meaninglessness of Metro politics, even from groups that might have made Metro politics more mean-ingful by their increased involvement. The weak popular interest in local campaigns and the low turnout on election day suggest that a large part of the public, though legally enfranchised, was poorly integrated into the Metro political system. Their exclusion, aside from whatever ethical judgments one might wish to make, created the opportunity for "a rebellion of alienated voters," such as occur in some factionless American cities.[10] These rebellions, because they are unpredictable and unsettling, must be considered dysfunctional to the system. Finally, if more citizens had found Metro politics meaningful, a popular commitment to the Metro form of government might have emerged.

An Open-Ended System. Only in one respect does factionless politics provide for a maximum flow of social messages to the political system. In structured electoral systems those interest groups that help the majority party or faction win the election will have better access to the decision makers and probably more influence over the policy outputs.[11] In unstructured elections the interest groups will have roughly equal access. Structured elections produce structured channels of access; unstructured elections produce open-ended policy-making systems. Structured elections, by incorporating certain elements into a majority coalition, produce in-groups and out-groups; unstructured elections produce legislatures that are responsive to the full range of groups intervening in policy-making politics.

This generalization on elections and access applied to the Metro case. One rough measurement of a group's access to Metro decision makers is its index of agreement with Metro policies (see Table 6.1). The measurement is rough because a low index may indicate a lack of access (an inability to alter the course of policy in the direction one desires), but a high index does not necessarily indicate access to or influence over public officials. The group may register a high index of agreement because it frequently endorsed policies that were going to be approved in any case. With these limitations in mind, the similar indices of agreement registered by all the general-purpose groups suggest roughly equal access. While the good government groups were somewhat more content than the liberal groups, the difference in the scores of these two blocs is small. The only out-groups were the neighborhood associations, and their consistent record of failure may be better explained by the prevailing respect for technical opinion than by the characteristics of local electoral politics. Metro elections, therefore, produced no obstacle to any group's expanding its policy-making role.

Metro's Political Elite: The Class and Ethnic Basis of Politics

The men who have the final say on all questions of Metro policy, the Metro councilors, may also be viewed as the Metro area's political elite. The important questions that must be asked of any ruling group relate to its social and ideological homogeneity and to its permeability. From what socio-economic groups are the decision makers drawn, and to what extent are they agreed in their general political outlook? How easy is it for outsiders to become part of this elite, and to what extent do the elite members put up barriers to invasion? These questions must be asked because the perspectives, experiences, and values that official decision makers bring to their offices are important parts of the policy-making process, and because these perspectives are not captured by the type of decision-making analysis undertaken in the preceding chapter. An official's internalized values may be a channel for the transmission of group attitudes and a mechanism for converting social issues into political issues, even in the absence of group pressures. One must ask not only who pressures the official but also who the official's reference groups are. In addition, internalized values explain why certain questions are not seen as problems and are not raised at all; understanding the background of decision makers permits us to deal with non-decisions and nonevents.[12]

The Social Background of Metro Decision Makers. In 1962, the Bureau of Municipal Research undertook a survey of the social characteristics and political attitudes of all individuals seeking local, elective office.[13] Since the BMR study found no differences in the characteristics of Metro councilors and municipal councilors, the results of the study may be treated as a portrait of both the Metro elite and the municipal elites. There also were no significant differences in the characteristics of successful and unsuccessful candidates—which in itself says a great deal about the unstructured, issueless character of Metro elections. The following discussion is based on the social characteristics of the winning candidates.

The bureau's data revealed that, despite the growing social diversity of the Toronto area, the political elite was drawn largely from the "old order" and was much less representative of the groups that entered the community after 1945. Table 7.2 at-

TABLE 7.2   The Social Characteristics of Metro's Population and Political Elite, 1961–1962

Social Characteristics	Metro Area		City of Toronto	
	Population[a]	Elite[b]	Population[a]	Elite[b]
Protestants	68.4%	77.0%	51.7%	68.0%
Catholics	29.5	7.0	34.7	5.0
English ancestry[c]	24.5	34.0	18.3	58.0
Middle-class occupations: managerial, proprietorial, sales, and clerical	13.2[d]	39.0[e]	9.9[d]	36.0[e]
Conservative Party supporters	47.5[f]	58.3[g]	44.4[f]	59.6[g]

[a] Based on Federal Census (1961) unless otherwise indicated.
[b] Based on Bureau of Municipal Research, *The Metro Politician*, 1962.
[c] Using Anglican Church membership as index.
[d] Percentage calculated on basis of total labor force, not total population.
[e] In classifying politicians, the most recently held private occupation was used.
[f] Based on the preference of voters (not the population at large) in the 1963 provincial election. It was thought that a provincial election would reveal, better than a federal election, the stable partisan preferences of Metro area voters. The 1963 election was selected because it stood closest in time to the BMR survey.
[g] Represents a percentage of municipal officials who were willing to indicate any party preference, not a percentage of all municipal officials. About one-third refused to cite any partisan loyalty.

tempts to demonstrate in rough fashion the political elite's over-representation of middle-class groups, Protestants, Conservative Party supporters, and persons of English descent (as measured by Anglican Church membership). This overrepresentation was more apparent in the City, where most of the "New Canadians" settled. The Metro political elite represented less the Toronto of 1962 than the Toronto of 1932—a tightly integrated, socially homogeneous, middle-class community, dedicated to the Crown and Empire, the Conservative Party, the Toronto *Telegram*, the Anglican Church, temperance, and Sunday blue laws. Under-represented in the 1962 political elite were Catholics, Italians and eastern Europeans, and persons of low income. (Also underrep-resented was the area's highest income group—those individuals earning over $25,000 a year.) The bureau's data, then, demon-strated the failure of the newer, ethnic groups to penetrate the political elite. The social homogeneity of the area's population had been dissolved by recent immigration, but the social homo-geneity of the local political leadership changed little.

This elite also was unresponsive to changes in the political complexion of the area. In the 1950s and 1960s, the partisan loy-alties of the Toronto area shifted from the Conservatives to the Liberals and New Democrats—although these shifts in party loyalty were more apparent at the federal than at the provin-cial level. In 1963 and 1965, the Conservatives from the metro-politan area failed to win any federal seats; but, in 1962, the Conservatives in Metro area government outnumbered the Lib-erals by almost 2 to 1.

Metro's Elite and the Politics of Consensus. The bureau's survey also found that there was a remarkable amount of agreement among local officials on the issues and that this consensus gen-erally embodied good government, middle-class ideals. Local government was consistently compared to a business, which had to be run efficiently by skilled managers so that costs could be minimized. In identifying the most pressing problems, the great majority of officials referred to "rising tax rates" and "rising debt charges." The BMR concluded that the officials' prevailing attitude was negative, that is, directed toward the minimizing of expenditures rather than the attainment of any substantive programs. But few officials carried their conservatism very far. Few thought that government interference in private enterprise was a serious problem, and no local official proposed cutting back a major program in order to reduce expenditures and curb taxes.

This consensus among Metro's elite on good government values was reflected in the political institutions and practices of the area: the high degree of professionalization in the Metro and municipal administrations, the legislators' deference to expert opinion and administrative leadership, the strong aversion to open partisan involvement in local politics, the widespread use of independent commissions, the fear of bossism and the continued support of the weak-mayor system, and the high level of honesty in government. Municipal reformers in Canada and the United States would probably rate Toronto area governments as clean and efficient.[14]

The prevalence of middle-class politicians and middle-class values was consistent with the area's low-pressure, loosely organized electoral politics. Toronto area elections were basically family quarrels, all occurring within the middle class and within the framework of middle-class values. The absence of dramatic conflict within the ranks of the political elite helped to strip area elections of their excitement and probably served to depress popular interest and participation.[15] Furthermore, working-class voters may have been apathetic because the middle-class issues had little salience for them. The social and attitudinal homogeneity of the Metro councilors facilitated the construction of legislative majorities, but only at the price of excluding major groups from direct representation in Metro's elite and at the price of making politics appear bland and uninteresting to many people. An important source of social differentiation was not being transmitted to the political system.

The sparsity of working-class and ethnic spokesmen within the political elite did not mean that these groups were excluded from politics or that their interests were not considered. Even middle-class politicians must win elections, and no City of Toronto politician could pursue his career without making appeals to the newer groups. Because some City politicians went further than others in their attempts to woo these lower-income groups, it is possible to discern working-class and good-government types within the ranks of middle-class candidates. Generally, the good-government type (e.g., Jean Newman, Ford Brand, Philip Givens) was praised for his administrative ability and his understanding of central planning and capital budgeting. His electoral strength usually lay in the northern, "silk stocking" parts of the City. The working-class politician was usually more colorful, less involved in the City's administrative business, and more scrupulous about his attendance at social gatherings and the celebration of ethnic-group holidays. The former type of politician more often tried to debate local issues; the latter would emphasize nonlocal issues like "the liberation of the Eastern European nations from Communist tyranny."

The development of these two roles within the ranks of middle-class City politicians sometimes structured Toronto elections. In 1964, when Philip Givens and Allan Lamport ran for mayor, the City's voters were given a clearcut choice between the two types of politician. For the most part, however, the degree of structuring on this basis was small and the articulation of class issues weak. Most City politicians avoided being placed in either category, in the hope of capturing both ethnic and good government support. In the 1964 City election, Labor endorsed Givens, the good government candidate. Moreover, one of the few Labor officials to hold a City-wide office, Ford Brand, won unanimous praise from the good government groups. Thus, the distinction between the two types of electoral roles was blurred, to say the least.

Working-Class and Ethnic Penetration of the Political Elite. It is reasonable to assume that class and ethnic issues would have been more pertinent to Metro politics if the Metro political elite had been less solidly middle class in its composition. The obvious question is why lower income groups did not pry their way into this political elite.

If the middle-class, Protestant groups in Metro constituted a political elite, they did not constitute a self-conscious elite, eager to protect its prerogatives and to exclude other groups from membership. The middle class ruled by tradition more than by conscious design. Because of Metro's unstructured elections, the elite was open-ended and easily permeable. Working-class and ethnic groups could have expanded their representation in the Metro elite through a more determined electoral effort.

That determined effort was not forthcoming. Only speculative hypotheses will be offered on the reasons for this lack of political aggressiveness. First, there is the evidence that lower-income groups generally participate less in politics. Also relevant is the natural lapse in time that occurs between an immigrant group's arrival in a community and that group's active intervention in local politics.[16] If the natural lag hypothesis is correct, ethnic demands for direct representation in Metro's elite will increase. An additional factor was the apparent willingness of Metro's ethnic and working-class leaders to defer to the "old order" and to press their political demands through the middle-class leaders. This deference, it seems to me, operated separately from the natural lag factor and may have inhibited an increase in the level of ethnic demands. Perhaps the working-class and ethnic leaders' acceptance of most middle-class values—a point discussed below—partially accounted for this satisfaction with the existing elite. Finally there was a matter of personalities. Toronto's newer groups did not find the type of flamboyant, popular leader capable of contesting a high office and galvanizing ethnic involvement in local politics.

There also were two important structural obstacles to lower-class penetration of the political elite. One obstacle, paradoxically, was Metro's unstructured elections. Parties or factions generally attempt to balance their slates of local candidates by placing at least one ethnic spokesman on the ticket. Newer groups or underdog groups often find the political party to be a channel for rapid political advancement. In factionless cities a candidate must raise his own funds and construct his own campaign organization. It often is some time before many members of a recently arrived ethnic community can piece together these resources. In one sense unstructured politics is easy to invade because there is no self-conscious in-group that seeks to exclude newcomers. In another sense unstructured politics is difficult to invade because so much is left to the individual candidate and because no electoral organization exists to coopt ethnic spokesmen. Unstructured politics can also be an obstacle to indigenous working-class groups. Where all the initiative rests with the individual, the electoral system favors middle-class candidates, that is, candidates with more time and money at their command.[17]

A second and perhaps less important obstacle was the spatial arrangement of Toronto's nine wards. Most of Toronto's wards were large, sprawling, and socially heterogeneous (see Figure 7.1). The average ward contained about 75,000 people. Wards 2, 3 and 4 each had some of the City's lowest income areas in its southern portions and some of the highest income areas in the northern portions. With the exception of Ward 8 (largely Italian) and Ward 9 (Toronto's "silk stocking" ward) the Toronto wards muted rather than represented the ethnic and economic differences in the City.

This ward pattern probably made conflict in the City Council easier to resolve and a unified City position on Metro issues easier to establish. Banfield and Wilson, in *City Politics*, note that aldermen in small-ward cities are often single-minded, militant fighters for the homogeneous interests of their respective wards.[18] In large-ward cities the aldermanic candidate must appeal to a variety of groups and must blur his public image. In small-ward cities most conflicts are resolved in the legislative chamber; in large-ward cities each alderman must resolve social conflicts within his own political style. In the large-ward case, conflicts are worked out during the election campaign within

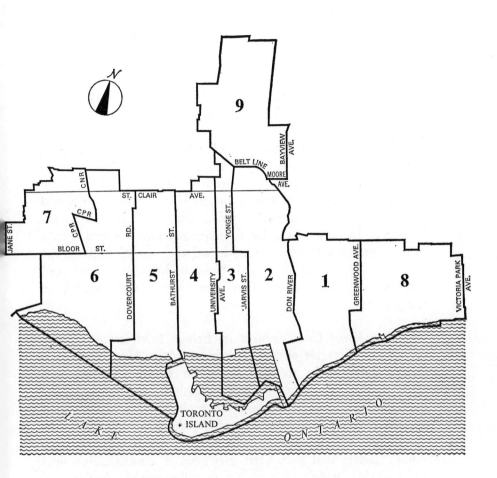

FIGURE 7.1   The City of Toronto's Large-Ward System

Source: The City of Toronto, *Municipal Handbook*, 1964

[205]

each ward, rather than after the election in the city council. Intralegislative negotiations are more successful in the large-ward city because the varied social structure of each alderman's constituency provides him with a certain amount of flexibility and autonomy.

But the small-ward pattern, while possibly increasing conflict in the municipal council, also increases the system's responsiveness to minority groups. Even Toronto's large wards would have been more receptive to ethnic penetration if these wards had coincided with, rather than divided, the City's natural neighborhoods. In each of the large, heterogeneous Toronto wards, the aldermanic candidates usually had their social roots in the middle-class parts of the ward. Since middle-class parts voted more heavily, candidates often concentrated their appeals in these areas.

The Functional Consequences of Ethnic Penetration. Despite the above obstacles ethnic representation in Metro's political elite seemed likely to increase. (The future of indigenous working-class representation will probably be determined by the extent of NDP involvement and success in Metro area elections.) In assessing the consequences of ethnic penetration for the Metro political system, one must first determine whether these ethnic leaders will have been socialized in middle-class values prior to their political emergence or whether these leaders will challenge the middle-class values.

If ethnic leaders challenge the middle-class values, as ethnic leaders do in many American and Canadian cities, one might expect less deference to administrative leadership, less emphasis on expertise and civil service procedures in the selection of administrative personnel, and greater support for open partisan involvement in local politics. The emergence of a new value scheme might produce new cleavages in the City bloc and might increase the social and attitudinal distance between most City and most suburban members of Metro Council. In the long run, this challenge to middle-class values might provoke a more

conscious attempt by middle-class groups to control local elections, a greater structuring of local elections, and an overall
increase in the intensity of electoral politics. Legislative conflicts would be more difficult to resolve, but Metro politics
might become more meaningful to many people.

There are, however, several good reasons for concluding that
this challenge to middle-class values will not occur. First, most
of the ethnic and working-class leaders in the 1950s and 1960s
apparently accepted these middle-class values. (I leave aside
the question of whether the rank and file in these classes also
accepted such values.) The Labour Council, the City aldermen recruited from Toronto's ethnic groups, the ethnic press,
and the two major newspapers oriented to a working-class and
ethnic clientele all accepted the major tenets of the good government, reform ideology.

Second, when ethnic and class tensions did penetrate the
political sphere, the source of these tensions were questions of
morality and personal style. Politicians recruited from the ethnic
groups, and working-class politicians within the ranks of the
middle class, would often focus their demands on a relaxation
of the Sunday blue laws and a relaxation of the regulations governing the consumption of alcohol. A contest between a working-class and good government politician often centered on the
sports-versus-culture issue—on whether the City needed an
expanded hockey arena or a center for the performing arts.

Nor would an increase in the importance of ethnic and working-class groups within the political elite necessarily mean a
strengthening of liberal–welfare values at the expense of good
government conservatism. In fact, two of Toronto's most prominent working-class politicians, Nathan Phillips and Allan Lamport, generally opposed new programs as too costly and urged
holding the line on the tax rate.[19] On the whole, however, ethnic
issues were not related to liberal-versus-conservative issues.

Assuming that campaign issues in the 1950s and 1960s gave
some indication of the status of ethnic group demands, those
demands had little to do with the major policy decisions facing

the Metro Council. If this is true, ethnic penetration would little alter the structure, style, or policy outputs of the Metro system.

Conclusions. High political consensus in the Metro area reflected high social consensus. Certain types of intergroup conflict, present in other communities, were not present in the Metro area's social structure. The Metro community lacked Negro–white conflict (in contrast to most American cities) and French–English conflict (in contrast to Montreal), because the demographic basis for such conflict was absent. The relatively harmonious state of relations between the "Anglo's" and "New Canadians" and between Labor and management removed two other potential sources of political conflict. Only a detailed exploration of the Metro social community would reveal whether this high degree of consensus is more apparent than real and, if real, what all the reasons for it are.

If there had been more social tension, Metro groups might have become more involved in politics, and the intensity of politics might have increased. At the same time, the highly unstructured Metro elections, the weak involvement of interest groups in policy-making politics, and the Metro elite's over-representation of certain groups and values were not conducive to the flow of issues from the social to the political sector. In the following section, moreover, I argue that, even if more social conflicts had been present, local beliefs about the nature of politics would have impeded the conversion of these tensions into political questions.

Furthermore, it is a mistake to treat social factors as necessarily independent variables. Perhaps collective-bargaining relations were relatively harmonious in the Metro area because Labor and business were not pitted against each other in the political arena. If Metro politics had been less dull or meaningless to the larger public, perhaps more segments of the community would have been encouraged to assert their viewpoints or to increase the level of their political demands. To an extent, political patterns have a life of their own. New groups may become socialized in the prevailing way of doing things in the political sphere and may adjust their political behavior accordingly.

Political Culture: A Deferential System

The culture of a political system may be defined as a set of basic beliefs about the nature of government and politics held by the vast majority of system members. I would exclude from this definition beliefs about trivial matters and beliefs that are lightly held. The culture of a system need not be the product of that system. In the Metro case, what seem to me to be the basic beliefs existed prior to the system's creation; these beliefs were brought to the system by the members. One may or may not include in this definition beliefs about the substance of policy. The following discussion includes only beliefs about the nature of politics itself, since these beliefs are more relevant to the theme of this chapter. One may or may not include the public at large in one's definition of system members. I include only political activists, since their values have the most immediate impact on the system and since I was better able to ascertain their beliefs than the beliefs of the larger public. Of course these comments are not intended to gloss over the continuing problems of definition or the difficult decisions about what beliefs to include and exclude from this political culture category.[20]

The essence of the Metro activists' beliefs about the nature of politics was the principle of deference to authority and leadership. Such beliefs help explain the willingness of the department heads to leave politics to the chairman, the ability of the chairman to maintain cabinet unity, the willingness of the Metro councilors to permit the chairman so significant a role and to go along so often with his leads, the deference of both legislators and interest group leaders to technical expertise, the willingness of interest group leaders on so many occasions to let the officials settle things, and the inclination of working-class and ethnic leaders to accept middle-class dominance. This deference would preserve much of the system's political tranquillity even in the face of increased social tensions.

This deferential culture appears to stem from a more general Canadian political culture, which in turn is an adaptation to North American experiences of the British political culture. The Metro system's links to that Canadian political culture help explain why Metro departs from the high-pressure, broker leadership pattern of politics evident in most American cities. If the following account of Canadian political culture is accurate, one would expect to find, in comparison to the United States, a less intense style of politics at all levels of Canadian government. The following account, it must be added, rests on the impressions of this author and other authors, since extensive survey data on what Canadians believe are not available.[21]

Attempts to define Canadian political culture and to distinguish it from the American have emphasized the greater respect in Canada for law and order and for persons in positions of authority; the lesser importance in Canada of individualism, experimentation, and a spirit of revolt, and the greater strength in Canada of an aristocratic or class tradition as opposed to an egalitarian tradition. These aspects of culture may produce in Canada, as they do in Great Britain, a willingness to let public policy matters be determined by the officials' greater understanding of the issues and to rely on the officials' self-restraint for the protection of one's rights.

Canadians, it seems, hold a unitary rather than pluralist view of the public interest. In the unitary view, informed persons in positions of authority, proceeding *in camera* and free of political pressures, search out the public interest. Canadians seem less willing than Americans to accept the notion that the public interest will emerge through the open agitation of issues and the open clash of opposing groups in a free political marketplace.

There are, however, several limits to the use of political culture as an explanation of the Metro system. These basic beliefs apparently needed an activating element. Again, one must resort to explanations in terms of personalities and unique events. If Gardiner had not exploited these beliefs, they might have remained latent. This same culture, for example, did not produce the same type of executive-directed system at the municipal level, where the activating element was absent. Nor does the Canadian political culture explain why Metro politics were more tranquil than politics in other Canadian cities—unless the Toronto area had absorbed more of the British tradition and less of the American tradition than western cities like Winnipeg and Vancouver.

Toward a Distinctive Theory of Local Politics

Chapters 6 and 7 proceeded on the assumption that Metro politics was less intense than politics in other Canadian and American cities and that only factors distinctive to Metro could explain this lesser intensity. Another explanation of Metro's low-pressure politics, which does not destroy the validity of the earlier explanations, is that local political systems are generally less competitive and intense than systems at higher levels of government. Students of American city politics, in emphasizing that broker leadership prevails at all levels of American government, have slurred over the distinctive characteristics of local politics. Studies by Dahl and others, which use local communities as a laboratory for the examination of democratic systems, also fail to note the differences between national and local democracies.[22]

The distinctive feature of local political systems, in comparison to national systems, is the weaker commitment of members to the local system's success and the greater degree of membership apathy about the local system's structure and outputs. The study of local politics may derive its major theoretical significance from the fact that it is concerned with minimally integrated systems. In accounting for this weak integration at the local level, the following explanations—some obvious, some requiring further testing—seem most relevant.

1. Political stakes at the local level are much smaller than at

the higher levels of government. The stakes may not seem smaller to groups and officials exclusively concerned with local issues, but groups that try to spread their influence across several levels of government will devote less of their political resources to local politics.

2. Many of the decisions taken by local government are so specific (e.g., to install a traffic light on a particular corner, to close a restaurant operating in violation of the health code, to increase the offer made to a property owner for land being expropriated by the city) that *individual* interests, but not *group* interests, are affected and aroused. It would be wrong to argue, as municipal reformers of sixty years ago did, that there are no issues in city government and that city government involves only administration. But it is correct to say that most decisions taken by municipal councils are on very specific questions, which at the higher levels of government would be decided by the administrative agencies.

3. Canadian and American cities rely heavily on the assistance and beneficence of senior governments for the solution of most urban problems. One of the urban political leader's most important tasks is extracting support and money from other governments. This reliance on external aid limits the range of conflict in city politics. All local actors agree that the city is not to blame for its worse dilemmas and that only the higher levels of government can provide solutions. Moreover, city politicians have an incentive to smother controversy and present a united front to other governments, so that the city's reputation and bargaining position will be enhanced.

4. Because local issues differ from national issues both in subject matter and in degree of specificity, the ideological framework used to assess national questions does not always apply to urban politics. Interest groups and parties may be uncertain about, or indifferent to, local issues because the groups do not know where to place such issues on a liberal–conservative spectrum. The groups may conclude that there is no politics at the local level, when in fact there is just a different brand of politics.

5. Few local decisions are final. Political actors may feel that they can always contest the issue when it reaches the stage of provincial or state approval. This attitude may be particularly prevalent in Canada, where provincial control of local actions is pervasive and where very little of consequence can be undertaken by a local government without provincial review and consent.

6. Many local interest groups are shoestring operations, so lacking in funds and organizational resources that they are qualitatively different from aggressive national groups, like the Canadian Labour Congress or the American Medical Association. Local groups are less likely to understand the issues, to relate the issues to group interests, or to draft alternative policies that would protect and enhance group interests. The competitive advantage that public administrators have, because of their access to information and staff resources, seems more significant at the local than the national level.

7. Compared to their national counterparts, local politicians appear less articulate, less involved in politics, and hence less able to play an assertive role in policy making. National, state and provincial politics siphon off a good deal of the political talent in Canada and the United States. Many of the assertive, able politicians who do enter local politics do not stay there very long. Most local councilmen, moreover, are part-time politicians, unwilling to devote their full energies to politics, not yet committed to a career as professional politicians, and sometimes using politics primarily to promote their private businesses.

8. Popular commitment to the community political system in no way approaches popular commitment to the national political system. One sociologist, Scott Greer, referred to American cities as "communities of limited liability."[23] If the citizen is basically unhappy with trends in his community, he is just as likely to move elsewhere as he is to voice political protest. If turnout in local elections and the extent of mass media coverage of local elections are any indication, the local government, far from being closest to the people, is the most remote. The local community is a social system whose membership changes freely

and frequently. Most of the members seem unconcerned with the future of the system.

9. Due to the greater specificity of local issues and the smaller scale of local government, face-to-face relations and personal influence within the legislature may be more important determinants of issue outcome than they are at the national level. The tact and sociability of particular councilmen will more often decide the fate of local issues than will the clash of groups or general principles.[24]

10. Cities sometimes attain a degree of social homegeneity rarely equaled at the national level. Toronto of thirty years ago is a case in point. All one-industry and two-industry towns offer further examples. A less differentiated social structure offers a less suitable basis for open-ended, pluralistic, competitive politics; such homogeneous communities tend to develop consensual, low-pressure politics.[25]

CHAPTER 8

ROLES
IN THE LEGISLATIVE
SUBSYSTEM

The substantive goal of this chapter is to describe how the Metro councilors came to define their roles in the Metro Council. After arguing that these roles were formed outside of the Council itself, I then speculate on why interaction with other councilors was not a more important influence over the legislator's behavior. The theoretical purposes of this chapter are twofold: to explore further the type of actor analysis mentioned in chapter 1, and to indicate the circumstances under which a legislature will *not* develop an informal system of structured relations.

The Metro Councilor: A Case Study in Role Definition

The Resulting Definition. The Metro councilor's role, described throughout this study, requires only a brief summary at this point. That role may be discussed in terms of two variables: the councilor's allocation of personal loyalty between Metro and other systems, and the councilor's allocation of time and involvement between Metro business and the proceedings of other systems.

The Metro councilor viewed himself as a municipal delegate attending an international conference. The councilor's major purpose at the conference was to ensure that his municipality received treatment on a par with the treatment accorded other municipalities. He was also to protect his municipality against unwelcome intrusions, like public housing projects, and against threats to its governmental powers. The councilor's major reference group was the municipality as a corporate entity. He had little loyalty to the Metro system and little interest in seeing it survive. The councilor did not view himself as a spokesman for particular interest groups in the area or as a broker of group demands, although he was prepared to transmit and defend neighborhood grievances on Metro policies.

If this weak loyalty had been accompanied by a strong involvement in Metro issues, there might have been intense conflict in Metro Council. But the councilor allocated most of his time and energies to municipal business. The result at the Metro level was a low-conflict, slack, and fluid pattern of legislative politics, in which the attitudes of councilors were seldom firmly fixed. Except on issues affecting a vital interest of his municipality, the councilor was willing to go along. Weak involvement also made the councilor highly amenable to the chairman's persuasive efforts. Debate in Council did change minds and voting intentions on specific policy proposals.

The recruitment of Metro legislators from the ranks of the municipal councils was designed to avoid Metro–municipal conflict. The Metro legislator, being a member of two systems, would presumably resolve intersystem conflicts within his own political personality. In fact no such role conflict occurred because the Metro legislator remained first and foremost a municipal politician.

The Process of Role Definition. The way in which individuals reach decisions about their appropriate role in a system can best be described by identifying the referent points that control these decisions. Table 8.1 presents a description of the Metro councilor's referent points. In discussing groups as referent points, a distinction should be made between "reference groups" —whose members provide standards and values for individual

TABLE 8.1 The Process of Role Definition: Referent Points for the Metro Councilors' Decisions on Legislative Role and Style

Reference Points	Extent of Influence on Councilor's Decisions
The Metro system a. Norms and role expectations	Little influence
b. Loyalty to system and functional needs of system	Little influence
Personality	Important determinant of style, i.e., degree of militancy and activism
Values not anchored in specific groups	Aspects of Canadian political culture and middle-class civic reform ideology help define role
Reference and interaction groups outside system	Provincial cabinet as reference group influences role
Interaction groups within system (excluding Metro Council)	Appointed and elected municipal officials exert both conscious and unconscious influence over style; neighborhood groups exert some influence over style
The Metro Council as interaction group	Little influence by either entire Council or bloc; behavior of a councilor's predecessor sometimes has some small influence over role; chairman influences specific votes but not roles or styles
Reference groups within system	Most important in role definition are the municipality as a corporate entity, the municipal voters, and the neighborhoods; City bloc looks to Toronto press; press and political parties also influence styles of ambitious councilors.

x but do not interact personally with x—and "interaction groups"—whose members maintain regular, face-to-face interaction with x. "Pressure" may be defined as a conscious and concerted effort to influence x; thus, pressure might be exerted by either type of group, although it probably would be exerted more by the interaction group. On the other hand both reference groups and interaction groups are capable of influencing individual x without the members consciously striving to do so or even being aware of their influence.[1]

First, it should be apparent from Table 8.1 that the attitudes of other Metro councilors were not important referent points for the individual councilor. Behavior patterns set by a councilor's predecessor did seem to have some influence over role definitions, mainly because these patterns were often the only specific guidelines available to the new councilor. On the whole, however, the emergence of a common role among a large number of Metro councilors is to be explained by the similar referent points of the councilors, not by interaction among these legislators in the Metro Council.

The obvious explanation of the Metro councilor's role definition was the statutory requirement that such councilors be recruited from the municipal councils. Candidates, for example, invariably ran for *municipal* office and treated Metro Council membership as an incidental perquisite of municipal office. Yet, we might ask, what prevented a candidate from emphasizing Metro office and treating his municipal position as incidental? Certainly Bill 80 did not compel, or even imply, that municipal office be given priority. The Metro councilor's reply would be that the voters were strongly committed to their respective municipalities and that candidates had to respect these commitments. But, if interest group statements and casual opinions expressed by voters during the campaigns are any indicator, the Metro councilor was far more concerned about municipal rights than was the electorate. At the least, one can say that the cues provided by the public were vague. It is conceivable that some candidate might have expressed strong support for the Metro system and still won election. The crucial question is why the Metro councilors were so willing to conclude, from the inadequate cues they received, that the public was committed to municipal autonomy.

The Metro councilor remained a municipal spokesman, it seems to me, mainly because of his internalized values and frame of reference. The typical Metro councilor had spent all his political career at the municipal level, first as a planning board member, then as a school trustee, and later as a municipal councilor. "The municipality as a governmental unit" was his most important reference group.

These predispositions were strengthened by his day-to-day interaction with elected and appointed officials at the municipal level. In quantitative terms this interaction remained far more significant than the councilor's interaction with any persons at the Metro level. The officials who dealt with the councilor on a daily basis were highly committed to municipal rights; it was easy for the councilor to conclude that everyone, including the voters, was similarly committed. Interaction with other Metro councilors was important only because it did not dispel this image.

In comparison to this pervasive, indirect influence, focused pressure by municipal officials had little effect on the Metro councilor's allocation of loyalties. As early as 1954, each Metro councilor had made it clear to his municipal council that he would not be an "instructed delegate." Since the Metro councilor defended municipal autonomy and shared their perspectives, municipal officials had little need of pressure.

My emphasis on internalized values is not intended to minimize the importance of the statutory provisions. Requiring that candidates run for both Metro and municipal office made it likely that candidates would emerge from municipal politics; it also ensured that Metro councilors would maintain regular interaction with municipal officials. In Metro Winnipeg, where the Metro councilors do not hold municipal office and where the Metro Council constituencies cut across municipal boundaries, the councilors represent more varied backgrounds and viewpoints and exhibit far less commitment to municipal rights.

Moreover, if the provincial officials had said that their eventual goal was to abolish municipal units, the councilors might have reassessed their values and reference groups. The councilors interpreted provincial caution to mean that Metro was little more than an experiment.

The Metro Toronto councilor allocated more of his time to municipal business because he derived greater personal gratification from his municipal role. He knew municipal business and the neighborhoods involved intimately. At the Metro level he was often frustrated by the technical and more general nature of the issues and by his need to rely on the chairman for background information. For fourteen of the twenty-four councilors, the municipal role was also more gratifying because it involved executive responsibilities, which most councilors seemed to enjoy more than legislative responsibilities. To these fourteen councilors, municipal achievements were *their* achievements, while Metro achievements were often publicly credited to the chairman and cabinet. Once the councilor decided to emphasize his municipal role, moreover, the Metro issues became even more difficult to digest, and the temptation to go along even more compelling.

Group pressures were more likely to occur at the municipal than the Metro level. Most of these pressures emanated from neighborhood groups and related to the detailed grievances of particular neighborhoods. The Metro councilor apparently concluded that his political future at the local level depended on his success in servicing neighborhood requests. An electoral challenger would sooner denounce the incumbent's policy on neighborhood grievances than the incumbent's behavior in Metro Council. In an indirect fashion, neighborhood pressures served to strengthen the Metro councilor's preoccupation with municipal business.

Direct pressure by municipal officials was more apparent in the allocation-of-time issue than in the Metro councilor's decisions about allocation of loyalty. A Metro councilor was seldom criticized by elected or appointed officials in his municipality for his stand on Metro policies, but he was more often criticized for devoting too much time to Metro business. The councilor was supposed to defend his municipality's vital interests, but he was vulnerable to criticism if he became engaged in issues or committee work not directly related to these vital interests. This overinvolvement, rather than the councilor's substantive views on Metro issues, was a frequent election issue.

The case of the City aldermen on the Metro Council illustrates the pressures at work in allocation-of-time decisions. In each Toronto ward the two candidates polling the largest number of votes were elected to the City Council, and the candidate topping the poll also obtained a seat on Metro Council. No aldermanic candidate, however, ran for Metro Council. The ward campaigns centered on neighborhood issues, most of which were within the jurisdiction of the Toronto City Council. If the top-ranking alderman became too interested in Metro business, he ran the risk of losing his neighborhood support by failing to devote enough time to grass-roots complaints. The second-ranking alderman, who was in a better position to focus on City Council business and keep his political fences in the ward well mended, often attempted to exploit the first-ranking alderman's overinvolvement in Metro business. Ironically, the goal of the second-ranking alderman was to top the poll in his ward and obtain the greater notoriety and salary that went with a seat on the Metro Council. Once on Metro Council, however, he too could alienate much of his neighborhood support. While it was unusual for incumbent aldermen to lose their seats on City Council, it was more common for the two aldermen in a ward to alternate the Metro seat between them, each having a turn at solidifying his neighborhood support and accusing the other of excessive attention to regional issues.

Finally, certain referent points, which might have challenged the councilor's almost exclusive preoccupation with municipal rights, were notable for their absence. The demands and expectations of general-purpose interest groups, working-class and ethnic groups, and groups external to the system played little part in the councilor's role-defining decisions.

Role and Style

Variations in the execution of a role may be referred to as the "styles" of the individual role-players. Whether variations in the behavior of legislators should be called differences in role or differences in style depends on how significant the variations are and whether these variations stem from different notions about the system and appropriate behavior within the system. Certain variations in the behavior of Metro councilors may be called "styles" because they occurred within the basic role orientation described above. In addition, these variations were overshadowed by the large degree of similarity in councilor behavior.

Activists and Part-Timers. Although all members of Metro Council were primarily committed to municipal business, some councilors took a more active part in Metro affairs than others. The activists were more likely to introduce motions, take an aggressive part in committee deliberations, and engage the Metro chairman in debate on the Council floor. The same individuals tended to be activists at the municipal and Metro levels; the activism of certain Metro councilors at the Metro level was achieved at the expense of their private, nonpolitical roles, not at the expense of their roles in the municipal systems. The activist and part-timer differed in their commitment to politics and to a full-time political career, not in their allocation of loyalty or time between Metro and the municipalities.

Activism sometimes presented a challenge to the chairman's leadership; but even the activist went along in a majority of cases. For reasons indicated below, the activist was mainly interested in identifying his name with certain causes and so was content to specialize in one or two issues. Furthermore, most activists specialized in policy areas—like Metro reform or public transit—where the technical inputs were ambiguous or nonexistent. In this way, activism was absorbed into the Metro system without any serious diminution in the overall influence of the chairman and cabinet.

The councilor's own personality, coupled with his political ambition, appeared to be the most important referent point for decisions on the activist style. But it was often difficult to determine whether personality determined ambition or *vice versa*. The activist sought higher office because he was interested in issues and was eager to have a greater impact on their outcome; but he also became interested in issues and causes in order to set his name apart from the other councilors and to attract the attention of the press and the political parties. Whether he wished to move up within the municipal hierarchy, as most activist City aldermen did, or wished to enter provincial politics, as most activist suburban reeves did, the activist had to demonstrate to certain groups that he was more than a time-server and more than a servicer of neighborhood grievances. The activist's key problem was creating this image without losing his neighborhood support.

Militants and Moderates. While each Metro councilor saw himself as a municipal spokesman, some councilors fought for municipal interests more vigorously than others. The militant came to Council prepared to fight. He insisted that his municipality was getting a raw deal from the Metro system and that other municipalities were benefiting more. He was less likely than his colleagues to support proposals put forward by the Metro chairman unless they were of direct benefit to his municipality. Often he would demand a *quid pro quo* in exchange for his vote. The militant was more likely to take his grievances to the Council floor or the press than to a department head or Council committee.

The moderate also was a defender of municipal interests. But, where no vital municipal interests were at stake, he more often supported the chairman's leads. The moderate was somewhat more flexible, more amenable to a bipartisan, compromise proposal, more inclined to process his grievances through the appropriate channels, and more willing to do his share of unspectacular committee work.

If the moderate's greater willingness to go along had reflected a commitment to the Metro system, militant and moderate would represent two distinct roles. But both the written evidence and the testimony of councilors in interviews with me indicate that the degree of a councilor's militancy reflected his personality, not his image of Metro. Some individuals preferred generating headlines and making accusations; others preferred quiet negotiations and harmonious personal relations. Moreover, it can be demonstrated that the range of difference between militant and moderate behavior was small, suggesting that these differences in behavior were variations within a single orientation.

One approximate indicator of militancy and moderation is the regularity with which individual members of Council supported the chairman's leadership. For each person serving on the Metro Council between 1953 and 1965, an index of support for the chairman's policies was constructed. Only major, nonunanimous votes, on which the chairman had taken a clear position, were used in the construction of this index.[2] The index itself represents the number of times an individual voted with the chairman divided by the total number of votes in which the individual participated. Thus, an index of support of 25 would indicate that a Council member, during the total length of his tenure on Council, supported the chairman 25 percent of the time. Obviously, the range of possible scores is 0 to 100. Table 8.2 presents the index of support for each individual serving on the Council between 1953 and 1965 and participating in more than ten major votes.

The support indices for members of the City bloc range from 51.4 to 90.9. More important, over half of the City officials were bunched in the 60 to 70 range. The range of support scores was somewhat wider in the suburban bloc—31.8 to 83.3—but this greater range was largely due to the low score of Reeve Oliver Crockford of Scarborough. More than half the suburban officials were bunched in the 65 to 75 range. All members of Council but two supported the chairman on more than 50 percent of these votes. This bunching of support scores between 60 and 75 suggests the narrow scope within which different styles operated.

Style and Group Pressures. The Metro councilor was largely free to pursue either the militant or moderate style, without worrying about interest group or voter reactions. The suburban neighborhood groups preferred suburban militants, and the general-purpose interest groups preferred moderates in both blocs; but statements of group preference were sporadic and casual. The Toronto newspapers praised militants in the City bloc and moderates in the suburban bloc, but did not make its electoral endorsements on this basis. Moreover, no Metro councilor appeared to suffer at the polls for having pursued one style or the other. The militancy or moderation of a Metro councilor was a campaign issue in only one election held during the thirteen-year period.

However, what scattered pressures there were on matters of style tended to encourage militancy. Municipal officials occasionally criticized a Metro councilor for not driving a hard enough bargain at the Metro level. Councilors were sometimes urged by municipal officials to be less submissive to the Metro chairman. In the 1960 election for mayor of Toronto, the one case in which style was an electoral issue, Controller Jean Newman was denounced by the incumbent mayor for having been lax in the defense of City interests at the Metro level. Moreover, all councilors, whatever their style, spoke in a more militant fashion about Metro issues when addressing their municipal councils than when addressing the Metro Council. Thus, municipal pressures may have set some limit to how moderate a councilor could be. A highly moderate councilor would not lose his municipal office, but he might strain his working relations with elected and appointed officials in his municipality.

Finally, one might note that the Toronto press, through its

TABLE 8.2   Variations in the Metro Councilors' Style: Degree of
Support for the Chairman's Policies, 1953–1965

Name	Constituency and Tenure	Index of Support for Chairman[a]
Suburbanites		
B. Nealson	Leaside, 1963–	83.3
R. Seagrave	Weston, 1953–54	81.0
W. Lewis	Etobicoke, 1953–56	80.0
V. Singer	North York, 1957–58	78.7
H. Clark	Weston, 1953–56	77.1
F. MacMahon	North York, 1953–56	76.5
C. Bick	Forest Hill, 1953–56	75.5
F. Hall	York, 1953–56	74.5
G. Bull	Weston, 1961–64	74.1
E. Pivnick	Forest Hill, 1963–	73.0
C. Tonks	York, 1957–60	72.3
C. Hiscott	Leaside, 1956–62	72.0
L. Simonsky	Forest Hill, 1957–62	71.6
D. Hague	Swansea, 1953 62	71.5
A. Harris	Scarborough, 1956	71.4
A. Campbell	Scarborough, 1957–	71.3
J. MacBeth	Etobicoke, 1963–	71.0
L. Ford	Long Branch, 1963–64	70.7
J. Strath	New Toronto, 1954	70.6
J. Mould	York, 1963–	70.0
F. Taylor	York, 1961–62	68.6
J. Holley	Weston, 1959–60	67.9
N. Goodhead	North York, 1959–64	67.1
O. Waffle	Etobicoke, 1957–63	65.8
J. Allen	East York, 1957–60	65.6
M. Curtis	Long Branch, 1953–62	64.9
H. Griggs	Mimico, 1961–	64.2
H. Simpson	East York, 1953–56	63.3
H. Burrell	Leaside, 1953–55	61.5
T. Davidson	East York, 1961–	60.5
W. Edwards	Mimico, 1955–60	58.3
A. Norris	Mimico, 1953–54	57.1
D. Russell	New Toronto, 1955–	56.9
W. Saunders	York, 1962	56.3
L. Kurata	Swansea, 1963–	51.7
L. Dickinson	Leaside, 1962	47.1
O. Crockford	Scarborough, 1953–55	31.8

[a] Only nonunanimous votes on important issues are included in this tabulation, and only individuals who cast more than ten votes on major nonunanimous issues are included.

TABLE 8.2 (continued)

Name	Constituency and Tenure	Index of Support for Chairman[a]
City Officials		
L. Saunders	Controller, 1953–54; Mayor, 1954	90.9
D. Balfour	Controller, 1954	87.5
C. Tidy	Ward 3, 1964	87.1
J. Gould	Ward 5, 1953–54	85.7
J. Newman	Ward 9, 1955–56; Controller, 1957–60	85.1
T. Wardle	Ward 8, 1963–	83.9
G. Ben	Ward 5, 1963–64	78.7
M. Robinson	Ward 6, 1953–60, 1963–64	75.4
M. Temple	Ward 7, 1959–60, 1963–	71.7
H. Menzies	Ward 5, 1961–62	71.4
R. Horkins	Ward 9, 1963–64	71.2
W. Davidson	Ward 7, 1953–58, 1961–62	70.1
W. Archer	Ward 3, 1959–63	70.1
W. Allen	Ward 1, 1953–55; Controller, 1959–61	69.4
P. Givens	Ward 5, 1955–60; Controller, 1963; Mayor, 1963–	69.4
D. Rotenberg	Ward 4, 1960–	68.9
R. Belyea	Ward 9, 1953–54; Controller, 1955	68.8
K. Waters	Ward 1, 1956–60	68.1
J. Cornish	Controller, 1956	66.7
K. Ostrander	Ward 9, 1961–62	66.7
A. Lamport	Mayor, 1953–54; Controller, 1963–64	66.1
F. Nash	Ward 9, 1957–60	65.8
F. Beavis	Ward 1, 1961–	64.9
R. Lipsett	Ward 8, 1953–54	62.3
M. Grayson	Ward 2, 1963–	62.3
A. Cranham	Ward 8, 1959–60	61.9
L. Reilly	Ward 9, 1954	61.5
A. Hodgins	Ward 8, 1961–62	60.9
A. Grossman	Ward 4, 1953–55	60.0
F. Brand	Controller, 1954–58	59.2
F. Clifton	Ward 6, 1961–62	58.1
W. Dennison	Ward 2, 1953–58; Controller, 1962, 1964–	56.3
D. Summerville	Ward 8, 1955–58; Controller, 1961–62; Mayor, 1963	56.1
H. Phillips	Ward 3, 1954–55	54.8
H. Orliffe	Ward 4, 1956–59	54.8
N. Phillips	Mayor, 1955–62	54.7
M. Birchard	Ward 2, 1959–60	54.5
M. Campbell	Ward 2, 1961–62	53.1
R. Parry	Ward 3, 1956–58	51.4

indirect and pervasive influence, probably accentuated the over-all militancy of many City officials.

Style and Constituency Characteristics. It may be argued that councilors were subject to so little pressure from their municipalities on questions of style because these councilors had already adapted their styles to the interests of their constituencies. If this were true, one would expect to find some correlation between the interests or social characteristics of a constituency and the style of its representatives on Council. One would expect to find all the councilors elected over a thirteen-year period by the same constituency pursuing a similar style. One reasonable hypothesis is that the outlying suburbs —with more grievances on Metro services—and the outlying, rapidly growing suburbs—with more serious demands to make of Metro in the construction field—would return more militant spokesmen than the suburbs largely content with things as they were.

Table 8.3 attempts to present quantitative evidence on the relation between style and constituency. An average index of support for the Metro chairman was constructed for each suburban municipality and for each City constituency. Leaside's 71.6 index, for example, indicates that mayors of Leaside serving on the Metro Council between 1953 and 1965 supported the Metro chairman's proposals 71.6 percent of the time. The range of support scores attained by the different mayors of Leaside, during 1953–1965, is included in order to demonstrate the degree of variation in style from one incumbent to another. Thus, one mayor of Leaside had as low a support score as 47.1, another mayor of Leaside had a score as high as 83.3, and the other mayors of Leaside were located within this range. The universe of votes on which these calculations are based is the same as that used in Table 8.2.

The table does reveal some slight relation between style and suburban constituencies. The greatest degree of support for the chairman came from three small, inlying suburbs: Weston, For-

TABLE 8.3 Political Styles and Metro Constituencies, 1953–1965

Constituency	Number of Incumbents Serving on Metro Council, 1953–1965	Average Index of Support for Chairman	Range of Personal Indices of Support[a]
Weston	5	75.4	67.9–81.0
Forest Hill	3	72.9	71.6–75.5
Leaside	4	71.6	47.1–83.3
Etobicoke	3	69.1	65.8–80.0
York	5	68.2	56.3–74.5
Scarborough	3	68.0	31.8–71.4
Swansea	2	67.4	51.7–71.5
North York	4	66.9	67.1–78.7
Long Branch	3	66.1	64.9–70.7
East York	3	62.8	60.5–65.6
Mimico	3	60.7	57.1–64.2
New Toronto	3	57.3	56.9–70.6
Ward 6	5	74.4	48.6–70.1
Ward 7	2	72.0	70.1–71.7
Controller	13	68.8	57.7–87.5
Ward 1	3	68.6	64.9–74.6
Ward 9	7	68.2	61.5–80.4
Ward 5	5	67.4	65.4–85.7
Ward 3	5	64.5	51.4–87.1
Ward 4	3	63.0	54.8–68.9
Ward 8	5	62.1	55.4–83.9
Mayor	5	60.5	54.7–90.9
Ward 2	5	53.8	53.1–70.1

[a] Only personal scores for councilors participating in ten or more votes are included in the figures on ranges.

est Hill, and Leaside. The six outlying suburbs—Etobicoke, Scarborough, North York, Long Branch, Mimico, and New Toronto—tended to register lower support scores than the in-lying suburbs.

But the table also suggests the limited importance of constituency as a determinant of style. The three, rapidly growing suburbs, with the most serious demands to make of Metro—Scarborough, North York, and Etobicoke—stood in the center of the suburban spectrum not at the militant pole. The most militant suburbs, the three Lakeshore municipalities, had no serious grievances outside of the TTC's fare zones; their militancy was mainly attributable to the long tenure and personal influence of Long Branch's militant reeve, Marie Curtis. Moreover, Table 8.3 reveals as much personal variation in style within each constituency as there was from one constituency to another. The range between the most militant and most moderate constituency was eighteen points on the support index. The range of personal variation within particular constituencies was greater than eighteen points in five of the twelve municipalities.

As Table 8.3 indicates, the variation in support scores among the City constituencies—53.8 to 75.4—was somewhat greater than the range in the suburban bloc. But if one excludes for the moment the militancy of Ward Two aldermen, the range of variation in the City bloc narrows to about fifteen points—60.5 to 75.4. Moreover, within each constituency but Ward Seven, there was a considerable range of variation in the styles of incumbents. This narrow range of variation from one constituency to another and the wide range of variation within constituencies discourage any generalizing about the impact of City constituencies on style.

If measured in terms of average income, the socio-economic characteristics of the Toronto wards were substantially the same. Only Ward 5, a low-income area, and Ward 9, a high-income area, stood apart from the other wards. But Wards 5 and 9, the two extremes in income, stood next to each other at the center of the bloc in terms of support for the chairman. The possibility that Ward 9 aldermen might prove more moderate than their City colleagues because the Ward was suburban-like in its social characteristics did not materialize. The aldermen from Toronto's lowest-income ward did not challenge the prevailing good government, middle-class values. Furthermore, the issues that Metro dealt with bore little relation to neighborhood interests. The alderman was even freer than the suburbanite to determine his style without reference to constituency.

Holding a City-wide constituency, as opposed to a ward constituency, did not appear to encourage any distinctive political style. Personality rather than constituency was the main referent point for decisions on style. The City controllers, on the average, were slightly more moderate than the rest of the City bloc; but the mayors of Toronto were slightly more militant. One may also assess the impact of City-wide constituency on style by examining the styles of City politicians who served first as alderman and later as controller or mayor. Five City officials served on Metro Council, over a period of years, as both ward and City-wide representatives. Of these five, four—Jean Newman, William Allen, Philip Givens, and Donald Summerville—maintained the same style as controller and, in the case of Givens and Summerville, as mayor that they had developed as alderman. In none of the four cases did the support score of these aldermen change more than six points after they had acquired a City-wide constituency. The exception to this rule was William Dennison, whose support score jumped from 48.6 as Ward Two alderman to 70.0 as City controller. Except for Dennison, aldermen carried their personal styles with them when they became controllers or mayors.

Legislative Systems as Referent Points

The preceding pages suggested that the councilor's interaction with other councilors had little effect on his behavior in Council. Councilor decisions about role and style were based on referent points lying outside the legislature. In the present section I hope to demonstrate the ineffectiveness of referent points lying within the legislature and to speculate on the conditions under which these points could have become more significant.

At the outset, three legislative referent points should be distinguished: the Metro chairman, the City and suburban blocs, and the entire Metro Council. Three types of influence might also be distinguished: influence over the councilor's basic orientation to the Metro system and to his role in that system, influence over the councilor's style, and influence over the councilor's voting behavior on specific outcomes. The following diagram summarizes my argument about the impact of these three referent points on each of these forms of behavior:

	Entire Metro Council	The Bloc	Metro Chairman
Role definition	Little	Little	Little
Style	Little	Little	Little
Voting on specific issues	Little	Some	Considerable

The arguments developed in the following pages are that the entire Council did not develop any norms or role expectations of its own to guide councilor behavior, that the City or suburban bloc was a slightly more significant referent point than the entire Council, that even bloc influence could not rival the influence of the chairman in affecting specific outcomes, and that no referent point within the legislature altered the councilor's basic orientation to the system and his part in it.

The extensive influence of the chairman over the councilor's decisions on specific proposals needs little further comment. This influence occurred without altering the councilors' notions about style and role—in fact, the chairman's influence was predicated on his accepting basic legislative orientations. The following pages focus first on the influence of the entire Council and then on the influence of the two blocs. Metro Council and the blocs will be referred to as "systems," although it is understood that Metro Council was a subsystem within the Metro government and that the blocs were subsystems within the Metro Council.

The Metro Council As a System. Legislatures, like any collection of individuals who interact on a regular basis, will develop some degree of normative integration. Legislatures may exhibit an *esprit de corps* that transcends party or factional lines and that unites all legislators against all outsiders. A legislature may develop norms and role expectations not contained in the formal rules, may teach these norms to new members, may exert informal social pressures on members straying too far from these norms, and may reward norm adherents with greater prestige and influence within the legislative system. Where an informal internal structure appears, the legislature as a whole becomes one referent point for the legislator's behavior.[3]

According to recent studies of the U.S. Congress, the norms of that institution encourage members to emphasize hard work in the committees rather than headline hunting, specialize in one or two areas of policy, defer to experience and long tenure in the system, forego an active part in floor debates during one's first term, respect and protect the prerogatives of the system against judicial and executive encroachments, go along with the party leadership whenever possible, and assume flexible, middle-of-the-road policy positions.[4] Most of these norms make an obvious contribution to the survival and stability of the legislative system; similar norms might be expected to appear in all well-integrated legislatures.

Metro Council achieved very little normative integration. There were no "norms," or "roles," defining those terms the way Parsons and most sociologists do.[5] There were no expressions of solidarity or of hostility to outsiders. What little influence the councilors had on each other's behavior did not cross bloc lines. There was no inner circle of norm adherents, whose influence operated without regard to bloc or faction. A well-integrated legislature probably would have preferred the moderate style, since this type of behavior was more conducive to the stability of the legislative system. Yet Metro Council did not consistently reward either militants or moderates.

There *were* some items of consensus in Council on how things should be done. Councilors agreed on the need for deference to leadership and expertise and on the importance of parity. The

Council believed that a member should give first loyalty to his municipality, that activists deserved more prominent positions in Council, and that a councilor could become either too militant or too moderate. These attitudes may be called Council norms—with two important qualifications. First, no social control mechanisms were used to enforce these norms, and no provisions were made for rewarding norm adherents. Second, these norms did not appear to change anyone's behavior or attitude. The Council norms emerged because a collection of individuals, forming their preferences independently of each other, happened to agree on certain points. The attitudes that formed the basis of these Council norms were brought to the Council and were little changed by the interactive processes of the Council. One might say that these attitudes were statistical norms that acquired some, but not all, the characteristics of social norms.

No councilor was ever criticized by his colleagues for violating any of the above norms—except for the norm on militancy and moderation. Only four councilors in thirteen years were censured by their colleagues for being either too militant or too moderate. In one case a councilor was removed from the Executive Committee; in two other cases removal was threatened. The fourth case involved only public criticism of the deviant. In all four cases the controls were wielded not by the entire Council but by one of the blocs. The extremist was criticized because his maverick tendencies had weakened bloc unity. Thus, it probably would be more accurate to call the attitude on militancy and moderation a "bloc norm" rather than a "Council norm."

If these Council attitudes had been norms in the sociological sense, the councilors' behavior would have been brought into line with the expectations implicit in these attitudes. The sociological literature is replete with examples of how group norms exert pressure on the individual and how the members' behavior converges on these norms.[6] One way of assessing the impact of Council's norms on legislative behavior is to note trends in the voting records of individuals who sat on Council over a period of years. Using the index of support for the Metro chairman, one might ask whether members, over the course of their terms on Council, moved toward the statistical center of Council's support scores, and whether councilors showed any increased support for the chairman, i.e., increased deference to leadership. To test these propositions I used the voting records of thirty councilors who had served on Council for four or more years. Each councilor's term was divided in half, and an index of support for the chairman was tabulated for each half term. All major votes were used in the tally. The Council's statistical center was defined as the average of all the personal support scores listed in Table 8.2.

Of the thirty councilors, thirteen stood further away from the Council center in the second half of their term than they had in the first; seventeen moved toward the center. Clearly there was no consistent tendency for councilors to move toward the center. Also lacking was evidence of increasing deference to the chairman. Of the thirty councilors, fourteen had a higher support score in their second half, while sixteen had a lower score.

If legislative behavior were being subordinated to normative expectations, one might expect to find signs of increasing Council unity. The "index of cohesion" is designed to measure the extent of voting agreement among a collection of individuals regularly casting recorded votes.[7] The index is obtained by subtracting the percentage of a group voting one way on an issue from the percentage voting the other way. The smaller percentage is always subtracted from the larger so that all figures on the index are plus figures. A score of 100 indicates perfect unity. If one is dealing with a number of votes, an estimate of the group's overall unity may be obtained by averaging its indices of cohesion on each vote.

An average index of Council cohesion was tabulated for each of Council's thirteen annual sessions. All major votes were used. The annual indices varied from 55.6 to 72.1. There was no trend toward greater—or lesser—cohesion. An increasing degree of cohesion would not necessarily indicate the emergence of normative integration in a group, but the existence and persistence of low cohesion imply that group norms and control mechanisms are minimal or nonexistent.

If the Council had become a more integrated system, it might have served as the mechanism for a transfer of loyalties. The councilors might have established some legislative solidarity that united both City and suburban officials against the outsiders in their respective municipalities. Clearly it was Gardiner's hope that mere membership on the Council, and interaction with other councilors, would produce more "Metro minded" officials.

In explaining why Gardiner's gradualist strategy did not succeed, it is difficult to avoid circular explanations. An integrated legislative system might have provided some counterweight to municipal loyalties, but the existence of strong municipal loyalties severely impeded the integration of the Metro Council. Of course, the Metro councilor was not unique in his attempt to represent a governmental unit before a federal or international assembly. What distinguished the Metro councilor from the U.S. senator or the United Nations delegate was the councilor's refusal to accept the very existence of the federal assembly. The Metro councilor, though willing to go along with the chairman's substantive proposals, consciously resisted the influence that Council membership might have on his basic orientations.

The Metro Council case suggests that regular interaction among a collection of individuals will not lead to the emergence of an informal social system if the individuals are determined to avoid such a system.

The City and Suburban Blocs As Systems. The public statements of Metro councilors suggest that the bloc was a more significant referent point for their behavior than was the entire Council. Typically the councilor would warn against the other bloc's domination of Metro Council and would deplore the lack of agreement within his own bloc. Bloc unity was a value that all councilors endorsed.

But these sentiments were not reflected in the councilors' voting behavior. Despite the councilors' avowals of bloc loyalty, the bloc was a disunited and weakly integrated system.

Table 8.4 presents the indices of cohesion for the City bloc, the suburban bloc, and the entire Council on three types of

TABLE 8.4   The Degree of Voting Unity in the City Bloc, the Suburban Bloc, and the Entire Metro Council, 1953–1965

		Indices of Cohesion		
Type of Vote	Number of Votes	Entire Council	City Bloc	Suburban Bloc
All major votes	437	65.4	77.2	72.1
All major nonunanimous votes	293	42.8	62.4	55.0
All factional votes	127	14.9	58.6	50.7

votes. The table considers cohesion on all major votes, on all major, nonunanimous votes, and on all factional votes. (For definitions of these phrases see Table 3.1 and the discussion of that table in chapter 3.) The index of cohesion of each bloc on all major votes exceeded 72.0, but this score was not substantially higher than the cohesion of the entire Council on these same issues. When Council unity declined, so did bloc unity. On factional issues, where bloc unity presumably would be most important, voting cohesion in each bloc fell close to the 50.0 mark. Apparently the cohesion of the two blocs was based more on the large degree of agreement in Council than on the bloc's own efforts to achieve unity. Over the course of Metro's thirteen years, neither bloc showed a trend toward greater cohesion.

One may also ask whether the belief in bloc unity drew councilors to the center of their respective blocs. Again, the voting records of councilors with long service on the Council were used and the term of each councilor divided in half. For each half-term and for each councilor, I compiled an index of bloc loyalty. This index represented the number of times a councilor had voted with a majority of his bloc divided by the councilor's total number of votes. All major votes were used. Of the thirty councilors, only thirteen—seven City officials and six suburban-ites—had higher bloc loyalty scores in the second half of their terms.

Nor did the councilors consistently move toward their bloc's average index of support for the chairman. Fifteen of the thirty councilors stood further away from their bloc's statistical center during the second half of their terms. In conclusion, bloc loyalty was a matter of consensus but not a guideline for legislative behavior and not a source of social pressures.

We need not conclude that the councilors' public statements were mere cant. These statements suggest that the bloc was a potentially significant social system; the crucial question is why this potential was not realized. Some answers will be provided by examining each bloc in turn.

The Suburban Bloc. The suburban officials may have been less vehement than the City officials in their praise of bloc unity, but the suburbanites still preached far more unity than they practiced. One major source of this incongruity between sub-urban attitudes and suburban behavior was the suburbanites' unwillingness to employ coordinating and control mechanisms. These officials refused to exert pressures on their colleagues. Some members even refused to attend the suburban caucuses that were convened from time to time. Since the suburban officials saw little of each other outside of the bimonthly Council meeting, they were protected from the unconscious influence that group members often have on each other. Bloc influence, like Council influence, was often viewed as a restraint on the expression of municipal interests. Thus, bloc unity was desirable but that unity had to emerge from the separate decisions of independent legislators.

Even if the suburban bloc had wanted to enforce norms, there were few rewards to dispense or sanctions to impose. The Council committees were not important. The only sought-after position was a seat on the Executive Committee. Moreover, in view of the chairman's control of floor proceedings and the Council norm on parity, a councilor could not be rewarded with better treatment or more public works for his municipality.

Another source of suburban disunity was the absence of stable and effective bloc leadership. Organized horizontally rather than hierarchically, the suburban bloc could not agree on who the appropriate leaders were. To many suburbanites, the institutionalization of leadership did not seem appropriate in a group of political equals. The reeves of the three large suburbs thought that they were the appropriate bloc leaders, but no other members of the bloc accepted this contention. Because of this dissensus on who should lead, a suburbanite consciously attempting to secure bloc unity was more often criticized than followed.

The suburbanites respected the intelligence and commitment to politics of certain activists within their bloc, but this respect did not produce a willingness to follow the activists' leads. The activist, it was thought, should be named to the Executive Committee, where his views would be heard and where his administrative abilities could be used to advantage. Thus, activists may be viewed as "norm adherents," who received slightly more rewards than did other councilors. Membership on the Executive Committee, however, did not make the activist a floor leader for the suburban bloc. For his own part the activist was usually less interested in leading his bloc than in leaving the Council. As the activist turned his attention to provincial politics and began adapting his behavior to the expectations of the parties and the newspapers, he would issue a barrage of proposals which he knew his suburban colleagues would ignore.

No activist in the suburban bloc could make a claim to bloc leadership unless he also held a seat on the Executive Committee. Without access to the information provided by administrators, the activist could be easily outdebated by the chairman or by any member of the committee. If suburban activists had been consistently elected and regularly returned to the Executive

Committee, stable bloc leadership might have emerged. The suburbanites could not pursue such a consistent policy because they did not fully control the election of suburban delegates to the committee. Since the entire Council named committee members, the City was sometimes able to caucus and agree on which suburban representative they would support. The City generally preferred the highly moderate, less aggressive, and less experienced members of the suburban bloc. Thus, the suburban bloc's most articulate and respected members were often deliberately excluded from the Executive Committee through the efforts of the City officials. The suburbanites could have checked this City strategem if they had been able to agree on their own committee nominees. But not all suburbanites would attend a caucus, and a natural consensus on the most respected activists rarely emerged.

Furthermore, the suburbanites did not use activism as their only criterion for committee membership. Bloc members thought that the suburban delegation should contain a rough balance between big and small suburbs and between eastern and western suburbs. The bloc also pursued a conscious policy of rotating committee membership so that a maximum number of suburban councilors had an opportunity to serve. While activists were more likely to be named, no activist was given an opportunity to accumulate influence, information, and other political resources. The roots of suburban leadership were periodically torn up.

Loss of the more articulate councilors to federal and provincial politics hampered the emergence of stable leadership in both blocs. But the suburban bloc experienced a more substantial turnover within the ranks of potential bloc leaders. An ambitious Toronto alderman could pursue his quest for higher office and still remain in City politics. An ambitious suburban reeve had nowhere to go but out of the municipal and Metro arena. Some of this turnover was inevitable. At the same time, perhaps more activists would have remained in Council if the suburbanites had developed clear leadership expectations and had consistently named activists to the Executive Committee.

The City Bloc: Sources of Cohesion. The City bloc had a greater potential for normative integration. Members of this bloc were also members of a separate system, the Toronto City Council. This other system provided for regular interaction among bloc members in the periods between Metro Council meetings. The City bloc at least had the institutionalized means through which influence and control could be brought to bear. The Toronto Council also provided City bloc members with clearly defined expectations on leadership. The same people who led in City politics, the mayor and the controllers, were expected to provide the leads on Metro issues. In line with this expectation the City bloc automatically named the mayor and controllers as City representatives on the Executive Committee.

The commitment to defending municipal interests, which made the suburbanites wary of bloc influence, served to strengthen the City's bloc unity. The suburbs differed in size, rate of population growth, municipal tax rates, construction needs, and satisfaction with Metro services. To the City official, however, maintaining bloc unity was synonymous with "getting the best deal for Toronto." Moreover, the large Toronto wards and the similarity in aldermanic constituencies, by discouraging the emergence of distinctive aldermanic styles, contributed to City unity.

The City bloc also exhibited some of the overt characteristics of well-integrated systems. City officials spoke more often than their suburban counterparts of the need for bloc unity. There was a more obvious *esprit de corps* within the City bloc, one indicator of which was the attempt by that bloc to find appointive offices for City politicians failing to secure reelection. In addition, the City frequently resorted to conscious coordination, or caucuses, in an attempt to produce a single City viewpoint on a particular issue.

The pervasive influence of the Toronto newspapers, aimed primarily at City officials, also contributed to consensus building with the City bloc.

It is true that City officials did not drift toward the center of the bloc over the course of their terms on Metro Council. Before concluding that City bloc influence was inconsequential, however, one must note that City officials, even before their appearance on Metro Council, interacted with members of the City bloc and probably acquired some of the City bloc's attitudes. City officials may have moved toward the center of the bloc prior to their formal membership in Metro Council.

The City Bloc: Sources of Disunity. The surprising fact about Council voting is not that the City bloc was more cohesive but that, in view of the above factors, the City's cohesiveness was only slightly greater than that of the suburbanites (see Table 8.4). Except on appointments to the TTC and the Executive Committee, the City's edge in cohesion was too slight to determine the outcome of issues or give the City bloc an upperhand.

The City did not realize its integrative potential because City officials shared the ambiguous suburban attitudes on bloc unity, social control, and leadership. There may have been a greater opportunity for unconscious, interpersonal influence in the City bloc, but there was an equal abhorrence of consciously applied control mechanisms. Like their suburban counterparts, the City officials revealed their respect for an activist by naming him to some significant position, not by following his leads on Metro policy. In addition, City officials, having decided to automatically name the mayor and controllers to the Executive Committee, lost their only source of rewards and sanctions. This rule on appointments to the Executive Committee was violated only once, when the City bypassed a controller and named a respected activist, Alderman William Archer.

The City bloc, like the suburban bloc, lost many of its talented members to provincial and federal politics before these individuals had served very long on Council. City activists were better able to pursue their ambitions and remain within municipal politics. An alderman who successfully made the leap to Toronto's board of control, however, usually did not secure enough votes to place among the two top-ranking controllers. Thus, moving up the City hierarchy meant interrupting one's tenure on

Metro Council, usually for about four to six years. Alderman Archer, for example, lost his seat on the Executive Committee and the Metro Council when he became a city controller; three years later, Controller Archer had not yet reappeared in Metro Council.

Other reasons for City disunity were unique to that bloc. City unity was not always sought because City leaders were undecided about whether to maximize City effectiveness in the Metro Council or to maintain an intransigent opposition to the Council's very existence.

A more divisive factor was the competition among City politicians for the same electoral positions. While the hierarchic form of organization aided City integration by providing clearly defined leadership expectations, that form of organization also produced institutionalized or structural strain among the City members. The career lines of the suburban officials did not overlap. The electoral ambitions of suburban officials would not encourage them to criticize their suburban colleagues in Council. In the City bloc, however, ambitious aldermen would denounce the leadership, and ambitious controllers would try to discredit the mayor. Criticisms of officials standing on the next highest rung of the ladder usually centered on their handling of City issues, but a residue of ill feeling inevitably carried over into Metro Council.

Aldermen expected the City's leadership to present a united front on Metro issues. That leadership, when uncertain or disunited, was clearly ineffective within the City bloc. The tendency for the mayor's electoral challengers to be recruited from the board of control, however, virtually precluded the issuance of unified leads. Moreover, the mayor's challengers were most likely to be one or both of the two top-ranking controllers, that is, the same controllers who sat on Metro Council and shared the mayor's bloc leadership. Relations between the mayor and the two controllers generally followed a set pattern in the period between elections. Following the election, there were statements about the need for bloc unity and unified City leadership. There were assurances that electoral politics would not be permitted to mar that unity. Acrimony between the mayor and one or both controllers began to build about six or eight months after the election and intensified as the next election approached.

The aldermen and the board of control also constituted separate subsystems within the Toronto City Council. In each subsystem the members were linked by common problems and grievances. Aldermen complained about not being given enough time and information on board proposals. The part-time politicians, the aldermen, all faced the problem of how to keep abreast of issues, win reelection, and at the same time maintain a private source of income. There was an obvious camaraderie among the aldermen. Periodically, aldermanic grievances would explode into a rebellion against the board of control. Although originating with City matters, these rebellions weakened the City bloc's unity in Metro Council.

There is impressionistic evidence that the City leaders were more effective in the City Council than as leaders of the City bloc in Metro Council, although only careful analysis of City Council voting could demonstrate or refute this notion. At the City level, the board spoke for the expert administrators; at the Metro level, it was the chairman who monopolized this crucial resource. At times the City's leadership was more effective in City than in Metro Council because the more respected controllers did not hold seats on Metro Council.

City disunity was often ascribed—by the press, for example —to the personalities of the men who served as mayor of Toronto between 1953 and 1965. Some of these men gave far greater attention to the ceremonial side of their office than they did to overseeing City administration or providing leadership. Frequent personal appearances before groups in the community often took precedence over floor leadership in either the City or Metro Council. Moreover, some of Toronto's mayors were ineffective floor leaders because they stood close to the militant or moderate poles of the City spectrum rather than near the center (see Table 8.2).

Clearly the factor of personality cannot be ignored. The structure of the Metro system would have been substantially different if Gardiner had been mayor of Toronto rather than chairman, or if Gardiner had been chairman and someone with the same aggressive personality had been Toronto's mayor. But there were also structural factors that encouraged the Toronto mayor to emphasize ceremonial duties over floor leadership. As newspaper criticisms of the individual mayors indicate, leadership expectations, though directed at the entire board, fell more heavily on the mayor. But the mayor's institutional resources did not enable him to meet these expectations. The newspapers might have periodically assessed the record of his administration, but the mayor actually had no more authority than any of the four controllers. The aldermen might have demanded leadership of the mayor but they were equally willing to follow the leads provided by any of the controllers. The mayor was effective in Council when he spoke for a united board, but he was expected to lead a board containing one or more political rivals. Of course, an insignificant office in the hands of an unusual individual can become significant, as the case of Gardiner and the Metro chairmanship demonstrated. The fact remains that the City bloc's leadership expectations were internally inconsistent and incongruous with the formal resources of the official expected to lead. Individual mayors retreated to the social and ceremonial aspects of their office in order to escape from the incongruities built into their leadership role.

CHAPTER 9

A FUNCTIONAL ASSESSMENT
OF THE METRO SYSTEM

The Problem of Functional Assessment

The functionalist approach provides some explicit and defensible criteria for gauging the success of a system's performance. Using this approach, one could identify those factors conducive or not conducive to a system's success and, in some cases, perhaps even prescribe reforms that would improve a system's performance. What functionalism cannot do, without importing values extrinsic to its approach, is judge the moral worth of a system. Thus, a functionalist-oriented author might indicate which factors limited the success of the Metro system and might suggest mechanisms that would overcome these limits, but he could not answer the claims of municipal officials that Metro was not worth preserving or enhancing.

In the discussion that follows, success will be defined as a system's ability to perform its integrative and adaptive functions to the satisfaction of relevant actors within and without the system. A relevant actor is one whose behavior and attitudes have direct implications for the system. Thus, success basically means winning the support of certain individuals. An unsuccessful system is one that suffers a withdrawal of support by its relevant public.

Successful integrative performance is the securing of enough internal support and unity to provide for a continuity in the system's structure and to permit the system to meet environmental demands. Successful adaptation may be defined as the attraction of sufficient external support to make survival and the securing of internal support possible. Attracting this external support requires that the system realize the tasks formally assigned to it, make some informal contributions to other systems, and solve problems to the satisfaction of problem-oriented actors located both inside and outside the system.

Thus, survival is one obvious measurement of success. The problem is defining survival and nonsurvival. The Parsonian definition, which equates survival with the continuance of a system's structure in close to its original form, makes no provision for orderly change.[1] If a system undergoes gradual but comprehensive change, at what point do we say that the original structure no longer exists? In a rapidly changing environment, moreover, the preservation of a system's original structure may not be conducive to that system's survival. Although not attempting to provide a definitive answer to the survival question, I would propose that survival be defined as a basic continuity in the name or identity, the internal structure, and the external relations of a system, so that whatever change the system experiences is orderly and gradual rather than abrupt or cataclysmic.

The minimal degree of integration and adaptation that a system must achieve in order to survive would depend on how comprehensive the system is. Total systems must make major efforts. In segmental systems, whose demands of the membership are small and whose survival is guaranteed by larger systems, little or no achievement could be required. The relative importance, but not the survival, of segmental systems is at stake.

The success of a system may be measured not only by its survival but by the extent of its development. Development will be defined as an increase in the level of a system's adaptive or integrative performance.[2]

The most significant expansion in a system's integrative capacity occurs when that system develops a normative basis of support. The transition from nonnormative to normative integration largely settles the integration or unity problem. Members begin to see the system as an end in itself rather than as an expedient and a useful means to some end. Behavior in the system becomes subject to norms, role expectations, and social control mechanisms. Since the system acquires a new legitimacy in the eyes of the members, these members begin to reallocate their time and loyalty in favor of the system. Members are more willing to smother controversy in order to preserve the system. As diffuse support for the system builds up, the members are more willing to go along with measures that do not directly benefit them or their constituents. The members also are more inclined to defend the system against external threats, to favor a continuance of the existing structure, and to see the system expand its powers and goals. The system will be less preoccupied with questions of unity and solidarity and more attentive to environmental demands. Once normative integration appears, the further development of the system can be measured by its comprehensiveness, that is, by the extent of membership behavior the system's norms attempt to control. A system may develop somewhat greater internal unity without making the leap into normative integration; but these are limits to how much internal solidarity can be secured without diffuse support for the system or normative controls on membership behavior.

One may take any of the indices of internal support—the members' satisfaction with policy outputs, their allocation of time and loyalty to the system, their willingness to defend the system against abolition or wholesale change—and convert them into indices of integrative development. Thus, an increase in any of the above indices would point to some integrative development in a system. This emphasis on individual attitudes may be supplemented with more objective or behavioral indices, like a growing rate of interaction among the members of a system, or an increasing degree of consensus in the voting behavior of the members.[3]

Objective and subjective indices may also be used to measure adaptive development. Such development may be defined as the increased satisfaction of external actors and of problem-oriented actors, both members and nonmembers, with a system's performance. At times these subjective attitudes may be directly gauged. Some objective indicators of adaptive development are:

1. An increase in the size and complexity of the system's structure, in the scope of its self-defined goals, and in its policy outputs—particularly in comparison to similar or competitive systems;
2. An increase in the tasks formally assigned to the system and in the level of tangible environmental inputs, like money, personnel, and physical resources;
3. The ability of a system to define new goals once its original goals or tasks are realized;
4. The willingness of a system to include in its revised goals more sophisticated and complex problems;
5. An increase in the system's autonomy or freedom from external controls.

The list could be expanded, but only those indices relevant to the Metro Toronto case were included.[4]

Increased role differentiation and structural specialization within a system's structure is an index of both adaptive and integrative development. Differentiation usually increases the ability of the system to absorb messages emanating from its physical environment, from other systems, and from actors within the system. Such systems are less likely than simple systems to ignore important problems or demands. But this differentiation also makes agreement within a system on specific outputs more difficult to reach. The key to sustained development appears to be the creation of coordinating mechanisms that preserve much of the system's earlier unity without curbing the development of more complex structures.[5]

Metro's Performance

Metro Toronto achieved a rudimentary level of integration during its early years. Nonnormative or calculative integration emerged. The system's most important members, the municipal officials, tolerated the Metro system because of their rough satisfaction with Metro's policy outputs. Municipalities were not free to withdraw, but the municipal officials on Metro Council could have brought Metro's policy-making process to a standstill. The degree of integration achieved was sufficient to avoid this breakdown in Council proceedings.

But integration did not develop beyond this point. No normative integration emerged. In 1965, municipal officials did not display any more support for the system and did not allocate any more of their time and energies to Metro business than municipal officials had in 1953. There were no indications of increasing unity or cohesion in Metro Council voting over the thirteen-year period. There were no signs that interaction at the Metro level was becoming either quantitatively or qualitatively more important to the Metro councilors.

Only one change occurred in the attitudes of municipal officials. In the early 1960s, the suburban officials demonstrated an increased willingness to defend the Metro system. This change in attitude, however, was not the product of participation in the system but of perceived changes in provincial attitudes. In 1953, suburbanites thought that the province might eventually dissolve Metro and return to the earlier arrangements. By the 1960s, it was clear that the Ontario cabinet would not consider such a course. Thus, most suburbanites grudgingly supported the Metro system as the least centralized form of government acceptable to the province. Their support of Metro, moreover, was designed mainly to head off City demands for total amalgamation. While not asking for Metro's abolition, suburbanites still favored returning some powers to the municipalities.

In summary, the gradualist notion that participation would beget support was disproven. Without provincial constraint, Metro could not have survived—in either 1953 or 1965.

From the province's point of view, the municipal officials were Metro's internal, relevant public. But one may include in this discussion of integrative performance some estimate of the extent to which Metro secured the loyalty and involvement of private groups in the community. The most important fact about the role of these groups was not their vague, inert support for the Metro system but their weak involvement in Metro politics. Compared to the broker leadership system, Metro incorporated a smaller range of groups and viewpoints in its policy-making process. This smaller range increased the opportunities for integration within the restricted circle of participants, but the existence of outsiders constituted a latent threat to this integration. If such groups had participated more fully in the system, moreover, the opposition of the municipal officials to Metro and the emphasis on structural or federal issues would have been either weakened or superseded. Of course, speaking of the system's failure to incorporate these groups does not necessarily mean that Metro's public officials, by pursuing somewhat different strategies, could have expanded group involvement. Group involvement rarely was sought by officials, but this policy usually resulted from the prior inclination of groups to stay uninvolved.

In the adaptive sphere Metro quickly achieved a role differentiation or an institutionalization of the problem-finding activity. This differentiation permitted the system to recruit respected technical men as department heads and to meet many of its assigned tasks. The system achieved a high enough rate of problem solving to retain the loyalties of these department heads, and the external reputation of these men helped build respect for the system among the professional associations and among technical officials at higher levels of government. Of those metropolitan problems cited by Ontario officials as the reason for Metro's creation, the problems requiring public construction were quickly met to the satisfaction of almost all relevant actors. One assigned task, the equalization of educational costs among the thirteen municipalities, was not met to the satisfaction of anyone supporting this goal. Other problems, as defined by problem-oriented actors, went unsolved because Metro did not have, and did not seek, adequate powers in these fields. The Metro system's limited control over municipal land-use decisions, and Metro's resulting inability to undertake comprehensive regional planning, is a case in point.

If one may use a system's annual expenditures as an index of that system's adaptive performance and importance, the Metro system, between 1953 and 1965, became more important in absolute terms, became more important relative to the area municipalities, but became less important relative to the province. Ontario's rate of expansion exceeded Metro's. Nor was there any decrease in the extent of external—provincial—control over the Metro system. The performance of *all* municipalities influenced provincial decisions on local autonomy and the allocation of powers between the two levels of government. However impressive its adaptive performance, Metro alone could do little to alter the basic trends in provincial–municipal relations.

Having achieved a quick breakthrough in the public works area, Metro proved unable to set new goals for itself. Metro's policy output continued to grow in quantitative terms, but most of this growth resulted from the elaboration of policies set in the early years. In the early 1960s, provincial administrators, academic observers, and professional organizations became increasingly critical of Metro's adaptive performance. It is reasonable to assume that cabinet officials were becoming increasingly restive, although there was no open break in cabinet unity.

The major reason for this impasse in problem solving was the limited integration of the system. By the 1960s, Metro had reached a point where it could not explore new problems without adding to its formal powers. But few members of the Metro Council wished to see the system strengthened. If, for example, welfare, urban renewal, and land-use planning had been Metro responsibilities, Council would have moved ahead with problem solving in these areas. Because these policy areas were municipal responsibilities, substantive problems in these areas became enmeshed in structural or federal questions. A change in either the integrative or adaptive level of a system need not be accompanied by a corresponding change in the other functional sphere. However, the Metro case suggests that a leveling off in the degree of integration will set limits to the extent of a system's adaptive development.

One way of summarizing Metro's performance is to note the distribution of satisfactions and dissatisfactions with that performance in 1965. Table 9.1 attempts this summary by noting the attitudes of six groups of actors toward thirteen proposed changes in the Metro system. An actor's willingness to support changes may be taken as an indicator of his dissatisfaction with the *status quo* and with Metro's performance. No attempt was made to weight issues according to how important the actors considered them, or to assess the intensity of an actor's feelings on issues. The table also gauges the actors' response to the 1966 Metro reorganization. Attitudes toward the *status quo* in 1965 and responses to the 1966 reforms are summarized by calculating "net satisfaction scores" for each group of actors.

The most obvious fact about the net satisfaction scores is the discontent of the adaptive-oriented actors. The cabinet's dissatisfaction is somewhat less than other adaptive-oriented actors mainly because the cabinet officials were unable to voice their discontents as freely as nonofficial actors. Within the Council, the City was the least contented group and the small, inlying suburbs the most contented. But no grouping in Council equaled the adaptive-oriented actors in the extent of its dissatisfaction. The table again indicates that democratic political systems are inclined to perform the integrative function better than the adaptive.

This table also spells out the conflict between adaptive and integrative leaders and indicates how this conflict produced an impasse in policy making. Almost any of the thirteen changes would have increased the net satisfaction of the adaptive actors; failing to act would have intensified the discontents of these actors. But a majority of the integrative leaders opposed all changes but two. Of the thirteen proposed changes, only a reduction in the number of municipalities and a greater Metro role in financing education would have increased the net satisfaction of both the integrative and adaptive actors.

[253]

TABLE 9.1 Sources of Support and Opposition to Changes in Metro Structure and Policies in 1965, and the Response to the 1966 Reorganization

	Integrative–Oriented Leaders			Adaptive–Oriented Leaders		
	City	Inner Suburbs	Outer Suburbs	General–Purpose Interest Groups	Metro Cabinet	External Technical Actors
Structural changes						
Abolish Metro and create one city	S(−)	O(+)	O(+)	S/O	O(+)	—
Reforms within Metro framework						
Popular election of chairman	O(+)	O(+)	O(+)	S/O	—	—
Popular election of councilors	O(+)	O(+)	O(+)	S/O	—	—
Reduce number of municipalities	S(+)	O(−)	S(+)	S(+)	—	—
Preserve City-suburban balance on Metro Council	S(−)	O(+)	O(+)	S/O	—	—
Preserve City-suburban balance on Executive Committee	S(+)	O(−)	O(−)	S/O	—	—

Policy changes to increase achievement

Public welfare	—	O(−)	O(−)	S(+)	S(+)	S(+)
Housing, urban renewal, redevelopment	S(−)	O(+)	O(+)	S(−)	S(−)	S(−)
Education	S(+)	O(−)	S(+)	S(+)	S(+)	S(+)
Land-use planning	O(+)	O(+)	O(+)	S(−)	S(−)	S(−)
Traffic control	O(+)	O(+)	O(+)	S(−)	S(−)	S(−)
Services in outer suburbs	O(+)	—	S(−)	S(−)	—	S(−)
Other: health, fire, libraries	S/O	O(+)	O(+)	S(−)	S(−)	S(−)
Net Satisfaction Score in 1965[a]	−1	+12	+7	−8	−5	−6
Net Satisfaction with 1966 Reforms[b]	+5	+4	+7	−2	−1	−2

[a] Number of changes opposed minus number favored
[b] Number of pluses after minuses have been subtracted

Symbols: S = Supported change O = Opposed change S/O = Took differing stands dash = Took no stand
plus = Provincial decision in accord with actors' views minus = Provincial decision not in accord with actors' views

Expanding Metro's Developmental Capacity

A sweeping reorganization of the system by provincial officials was the most obvious way to break this impasse. Before considering provincial reform, two other possibilities should be noted.

The Metro chairman might have tried to break the impasse by linking together certain municipal grievances and securing Council approval of a package plan. Thus, one might have joined Metro participation in urban renewal with expansions in suburban services. Such a strategy would have meant applying the notion of parity more broadly than Gardiner originally intended. By bringing service programs into parity considerations, this strategy would also have required greater Metro Council control of some independent commissions. Moreover, since the small, inlying suburbs had no serious grievances, any strategy to break the deadlock would have required the chairman to rely on a coalition of officials from the City and the outlying suburbs, in direct violation of Gardiner's notion about the need for *ad hoc*, fluid, and consensual majorities. Finally, this type of strategy would have demanded a more ambitious image of the chairman's floor-leading role than Allen seemed to hold.

Another potential source of change, other than provincial reorganization, was the likelihood that political parties, ethnic groups, and perhaps organized Labor would increase their involvement in Metro politics. The intervention of new actors, rather than "solve" the deadlock, probably would dissolve it, by introducing new issues, new sources of loyalty, and new lines of division. Structural or federal issues, the major obstacles to problem solving in certain policy areas, would become far less important.

In 1963, the provincial cabinet, prompted mainly by the City's renewed campaign for total amalgamation, appointed a Royal Commission on Metro Toronto. This process of review culminated in a reorganization of the Metro system, approved by the Ontario legislature as Bill 81 in May, 1966. Rather than speculate on all the possible structural reforms that might have broken the Metro deadlock, the following discussion will deal only with reforms that were seriously considered during the 1963–1966 period.

Obviously, the integration problem could have been largely solved by abolishing Metro and creating one unified city for the area. But the province quickly rejected this possibility, for the same reasons that had prevailed in 1953. Total amalgamation would stir strong resentment elsewhere in the province, create a government rivaling the province in size and importance, and possibly lay the groundwork for the emergence of a unified City bloc in the provincial legislature. Amalgamation would certainly be denounced by the twelve suburbs and might weaken Conservative Party strength in that area. There is an obvious paradox in the provincial concern over suburban opposition. If the Metro system had secured more integration and had created the metropolitan spirit of which Gardiner often spoke, abolition of the Metro system would have been more seriously considered by the provincial politicians. Metro's failure to attain a greater degree of integration ensured the survival of that system!

Of all those proposals urging revisions in the federal structure, three received major attention before being rejected: a proposal to have the Metro councilors directly elected, a proposal to have the Metro chairman elected in the area at large, and a proposal to transfer several important powers from the municipal to the Metro level. The Royal Commission accepted the first, but rejected the second and third. The province rejected all three. Although the question is an academic one, one might ask what effect these reforms would have had on the Metro deadlock.

The transfer of powers to the Metro level, in all likelihood, would have greatly facilitated problem solving. Certain substantive problems would have been separated from structural or federal issues.

The direct election of Metro councilors might have made the councilors more inclined to seek reelection on the basis of their record at the Metro level, to support the Metro system at least as much as they supported the municipal unit, and to devote most of their political time to Metro business. Direct election appears to have had these effects in the Metro Winnipeg system. But the Royal Commission's proposals differed from the Winnipeg plan in two respects. First, none of the newly created Metro Council constituencies would cross municipal boundaries. Second, in order to avoid conflict between the two levels of government, the commission proposed that Metro councilors also hold seats on their respective municipal councils. Thus, the Metro councilors would continue to interact on a regular basis with municipal officials and might continue to see the municipality as their crucial reference group. The Metro councilor's decisions about reference groups would also hinge on his career aspirations. If he looked to a career in provincial or federal politics, he would be more "Metro minded" than if he hoped to become the mayor of his municipality. On the whole, however, a directly elected councilor would probably assign somewhat more loyalty and time to the Metro system than a councilor recruited from the municipal councils.

Thus, the direct election of Metro councilors would probably increase the level of integration and the rate of problem solving within the Metro Council. But the support given to Metro by a Metro councilor, and the resulting expansion in the Metro system, would be sharply criticized by municipal officials. Greater integration within the Council would be secured only at the price of increased municipal dissatisfaction with the system's performance. These municipal officials could no longer disrupt Council proceedings or bring Metro's policy-making process to a standstill, but they could press their attack at the provincial level and perhaps force another Metro reorganization. On the other hand, direct elections would also expand the size of the Metro system's relevant public. The municipal officials, though still important, could no longer claim to be the only actors who spoke for the electorate. The net effect of direct elections on Metro's long-range integrative problem would depend on how much weight the province gave to the opinion of municipal officials and the opinion of Metro councilors.

Having councilors directly elected, though expanding Metro's developmental capacity over the long run, might increase the incidence of Council conflict over the short run. More demands would be made of the chairman by Metro legislators. The councilors probably would be more involved in Metro business and less willing to go along.

A higher level of commitment among the councilors might produce a greater incidence of legislative conflict and perhaps stalemate. But this increased commitment could have the opposite effect if the chairman's ability to coordinate legislative behavior were increased accordingly. The direct election of the chairman and some expansion of his formal powers might enhance the chairman's ability to build majorities. In other words, Gardiner's reliance on informal powers and purely intralegislative influence was effective in a low-pressure, low-involvement Council. Increasing the level of commitment without also increasing the means of coordination would probably lead to a reduction in Metro's policy output. Increasing both commitment and coordination would permit Metro to expand significantly its policy output.

In 1965, several adaptive-oriented actors, eager to see Metro expand, nevertheless opposed the direct election of Metro councilors, unless the province also agreed to provide for a stronger, popularly elected, Metro chairman. These actors, though unhappy with the *status quo*, implied that they would rather see a perpetuation of low-pressure Council politics than the appearance of a more intense—but also uncoordinated and unpredictable—brand of Council politics.

The provincial cabinet seemed convinced that the direct election of Metro councilors and the Metro chairman would encourage open partisan intervention in Metro area politics. The large size of the Metro constituencies would probably encourage candidates to seek more extensive party assistance. Most cabinet officials opposed partisan local politics in principle and feared that party intervention in the Metro area might set a precedent for other Ontario cities. In addition, some cabinet members apparently feared that one of the opposition parties would capture control of the Metro Council. Even if the Conservative Party were to capture control, Conservative Metro councilors might become a pressure group within the party, embarrassing the provincial leadership with their demands on Metro's behalf. A popularly elected Metro chairman, openly affiliated with one of the political parties, could not help but be a source of irritation and embarrassment to the premier. If the chairman were a Liberal or New Democrat, he would be a regular critic of the premier. If the chairman were a Conservative, he could become the head of a Metro bloc within the party.

No official at the provincial or local level favored an increase in the formal powers of the chairman, unless provision were also made for his popular election. Thus, once the province had decided against popular election of the chairman, an increase in formal powers was necessarily ruled out. The chairman, of course, could continue to exert his *de facto* leadership, but officially vesting these powers in a nonelective official was seen as inappropriate. Moreover, to provide statutory recognition of the chairman's chief administrator and floor leader roles would mean challenging Ontario's weak mayor tradition. The cabinet was not intensely committed to that tradition but, at the same time, was reluctant to create a strong mayor precedent for other Ontario cities. Finally, a popularly elected Metro chairman with the formal powers of a strong mayor and with control over a bureaucracy larger than those of most Canadian provinces would become the second most important politician in Ontario. Such a strong chairman would force the premier to share the political spotlight and the attention of the news media.

As for the proposal to transfer major municipal programs to the Metro level, the province could not have accepted this reform without destroying the rationale for a federal system. If the municipalities were to be stripped of every significant power, the obvious question was why the municipal units were retained at all.

In view of the above considerations, it is not surprising that the 1966 reorganization provided for minimal changes in the system. Retained were the federal form of government, the recruitment of Metro councilors from the municipal councils, the appointment by Council of a chairman with no significant formal powers, and most other features of Bill 80. The number of municipalities was reduced from thirteen to six, the size of the Council was expanded, and the basis of municipal representation on Metro Council was altered. The new municipalities and their representation on Metro Council were as follows:

City of Toronto (to include the City of Toronto, Forest Hill, and Swansea)	12 seats
North York (unchanged)	6 seats
Scarborough (unchanged)	5 seats
Etobicoke (to include Etobicoke, Mimico, New Toronto, and Long Branch)	4 seats
York (York and Weston)	3 seats
East York (East York and Leaside)	2 seats
Total	32 seats

Toronto's demand for a continued even division of seats between City and suburbs was rejected. However, an even division was retained on the Executive Committee, whose composition was now defined in provincial statute rather left to the Council. The size of the committee was expanded to eleven, but the manner of electing committee members was unchanged. Each suburban delegation would include the mayor or reeve of that municipality. In those suburbs with boards of control, the delegation would include all or some of the controllers. In the other suburbs, the delegation would be completed by the addition of members appointed by and from the municipal councils. (The North York delegation would include the mayor, the four controllers, and one councilor named by the municipal council.) The composition of the City's delegation was left unchanged.

The 1966 Act decreed only one change in the distribution of powers between the Metro and municipal levels. Welfare, or public assistance, was transferred to the Metro level.

Finally, a dramatic change was enacted in the field of education. The federal structure was retained, but the Metro School Board was given power to levy one school tax rate for the entire area and to assume virtually complete control over the fiscal decisions of the local boards. The Metro School Board, then, was given the means to realize its equalization task. The number of local boards was reduced to six, and the basis of municipal representation was changed accordingly. Here, as in Metro Council, the City's representation fell below the 50 percent mark. Although the province added its assurance that local boards would continue to control policy, most school officials doubted whether this local autonomy could coexist with centralized control of expenditures. Amalgamation, behind a façade of federalism, seemed likely to emerge in the educational sphere.

In summary, the provincial reforms emphasized the two points —reduction in the number of municipalities and a greater Metro role in financing education—on which almost all Metro actors had been agreed (see Table 9.1). The strategy of this reorganization appeared to be finding the least common denominator.

These reforms are not likely to change any basic features of the executive-directed system. Although Council's size and composition are altered, neither the entire Council nor any bloc within the Council is likely to emerge as an integrated social system and a more significant referent point for legislative behavior. Replacing twelve independent reeves with five municipal blocs may clarify the internal structure of the suburban bloc. Perhaps the five reeves will emerge as the recognized suburban leaders. Within each municipal bloc, however, the reeve's leadership probably will be challenged by ambitious controllers or councilors. An opportunity to increase the coherence of the City bloc's leadership was lost when the province rejected a proposal to include all four controllers in the Toronto delegation. During 1966, a great deal was said in the Metro area about the City's loss in representation and the possibility of suburban domination in future Metro Councils. But domination would require the emergence of an integrated suburban bloc, and such a development seems no more likely to occur under the new arrangement than under the old. A larger Council may have to restrict its floor debates and rely even more on leadership. Thus, the expansion in size may add, marginally, to the chairman's influence.

Aside from the areas of education and public assistance, where breakthroughs will undoubtedly occur, the reforms seem unlikely to expand Metro's capacity for development. The Metro councilor's basic orientation to the system, and his hostility to further development, remain intact. An examination of the responses to provincial reforms, as described in Table 9.1, reveals that integrative leaders were accommodated more than adaptive leaders. The integrative or political leaders, who were more satisfied at the outset of reform, registered a net satisfaction, or plus score, with the 1966 reorganization. The adaptive leaders, far less satisfied prior to reform, found more to criticize than praise in the 1966 reorganization. Bill 81, therefore, did little to eliminate or lessen the gap between adaptive and integrative leaders. The adaptive leaders will continue to advocate an expanded rate of problem solving; the integrative leaders will continue to oppose any venture into new policy areas.

This impasse will be broken only by the appearance of new actors and new issues or by the construction of a Council majority behind some multifaceted, package plan. In an indirect fashion, the 1966 reforms may improve the Metro chairman's ability to achieve a breakthrough in Council. First, the mere fact that reform was completed and is not likely to be considered again for at least five years may encourage the Metro councilors to temporarily lay aside their grievances and cooperate with the chairman. Metro, in 1966, was entering the first phase—the most harmonious phase—of the five-year cycle described in chapter 3. Second, the 1966 reforms may convince City officials that amalgamation will never be imposed by provincial statute. In the early 1960s, City officials had insisted that Metro be abolished not expanded. After 1966, the City may return to its earlier view that steady expansions in Metro's power will introduce total amalgamation through the back door.

NOTES

CHAPTER I

The Uses and Limits of Functional Theory

1. This view of theory is one that Ernest Nagel calls the "instrumentalist" view; see *The Structure of Science* (New York and Burlingame, Harcourt, Brace, and World, 1962), pp. 129–40.

2. The literature on local government outside the United States is mainly devoted to descriptions of formal institutions and suggestions for change. See, for example, William Robson, ed., *Great Cities of the World* (Rev. ed.; London, Allen and Unwin, 1957); and Harold Alderfer, *Local Government in Developing Countries* (New York, McGraw-Hill, 1964). There are, however, increasing efforts to see local governments in behavioral and political terms. See J. Bulpitt, "Party Systems in Local Government," *Political Studies*, XI (Feb., 1963), 11–35; Fred Burke, *Local Government and Politics in Uganda* (Syracuse, Syracuse University Press, 1964); Guy Bourassa, "Les Elites Politique de Montréal: de L'Aristocratie à La Démocratie," *Canadian Journal of Economics and Political Science*, XXXI (Feb., 1965), 35–51; Herbert Werlin, "The Nairobi City Council: A Study in Comparative Local Government," and J. David Greenstone, "Corruption and Self-Interest: A Comment on Local Politics in East Africa," both appearing in *Comparative Studies in Society and History*, VIII (Jan., 1966), 181–210. Of course there are some nations where local government is part of the national administration or where so little power is given to the local unit that such local systems may be hardly worth studying. Where the regime is unstable or where local autonomy runs contrary to the modernizing and planning goals of the national elite, local self-government may be more a promise and an ideology than a practice. See, for example,

Robert Fried, *The Italian Prefects* (New Haven, Yale University Press, 1963); Fred Riggs, *Administration in Developing Countries* (Boston, Houghton Mifflin, 1964), pp. 365–96; and Reinhard Bendix, *Nation-Building and Citizenship*, (New York, Wiley, 1964), pp. 215–98. In Canada the descriptive–prescriptive approach prevails. My statements about Canadian cities outside of the Toronto area are based on the Winnipeg, Montreal, and Vancouver newspapers. I have also gained a great deal from my conversations with knowledgeable persons in this field, particularly Guy Bourassa, Lionel Feldman, Albert Rose, and Thomas Plunkett.

3. The initial and most comprehensive statement of Parsons' theory is to be found in Talcott Parsons and Edward Shils, eds., *Toward a General Theory of Action* (Cambridge, Harvard University Press, 1951), Part II; and T. Parsons, *The Social System* (New York, The Free Press, 1951). In *The Structure of Social Action* (New York, The Free Press, 1937), Parsons traces the origins of his theory to Durkheim, Pareto, and Weber. More recent formulations of his theory are to be found in T. Parsons and Neil Smelser, *Economy and Society* (New York, The Free Press, 1956), particularly pp. 46–84; and T. Parsons, "General Theory in Sociology," in Robert Merton *et al.*, *Sociology Today* (New York, Basic Books, 1959), pp. 3–38. Essays by Parsons of particular interest to political scientists include: " 'Voting' and the Equilibrium of the American System," in Eugene Burdick and Arthur Brodbeck, eds., *American Voting Behavior* (New York, The Free Press, 1959), pp. 80–120; and "Authority, Legitimation, and Political Action," "The Distribution of Power in American Society," "Social Strains in America," "A Sociological Approach to the Theory of Organizations," and "Some Ingredients of a General Theory of Formal Organizations," all reprinted in T. Parsons, *Structure and Process in Modern Societies* (New York, The Free Press, 1960), pp. 16–96 and 170–247. Robert Merton demonstrates that the functionalist approach can be separated from many specific aspects of the Parsonian framework. See "Manifest and Latent Functions," in R. Merton, *Social Theory and Social Structure* (Rev. ed.; New York, The Free Press, 1957), pp. 19–84. An approach that resembles Parsons' in many respects is contained in George Homans, *The Human Group* (New York, Harcourt, Brace, 1950).

4. For configurationism see A. L. Kroeber, *Configurations of Culture Growth* (Berkeley and Los Angeles, University of California Press, 1944); and Parsons, *The Social System*, pp. 488–90.

5. See Parsons, "General Theory in Sociology," in Merton *et al.*, *Sociology Today*, pp. 3–38.

6. *Ibid.* See also Parsons and Smelser, *Economy and Society*, pp. 51–84. In the essay appearing in the Merton volume, Parsons notes some similarities between his more recent framework and the approach pursued in David Easton, "An Approach to the Analysis of Political Systems," *World Politics*, IX (April, 1957), 383–400.

7. Semantic confusion in the field of functional analysis is carefully explored in Merton, *Social Theory and Social Structure*, pp. 20–25. But at a later point (p. 121) Merton equates a functionalist explanation of social deviation with a sociological, as opposed to a psychological, explanation.

8. Merton, *Social Theory and Social Structure*, p. 121.

9. Parsons traces his roots to the classical sociological tradition in *The Structure of Social Action*. Some critics of functionalism insist that it is not really a distinctive theory. Kingsley Davis, for example, equates functionalism with the major sociological tradition and minimizes Parsons' and Merton's contributions to that tradition; see "The Myth of Functional Analysis as a Special Method in Sociology and Anthropology," *American Sociological Review*, XXIV (Dec., 1959), 757–73.

10. The link between recent, sociological, functionalism and the earlier, anthropological, brand of functionalism is traced in Merton, *Social Theory and Social Structure*, pp. 22–37.

11. A major contribution of David Truman's *The Governmental Process* (New York, Knopf, 1951) was to help reorient political science in a sociological direction and to suggest that politics was the study of certain types of social structures. The major influence on Truman, however, was not functionalism but the small-group and social-psychological literature. Some recent studies by political scientists, which to some degree show the influence of Parsons, are: George Modelski, "Agraria and Industria: Two Models of the International System," *World Politics*, XIV (Oct., 1961), 118–43; Leonard Binder, *Iran* (Berkeley and Los Angeles, University of California Press, 1962); William Mitchell, *The American Polity* (New York, The Free Press, 1962); Richard Fenno Jr., "The House Appropriations Committee as a Political System: The Problem of Integration," *American Political Science Review*, LVI (June, 1962), 310–24; Theodore Lowi, "Toward Functionalism in Political Science," *American Political Science Review*, LVII (Sept., 1963), 570–83; David Apter, *Ghana in Transition* (New York, Atheneum, 1963); Fred Riggs, *Administration in Developing Countries*, especially pp. 19–31; and Joseph LaPalombara, *Interest Groups in Italian Politics* (Princeton, Princeton University Press, 1964). See also the works by Karl Deutsch and Ernst Haas cited in note 34. An assess-

ment of how political scientists have used and could use Parsonian analysis is explicitly undertaken in Robert Holt, "A Proposed Structural Functional Framework for Political Science," and William Flanigan and Edwin Fogelman, "Functionalism in Political Science," both appearing in Don Martindale, ed., *Functionalism in the Social Sciences* (Philadelphia, The American Academy of Political and Social Science, 1965), pp. 84–126. Of four recent attempts at general theory in the field of political science. Almond and Apter appear to be most heavily influenced by Parsons. Deutsch acknowledges a debt to functionalism but is more influenced by cybernetics. Easton pursues a "general systems" approach but quickly dismisses functionalism. See David Apter, "A Comparative Method for the Study of Politics," *American Journal of Sociology*, LXIV (Nov., 1958), 221–37; Gabriel Almond, "A Functional Approach to Comparative Politics," in G. Almond and J. Coleman, *The Politics of Developing Areas* (Princeton, Princeton University Press, 1960), pp. 3–65; Karl Deutsch, *The Nerves of Government* (New York, The Free Press, 1965); and David Easton, *A Systems Analysis of Political Life* (New York, Wiley, 1965).

12. Parsons' influence on the study of comparative government may be seen in the works by Apter, Almond, LaPalombara, Riggs, and Holt cited in the above note.

13. Parsons only briefly deals with social change in *The Social System* (ch. 11) and in *Toward a General Theory of Action* (pp. 230–33); but he returns to the problem of change in "Evolutionary Universals in Society," *American Sociological Review*, XXIX (June, 1964), 339–57. Functionally oriented studies of social change should lay to rest the charge that structural functionalism is necessarily static. See Neil Smelser, *Social Change in the Industrial Revolution* (Chicago, University of Chicago Press, 1959); and S. N. Eisenstadt, *The Political Systems of Empire* (New York, The Free Press, 1963).

14. See Lewis Coser, *The Functions of Social Conflict* (New York, The Free Press, 1956), ch. 1. Parsons' relative neglect of change and conflict is examined in Ralf Dahrendorf, *Class and Class Conflict in Industrial Society* (Stanford, Stanford University Press, 1959), ch. 5.

15. Excellent general statements of what I have called the war theory of politics can be found in Charles Merriam, *Political Power* (reprinted by the Free Press in 1950); and Pendleton Herring, *The Politics of Democracy* (New York, W. W. Norton, 1940). Also in this tradition are Harold Lasswell and Abraham Kaplan, *Power and Society* (New Haven, Yale University Press, 1950); and Robert Dahl, *Modern Political Analysis* (Englewood Cliffs, N.J., Prentice-Hall, 1963), particularly ch. 5 and 7. Some of the shortcomings of

this emphasis on power and conflict are noted in Deutsch, *The Nerves of Government*, ch. 7; and Mitchell, *The American Polity*, pp. 142–43. I discussed conflict and normative integration in a specific context; see H. Kaplan, *Urban Renewal Politics* (New York, Columbia University Press, 1963), pp. 166–72. The so-called group approach developed by David Truman in *The Governmental Process* seems to me to involve two distinct ideas. One idea is that the study of interest groups is vital to an understanding of all aspects of American political life. This statement is an empirically verfiable proposition about politics in the United States; either interest groups are or are not as important as Truman says they are. At the same time, Truman is arguing that small-group and social-psychological theory is essential to an understanding of politics and that politics can be best studied as the operation of particular types of social structures. This second idea is less an empirical proposition than a research strategy, to be judged on the basis of its utility in concrete research. The first approach, which appears to have drawn most of the criticism, places Truman firmly in the Merriam-Herring camp; the second approach represents an attempt to import sociological concepts to political science.

16. Mitchell, *The American Polity*, pp. 142–43. David Truman does consider, briefly, the problem of what holds the American system together; see *The Governmental Process*, pp. 508–24.

17. For an attempt to define the distinctive features of non-Western politics and an implicit rejection of models used to study American politics, see Lucian Pye, "The Non-Western Political Process," *Journal of Politics*, XX (Aug., 1958), 468–86.

18. Parsons, "The Distribution of Power in American Society," in *Structure and Process in Modern Societies*, pp. 199–225.

19. Max Weber, for example, was interested in how legal–rational institutions and values emerged, and Parsons derives much of his approach from Weber. See Parsons, *The Structure of Social Action*, pp. 640–99; and *The Social System*, pp. 101–36.

20. Merton, *Social Theory and Social Structure*, p. 311; David Truman, *The Congressional Party* (New York, Wiley, 1959), pp. 95–99 and *passim.*; and Robert Dahl, *Who Governs?* (New Haven, Yale University Press, 1961), pp. 271–75. For organizational "slack" see James March and Herbert Simon, *Organizations* (New York, Wiley, 1958), p. 126. The distinction between instrumental and expressive or consummatory orientations plays an important part in Parsons' framework, but he dismisses the possibility that a system might be based largely on instrumental orientations; see Parsons, *The Social System*, pp. 36–51.

21. Overlapping membership, divided loyalties, role conflict, and

choices among reference groups are important parts of Truman's and Merton's formulations. Here, Merton's more cautious approach to the study of entire systems and his recognition of the diversity and malintegration in systems provide important qualifiers to Parsons' model. See Merton, *Social Theory and Social Structure*, ch. 8 and 9; and Truman, *The Governmental Process*, pp. 157–67, 336–43, 520–24, and *passim*. Parsons considers the problem of multiple group membership in one of his essays but has not accorded this notion an important place in his general scheme. See Parsons, " 'Voting' and the Equilibrium of the American Political System," in Burdick and Brodbeck, eds., *American Voting Behavior*, pp. 80–120.

22. In making the goal-setting or policy-making process the core of my approach to political systems, I follow Almond and Easton; see Almond and Coleman, *The Politics of Developing Areas*, pp. 3–65; and Easton, *A Systems Analysis of Political Life*. Of course, such an approach does not rule out consideration of institutionalized values or political culture.

23. Parsons' lesser interest in quantification also stems from Weber. See *The Structure of Social Action*, pp. 581–86. While there are undoubtedly differences in emphasis and methodology between functionalists and behaviorists, there does not seem to me to be any inherent conflict between Parsons' approach and the use of quantification or the development of indices based on overt behavior. Karl Deutsch, for example, appears to be committed to both approaches. See Deutsch's articles in Philip Jacob and James Toscano, eds., *The Integration of Political Communities* (Philadelphia and New York, Lippincott, 1964). The clash between the functionalist and the behaviorist point of view is emphasized in Don Martindale, *The Nature and Types of Sociological Theory* (Boston, Houghton Mifflin, 1960), Parts V and VI; and Maurice Natanson, ed., *Philosophy of the Social Sciences* (New York, Random House, 1963), Part III.

24. To Parsons "equilibrium" is synonymous with normative integration. Another approach equates "equilibrium" with stability in rates and forms of interaction. See Parsons, *The Social System*, ch. 7. For the interactionist definition, see Homans, *The Human Group*, pp. 301–5 and *passim.*; and Truman, *The Governmental Process*, pp. 26–32. Both Parsons and the interactionists assume that attempts will be made by system members to restore an equilibrium once it is disrupted. Another notion of equilibrium is presented in ch. 5 of this study; see note 2.

25. See Merton's discussion of types of groups in *Social Theory and Social Structure*, pp. 310–26. March and Simon relate the level

of necessary "inducements" in an organization to the level of desired "contributions"; see *Organizations,* pp. 83 and 122. Amitai Etzioni discusses the "scope" of an organization and the degree of "compliance" required in *A Comparative Analysis of Complex Organizations* (New York, The Free Press, 1961), pp. 160–72.

26. Relevant to this point is Lewis Coser's discussion of the "group binding" effects of conflict; see *The Functions of Social Conflict.*

27. My discussion of the two levels of analysis, and my use of terms, has been influenced by J. D. Singer, "The Level of Analysis Problem in International Relations," *World Politics,* XIV (Oct., 1961), 77–92; and the commentary on this question in Ernst Haas, *Beyond the Nation State* (Stanford, Stanford University Press, 1964), ch. 3.

28. The notion of "referent points" is obviously derived from "reference groups" but I include as "referent points" individual personality and internalized values not anchored to any specific group. For reference groups, choice among reference groups, and the related problem of role definition, see Merton, *Social Theory and Social Structure,* ch. 8 and 9, but particularly pp. 301–8; and Truman, *The Governmental Process,* particularly pp. 332–43. The distinction between "reference groups" and "interaction groups" is made in R. H. Turner, "Role-Taking, Role Standpoint, and Reference-Group Behavior," *American Journal of Sociology,* LXI (Nov., 1956), pp. 316–28. For personality as a referent point for legislative behavior, see James Barber, *The Lawmakers* (New Haven, Yale University Press, 1965). Parsons devotes only a passing glance to this whole problem; see *The Social System,* p. 292. The links that Parsons provides between macro and micro analysis—socialization, internalization, and social control—do not seem to me to exhaust the problem; see Parsons, *The Social System,* ch. 6 and 7.

29. Most political scientists adopt a broader definition of "role" than that used by Parsons and most sociologists. For example, the legislative roles described by political scientists meet few of the criteria set down by Parsons. For the sociological definition of role, see Parsons and Shils, *Toward a General Theory of Action,* pp. 191–97; Theodore Sabin, "Role Theory," in Gardner Lindzey, ed., *Handbook of Social Psychology* (Reading, Mass., Addison-Wesley, 1954), pp. 223–58; and Michael Banton, *Roles* (New York, Basic Books, 1965). The political scientists' use of "role" in the study of legislatures can be seen in Oliver Garceau and Corinne Silverman, "A Pressure Group and the Pressured: A Case Report," *American Political Science Review,* XLVIII (Sept., 1954), 672–91; Heinz

Eulau *et al.*, "The Role of the Representative: Some Empirical Observations on the Theory of Edmund Burke," *American Political Science Review*, LIII (Sept., 1959), 742–56; Frank Sorauf, *Party and Representation* (New York, Atherton, 1963), pp. 121–46; and James Barber, *The Lawmakers.*

30. "Contributions" are discussed in Parsons and Smelser, *Economy and Society*, pp. 46–51.

31. My definition is largely in accord with that of Parsons and Almond; see Parsons and Smelser, *Economy and Society*, pp. 47–48; and Almond and Coleman, *The Politics of Developing Areas*, p. 7.

32. For example, Key traces the growth in federal power to the weak performance of the state governments; see V. O. Key Jr., *American State Politics* (New York, Knopf, 1957), ch. 1.

33. My discussion of functions and role differentiation is similar to the argument presented in Robert Bales, "The Equilibrium Problem in Small Groups," in Talcott Parsons *et al.*, *Working Papers in the Theory of Action* (New York, The Free Press, 1953), pp. 111–61; R. Bales and P. E. Slater, "Role Differentiation in Small Decision-Making Groups," in T. Parsons *et al.*, *The Family, Socialization, and Interaction Process* (New York, The Free Press, 1955), pp. 295–306; and T. Parsons, "Some Ingredients of a General Theory of Formal Organizations," in *Structure and Process in Modern Societies*, pp. 56–96. Since goal attainment is the major contribution of political systems to the entire society, these analyses of task-oriented systems seem particularly relevant to political science. See also George Homans' distinction between the "internal" and "external" aspects of group life in *The Human Group*, ch. 4–6.

34. Karl Deutsch *et al.*, *Political Community and the North Atlantic Area* (Princeton, Princeton University Press, 1957); Jacob and Toscano, eds., *The Integration of Political Communities;* Ernst Haas, *The Uniting of Europe* (Stanford, Stanford University Press, 1958); and Haas, *Beyond the Nation State.* "Integration" as a process has also been used to study "nation building." See Karl Deutsch and William Foltz, *Nation-Building* (New York, Atherton, 1963). My distinction between normative and nonnormative integration parallels Etzioni's distinction between "normative" and "calculative" organizations in *A Comparative Analysis of Complex Organizations*, p. 10 and *passim.* See also David Easton's distinction between "diffuse" and "specific" support in *A Systems Analysis of Political Life*, ch. 10. Easton's use of these phrases are not to be equated with Parsons' use of the same phrases in discussing role orientations.

35. The transition from nonnormative to normative integration is described as "the emergence of political community" in the works by Deutsch and Haas cited in note 34.

36. The spiraling character of systemic changes was noted in Homans, *The Human Group*, p. 450 and *passim*. I pointed out this spiral in a study of an administrative organization; see H. Kaplan, *Urban Renewal Politics*.

37. That no permanent solution can be found to functional problems is implied or openly stated by the studies cited in note 33.

38. Deutsch, *The Nerves of Government*, ch. 13.

39. My use of the phrase "role differentiation" does not imply that complex role structures necessarily emerge from the bifurcation of simpler structures. This process of bifurcation is described in Smelser, *Social Change in the Industrial Revolution*, and is discussed in Amitai Etzioni, "The Epigenesis of Political Community at the International Level," *American Journal of Sociology*, LXVIII (Jan., 1963), 407–21. The ways in which a differentiated role structure aids a system's performance are stressed in S. N. Eisenstadt, "Bureaucracy and Political Development," in Joseph LaPalombara, ed., *Bureaucracy and Political Development* (Princeton, Princeton University Press, 1963), pp. 96–119; S. N. Eisenstadt, "Social Change, Differentiation, and Evolution," *American Sociological Review*, XXIX (June, 1964), 375–85; and Paul Diesing, *Reason in Society* (Urbana, University of Illinois Press, 1962), pp.176–98.

40. Almond and Coleman, *The Politics of Developing Areas*, p. 16; and Bernard Cohen, *The Political Process and Foreign Policy* (Princeton, Princeton University Press, 1957).

41. It seems to me that Almond's four "input functions" are more "activities" (as I define the phrase) than "functions" (my definition). Thus, my list of activities closely follows Almond's list. See Almond and Coleman, *The Politics of Developing Areas*, pp. 16–20.

42. My discussion of influence, here and in ch. 6, relies on Dahl, *Who Governs?*, particularly ch. 8 and 12; and Dahl, *Modern Political Analysis*, pp. 39–54

43. The dangers of focusing too narrowly on the policy-making process are noted in Robert Agger *et al.*, *The Rulers and the Ruled* (New York, Wiley, 1964), pp. 67–68. My distinction between specific and pervasive influence is further explored in ch. 6 of this study.

44. In *The Rulers and the Ruled*, Agger and others argue for less reliance on a simple pluralist–elitist continuum in studying local political systems. I do not make extensive use of the framework employed in that study for two reasons. First, some of the proposed variables, like whether a political elite uses illegitimate sanctions to pervert the electoral process, do not seem particularly important in the study of large North American cities. Another major variable is whether the political elite in a community agree or disagree on

ideology. The authors go on to define ideology as a comprehensive world view or political *weltanshauung*. Defining the term in this way, I doubt whether any North American city has "ideological" divisions. Second, although the authors argue for a more complex framework, they remain primarily interested in the question of how democratic a local system is. I am not quarreling with this interest, only arguing that there are other aspects of political system that also deserve study. For the debate between elitists and pluralists see Nelson Polsby, "How to Study Community Power: The Pluralist Alternative," *Journal of Politics*, XXII (Aug., 1960), 474–84; N. Polsby, *Community Power and Political Theory* (New Haven, Yale University Press, 1963); Agger *et al., The Rulers and the Ruled*, pp. 73–124, and 524–27; and William D'Antonio and Howard Ehrlich, *Power and Democracy in America* (Notre Dame, Notre Dame University Press, 1961), pp. 25–89.

45. Although my business elite model is an ideal type, the following studies described local systems that more or less adhere to this model: Robert and Helen Lynd, *Middletown* (New York, Harcourt, Brace, 1929); Robert and Helen Lynd, *Middletown in Transition* (New York, Harcourt, Brace, 1937); Floyd Hunter, *Community Power Structure* (Chapel Hill, University of North Carolina Press, 1953); Carol Estes Thometz, *The Decision Makers* (Dallas, Southern Methodist University Press, 1963). Other studies in this vein are summarized in William Form and Delbert Miller, *Industry, Labor, and Community* (New York, Harper and Brothers, 1960).

46. For broker leadership in large U.S. cities see Martin Meyerson and Edward Banfield, *Politics, Planning, and the Public Interest* (New York, The Free Press, 1955); James Wilson, *Negro Politics* (New York, The Free Press, 1960); Wallace Sayre and Herbert Kaufman, *Governing New York City* (New York, Russell Sage Foundation, 1960); Edward Banfield, *Political Influence* (New York, The Free Press, 1961); Robert Dahl, *Who Governs?;* Roscoe Martin, Ralph Munger *et al., Decisions in Syracuse* (Bloomington, Indiana University Press, 1961); Oliver Williams and Charles Adrian, *Four Cities* (Philadelphia, University of Pennsylvania Press, 1963); Edward Banfield and James Wilson, *City Politics* (Cambridge, Harvard and M.I.T. Press, 1963); Theodore Lowi, *At the Pleasure of the Mayor* (New York, The Free Press, 1964); Edward Banfield, *Big City Politics* (New York, Random House, 1965); and S. J. Makielski, *The Politics of Zoning* (New York, Columbia University Press, 1966). More general accounts of broker leadership politics in the American context are presented in William Mitchell,

The American Polity, ch. 13; and James March, "The Business Firm as a Political Coalition," *Journal of Politics*, XXIV (Nov., 1962), 662–678

47. Banfield and Wilson, *City Politics*, p. 311.
48. Banfield, *Political Influence*, pp. 284–85.
49. Sayre and Kaufman, *Governing New York City*, pp. 716–19.
50. Duane Lockard, *The Politics of State and Local Government* (New York, MacMillan, 1963), p. 143.

51. My use of the terms "executive directed" or "executive centered" does not mean that the Metro system contains the "executive centered coalition" described by Dahl in *Who Governs?*, ch. 17.

52. Sayre and Kaufman assess the New York pattern in *Governing New York City*, pp. 720–25. A discussion of the New York City reform movements can be found in that book as well as in Lowi, *At the Pleasure of the Mayor*, pp. 175–211. For the role of the party machine, see Wilson, *Negro Politics;* Banfield, *Political Influence;* and Martin, Munger et al., *Decisions in Syracuse*, particularly pp. 306–11 and 326–27. A coalition built around the mayor is described in Dahl, *Who Governs?;* and a coalition built around a politician-administrator is described in Kaplan, *Urban Renewal Politics.*

CHAPTER 2

The Metro System: Origins and Initial Development

1. The origins and early years of Metro Miami and Metro Nashville are described in Edward Sofen, *The Miami Metropolitan Experiment* (Bloomington, Indiana University Press, 1963); T. J. Wood, "Dade County, Unbossed and Erratically Led," *The Annals of the American Academy of Social and Political Science*, CXXXV (May, 1964), 64–71; Daniel Grant, "Urban and Suburban Nashville: A Case Study in Metropolitanism," *Journal of Politics*, XVII (Feb., 1955), 82–99; Daniel Grant, "Metropolitics and Professional Political Leadership: The Case of Nashville," *The Annals of the American Academy of Social and Political Science*, CXXXV (May, 1964), 72–83; Daniel Grant, "A Comparison of Predictions and Experience with Nashville 'Metro,'" *Urban Affairs Quarterly*, I (Sept., 1965), 35–54. My remarks on Metro Winnipeg are based on primary sources, mainly the Winnipeg *Free Press* and Winnipeg *Tribune.*

2. An elaborate description of the Toronto area's development and problems seems unnecessary, since the Toronto experience runs true to the North American pattern and since that pattern has been described at length in other studies. A good deal of the literature on

metropolitan development and problems is summarized in John Bollens and Henry Schmandt, *The Metropolis* (New York, Harper and Row, 1965), particularly ch. 1–6, 9–12.

3. The American metropolitan reform movement is described in Victor Jones, *Metropolitan Government* (Chicago, University of Chicago Press, 1942); Scott Greer, *Metropolitics* (New York, Wiley, 1963); and Bollens and Schmandt, *The Metropolis*, ch. 16.

4. Home-rule traditions in the U.S. are described in Charles Adrian, *Governing Urban America* (2d ed.; New York, McGraw-Hill, 1961), pp. 180–88. For the Canadian tradition see Donald Rowat, *Your Local Government* (Toronto, MacMillan, 1955), ch. 1 and 8.

5. Metropolitan reform has made the least headway in those provinces controlled by the rural-based Social Credit Party. See Harold Kaplan, *The Regional City* (Toronto, The Canadian Broadcasting Corporation, 1965). Urban–rural conflict in American states has been the subject of many studies; for example, Malcolm Jewell, ed., *The Politics of Reapportionment* (New York, Atherton, 1962). The strength of the Conservative Party in the Metro Toronto area has been steadily declining, but Conservative majorities in the provincial legislature have remained large. An adequate—or even inadequate —study of Ontario politics has yet to be written. Some basic information on Ontario politics may be derived from Dennis Wrong, "Ontario Provincial Elections, 1934–1955; A Preliminary Survey of Voting," *Canadian Journal of Economics and Political Science*, XXIII (Aug., 1957), 395–403; L. S. Grossman, "Safe Seats: The Rural–Urban Pattern in Ontario," *Canadian Journal of Economics and Political Science*, XXIX (Aug., 1963), 367–71; and F. F. Schindeler, "Legislative–Executive Relations in Ontario," PhD. dissertation (unpublished), University of Toronto, 1965.

6. Canadian and Ontario attitudes on municipal government are described in Donald Rowat, *Your Local Government*, ch. 1 and 2; and K. G. Crawford, *Canadian Municipal Government* (Toronto, University of Toronto Press, 1954), ch. 2 and 3. British Columbia is the only province influenced by the American strong mayor plan. To use Herbert Kaufman's phrases, Canadians emphasize "representativeness" and "neutral competence" over "executive coordination"; see *Politics and Policies in State and Local Governments* (Englewood Cliffs, N. J., Prentice-Hall, 1963), pp. 44–51.

7. Examples of the politics-of-administration approach are Pendleton Herring, *Public Administration and the Public Interest* (New York, McGraw-Hill, 1936); Avery Leiserson, *Administrative Regulation* (Chicago, University of Chicago Press, 1942); Philip Selznick,

TVA and the Grass Roots (Berkeley and Los Angeles, University of California Press, 1949); Herbert Simon *et al.*, *Public Administration* (New York, Knopf, 1950), ch. 18 and 19; David Truman, *The Governmental Process* (New York, Knopf, 1951), ch. 14; Arthur Maas, *Muddy Waters* (Cambridge, Harvard University Press, 1951); Marver Bernstein, *Regulating Business by Independent Commission* (Princeton, Princeton University Press, 1955); J. Leiper Freeman, *The Political Process* (Garden City, N.Y., Doubleday, 1955); Grant McConnell, *The Decline of Agrarian Democracy* (Berkeley and Los Angeles, University of California Press, 1959); Wallace Sayre and Herbert Kaufman, *Governing New York City* (New York, Russell Sage Foundation, 1960), ch. 8–10; Victor Rosenblum, "How to Get Into TV: The Federal Communications Commission and Miami's Channel 10," in Alan Westin, ed., *The Uses of Power* (New York, Harcourt, Brace, and World, 1962), pp. 173–228; Emmette Redford *et al.*, *Politics and Government in the United States: National State and Local Edition* (New York, Harcourt, Brace, and World, 1965), ch. 21.

8. For role differentiation see note 39 to ch. 1.

9. Etzioni emphasizes Barnard's distinction between efficiency and effectiveness and notes the tendency for organizations to stress internal over external needs. See Chester Barnard, *The Functions of the Executive* (Cambridge, Harvard University Press, 1938); Amitai Etzioni, "Two Approaches to the Study of Organizational Effectiveness," *Administrative Science Quarterly*, V (June, 1960), 257–78; and Amitai Etzioni, *A Comparative Analysis of Complex Organizations* (New York, The Free Press, 1961), ch. 4.

CHAPTER 3

The System's Performance

1. For the distinction between "hard" and "soft" programs and for many other insights into Metro's policy output, I am indebted to Frank Smallwood, *Metro Toronto: A Decade Later* (Toronto, Bureau of Municipal Research, 1963); and Albert Rose, "A Decade of Metropolitan Government in Toronto," *Buffalo Law Review*, XIII (Spring, 1964), 539–56.

2. Interaction analysis and the Parsonian emphasis on subjective variables, like "values," are discussed in note 23 to ch. 1. The small-group literature has documented the tendency for regular interaction to produce greater agreement in the attitudes or sentiments of the

interacting individuals. See, for example, George Homans, *The Human Group* (New York, Harcourt, Brace, 1950), pp. 110–19 and *passim*.

3. "Urban renewal" in this context means clearance and/or rehabilitation projects which may or may not include public housing. Since federal involvement in renewal projects not involving public housing was minimal during the 1950s, the expense to Metro *was* an issue in the renewal field, though not in the public housing field. The development and current status of federal housing legislation in Canada is described in "The Role of Private Enterprise in Urban Renewal," a study conducted by Murray V. Jones for the Metropolitan Toronto Planning Board, March, 1966, pp. 14–63.

4. Some of the early community studies were Robert and Helen Lynd, *Middletown* (New York, Harcourt, Brace, 1929); W. Lloyd Warner et al., *Democracy in Jonesville* (New York, Harper, 1949); and Floyd Hunter, *Community Power Structure* (Chapel Hill, University of North Carolina Press, 1953). The need to reassess the role of public administrators in local political systems is recognized by M. Kent Jennings in "Public Administrators and Community Decision Making," *Administrative Science Quarterly*, VIII (June, 1963), 18–43.

5. W. Sayre and H. Kaufman, *Governing New York City* (New York, Russell Sage Foundation, 1960), ch. 8–10. For "clientelism" and "departmentalism" at the higher levels of American government, see Marver Bernstein, *Regulating Business by Independent Commission* (Princeton, Princeton University Press, 1955); Richard Fenno Jr., *The President's Cabinet* (Cambridge, Harvard University Press, 1954).

6. Sayre and Kaufman, *Governing New York City*, p. 303.

7. Canadian political culture is discussed more fully in ch. 7; for my sources see note 21 to that chapter. For evidence of departmentalism and clientelism in a parliamentary-cabinet system, see Richard Rose, *England* (Boston, Little, Brown, 1964), pp. 131–35 and 197–99.

8. For sources on Nashville, Miami, and Winnipeg see note 1 to ch. 2.

9. For the Haas, Deutsch, and Etzioni studies on international federations, see note 34 to ch. 1. The parallel between metropolitan and international organizations is explicitly examined in Phillip Jacob and James Toscano, eds., *The Integration of Political Communities* (Philadelphia and New York, Lippincott, 1964).

10. K. Deutsch et al., *Political Community and the North Atlantic Area* (Princeton, Princeton University Press, 1957), pp. 5–7.

11. In his reliance on personal skills rather than formal authority, the chairman's legislative role resembles that of floor leaders in the U.S. Congress. A crucial difference is the chairman's greater reliance on bipartisan support. See David Truman, *The Congressional Party* (New York, Wiley, 1959), ch. 4 and 6. Gardiner's use of breathing spells resembles the vacillation between instrumental and affective requirements noted in small groups; see Robert Bales, "The Equilibrium Problem in Small Groups," in T. Parsons *et al.*, *Working Papers in the Theory of Action* (New York, The Free Press, 1953), pp. 111–61.

12. David Truman noted that a dispersion of powers often reduces the intensity of politics; see "Federalism and the Party System," in Arthur MacMahon, ed., *Federalism: Mature and Emergent* (New York, Doubleday, 1955), pp. 115–36.

13. The notion of "gatekeeper" is developed in David Easton, *A Systems Analysis of Political Life* (New York, Wiley, 1965), pp. 87–99.

14. The Gardiner strategy might be added on to Haas's list of the techniques through which conflict in international organizations is resolved. See Ernst Haas, "International Integration: The European and Universal Process," *International Organization*, XV (Autumn, 1961), particularly pp. 367–68.

15. In this section, and at other points in the study, I ask "what would happen if" questions. This process of subjecting a system to mental experiments is described by Parsons in *The Structure of Social Action* (New York, The Free Press, 1937), pp. 610–22; and applied by Parsons in *The Social System* (New York, The Free Press, 1951), ch. 10.

16. Charles Merriam uses the phrase "credenda and miranda of power" in his *Political Power* (New York, The Free Press, 1950), ch. 4. Parsons considers the same phenomena under the concept of "expressive symbolism"; see *The Social System*, ch. 9.

17. The "factional vote" is similar to the "party vote" used in studies of legislative behavior in partisan legislatures. A discussion of this and other techniques of voting analysis can be found in the Appendix to Truman's *The Congressional Party*, pp. 320–30.

18. This argument owes a good deal to David Apter's discussion of "institutional transfer" in *Ghana in Transition* (New York, Atheneum, 1963). Apter treats anarchy and apathy as two alternative consequences of unsuccessful transfer. Apathy might be more likely to result in segmental systems where the members can always increase their involvement in some other segmental system; see note 21 to chap. 1.

CHAPTER 4

The System's Performance (continued)

1. A policy subsystem may contain several formal units of organization, like an administrative agency and a legislative committee. Although these units may be treated as subsystems, the policy subsystem is larger than, and includes, these formal subsystems. The entire legislature may participate in all policy areas, but the legislators will often hold different attitudes and pursue different forms of behavior in each of these policy subsystems. These variations in legislative behavior and attitude constitute a major reason why each policy subsystem develops distinctive features. Any study of a particular policy area assumes that the area forms a definable subsystem. See, for example, Harold Kaplan, *Urban Renewal Politics* (New York, Columbia University Press, 1963), ch. 8. Such subsystems are particularly important when they exist within a larger decentralized system. For descriptions of U.S. urban political systems as holding companies for semi-autonomous subsystems, see Wallace Sayre and Herbert Kaufman, *Governing New York City* (New York, Russell Sage Foundation, 1960), ch. 9; Edward Banfield, *Political Influence* (New York, The Free Press, 1961), ch. 8; Robert Dahl, *Who Governs?* (New Haven, Yale University Press, 1961), Book III; and Theodore Lowi, *At the Pleasure of the Mayor* (New York, The Free Press, 1964), ch. 9. The independence of policy subsystems at the national level is discussed in J. Leiper Freeman, *The Political Process* (Rev. ed.; New York, Doubleday, 1965).

2. Theodore Lowi systematically states some of the differences between policy subsystems within the American national political system, but does not note the impact of national style on all these subsystems; see, "American Business and Public Policy: Case Studies and Political Theory," *World Politics*, XVI (July, 1964), 677–715.

3. See studies by Sayre and Kaufman, Dahl, Banfield, and Lowi cited in note 1.

4. This evolutionary model emerged from my inquiry into the origins of planning programs in American and Canadian cities, but the model seems to fit the emergence of many welfare programs as well. See Robert Walker, *The Planning Function in Urban Government* (Chicago, University of Chicago Press, 1941); Arthur Schlesinger Jr., *The Coming of the New Deal* (Boston, Houghton Mifflin, 1958); Maurice Bruce, *The Coming of the Welfare State* (London, Batsford, 1961); and Ashley Foard and Hilbert Fefferman,

"Federal Urban Renewal Legislation," in James Wilson, ed., *Urban Renewal: The Record and the Controversy* (Cambridge, M. I. T. Press, 1966), pp. 71–125.

5. For the crisis in public assistance programs, and specifically the controversy over the Newburgh Plan, see Edgar May, *The Wasted Americans* (New York, Harper, 1963). For the recent re-evaluation of urban renewal and related housing programs, see Wilson, *Urban Renewal: The Record and the Controversy*, particularly Part VII.

6. The popularity of public works programs has been explicitly noted in H. Simon *et al.*, *Public Administration* (New York, Knopf, 1950), p. 420; and Kaplan, *Urban Renewal Politics*, pp. 179–80. James March and Herbert Simon note that one's loyalty to an organization is often greater if the organization has an observable product; see *Organizations* (New York, Wiley, 1958), p. 75. The political appeal of public works may also be inferred from studies of construction agencies; see Arthur Maas, *Muddy Waters* (Cambridge, Harvard University Press, 1951); Sayre and Kaufman, *Governing New York City*, ch. 9; and Robert Wood, *1400 Governments* (Cambridge, Harvard University Press, 1961), ch. 4.

7. The sum-zero game is defined in Talcott Parsons, "The Distribution of Power in American Society," *Structure and Process in Modern Societies* (New York, The Free Press, 1960), pp. 199–225.

8. As a further illustration of the "universal traits" in a particular policy area, I might add that the transit debate in the Metro area restated the arguments being voiced throughout North America and Western Europe; see Great Britain, Ministry of Transport, *Traffic in Towns* (London, H.M.S.O., 1963); and Lyle Fitch and associates, *Urban Transportation and Public Policy* (San Francisco, Chandler, 1964).

9. For regulatory politics in the U.S. see Marver Bernstein, *Regulating Business by Independent Commission* (Princeton, Princeton University Press, 1955); Victor Rosenblum, "How to Get into TV: The Federal Communications Commission and Miami's Channel 10," in Alan Westin, ed., *The Uses of Power* (New York, Harcourt, Brace, and World, 1962), pp. 173–228.

10. The problems of economic and physical planning within the context of American politics are emphasized in Bernstein, *Regulating by Independent Commission;* Emmette Redford, *American Government and the Economy* (New York, MacMillan, 1965), particularly p. 65; and Alan Altshuler, *The City Planning Process* (Ithaca, Cornell University Press, 1966), ch. 7. For a more general discussion of planning and democracy see Robert Dahl and Charles Lindblom,

Politics, Economics, and Welfare (New York, Harper and Row, 1953), pp. 277ff. Myron Weiner's study of India provides some perspective to the foregoing accounts. Weiner notes that the compatibility of planning and democratic politics depends largely on the nature of the demand-inputs in the particular political system; see *The Politics of Scarcity* (Chicago, University of Chicago Press, 1962), p. 234.

11. Professor Albert Rose of the University of Toronto's School of Social Work made the point about Metro's early years in commenting on an earlier version of this study.

12. The "gradualists" are also referred to as "functionalists" in the literature on international organization, but I have deliberately avoided using the latter phrase in this context. The gradualist position is defended by Amitai Etzioni in "The Dialectics of Supranational Unification," *American Political Science Review*, LVI (Dec., 1962), 927–35; "The Epigenesis of Political Community at the International Level," *American Journal of Sociology*, LXVIII (Jan., 1963), 407–21; "European Unification. A Strategy for Change," *World Politics*, XVI (Oct., 1963), 32–51. A careful and more skeptical appraisal of the gradualist approach is contained in Ernst Haas, *Beyond the Nation State* (Stanford, Stanford University Press, 1964).

13. For "spillover" see Haas, *Beyond the Nation State*, pp. 407–14 and *passim*.

14. If this theory, often referred to in Metro as the "honeymoon" theory, were correct, one would find increasing dissensus in Council voting over the thirteen-year period. I found neither increasing harmony nor increasing conflict in Council voting. See ch. 8 for data on this point. The "honeymoon" notion may be seen as the opposite of the "gradualist" theory.

15. My definition of a successful administrator as one who wins the support of his subordinates is derived from the Barnard-Simon model of administrative organizations. See March and Simon, *Organizations*, pp. 84–88. Of course, this test is not the only criterion for successful administrative leadership.

16. I return to this point in ch. 8, where the nature of bloc leadership is more fully described.

17. It seems reasonable to assume that most individual chairmen would prefer the command aspects of their role to the negotiating aspects. Matthew Holden makes this point with reference to mayors serving on advisory metropolitan commissions; see "The Governance of the Metropolis as a Problem in Diplomacy," *Journal of Politics*, XXVI (Aug., 1964), 627–47.

CHAPTER 5

Independent Policy-Making Subsystems

1. For the structural–functional approach to formal organizations, see Philip Selznick, "Foundations of the Theory of Organization," *American Sociological Review*, XIII (Feb., 1948), 25–35; Talcott Parsons, "A Sociological Approach to the Theory of Organizations," and "Some Ingredients of a General Theory of Formal Organizations," both reprinted in *Structure and Process in Modern Societies* (New York, The Free Press, 1960), pp. 16–96. This approach, it seems to me, fuses the concern of most organization theorists with the internal, vertical, and psychological aspects of formal organizations and the concern of the administration-as-politics school with organization-environment relations. Some examples of the latter school are presented in note 7 to ch. 2. "Organization theory" includes James March and Herbert Simon, *Organizations* (New York, Wiley, 1958); Amitai Etzioni, *A Comparative Analysis of Complex Organizations* (New York, The Free Press, 1961); and Michel Crozier, *The Bureaucratic Phenomenon* (Chicago, University of Chicago Press, 1964). Discussions of how the structural–functional approach to complex organizations relates to other approaches can be found in: A. Etzioni, "Two Approaches to Organizational Effectiveness," *Administrative Science Quarterly*, V (June, 1960), 257–78; and Ernst Haas, *Beyond the Nation State* (Stanford, Stanford University Press, 1964), ch. 4. Criticisms of the structural–functional approach can be found in Henry Landsberger, "Parsons' Theory of Organizations," and William Foote Whyte, "Parsons' Theory Applied to Organizations," both in Max Black, ed., *The Social Theories of Talcott Parsons* (Englewood Cliffs, N.J., Prentice-Hall, 1962), pp. 214–67.

2. The notion of policy equilibrium is presented in Samuel Huntington, "Equilibrium and Disequilibrium in American Military Policy," *Political Science Quarterly*, LXXVI (Dec., 1961), 481–502; and in March and Simon, *Organizations*, p. 86.

CHAPTER 6

The Social Context of Metro Politics

1. The early community studies, executed mainly by sociologists, are cited in note 4 to ch. 3. Studies that found business elites are cited in note 45 to ch. 1.

2. For a general discussion and review of the literature on community politics and social structure, see Peter Rossi, "Power and Community Structure," *Midwest Journal of Political Science*, IV (Nov., 1960), 390–401; Nelson Polsby, *Community Power and Political Theory* (New Haven, Yale University Press, 1963); and Wallace Sayre and Nelson Polsby, "Political Science and the Study of Urbanism," in Philip Hauser, ed., *The Study of Urbanization* (New York, Wiley, 1965).

3. David Truman, *The Governmental Process* (New York, Knopf, 1951), pp. 104–6 and *passim*.

4. Philip Jacob and James Toscano, eds., *The Integration of Political Communities* (Philadelphia and New York, Lippincott, 1964), particularly ch. 1.

5. This table was suggested to the author by a similar table appearing in Karl Deutsch and Lewis Edinger, *Germany Rejoins the Powers* (Stanford, Stanford University Press, 1959), pp. 204–16.

6. For ethnic and middle-class politics see Banfield and Wilson, *City Politics* (Cambridge, Harvard and M.I.T. Press, 1963), especially chs. 3, 9, 10, 11, 12, 20, and Conclusions, and the studies cited therein.

7. The early rivalries of the *Star* and the *Telegram* and the postwar changes in the *Telegram* are noted in Ross Harkness, *Joseph E. Atkinson of the Star* (Toronto, University of Toronto Press, 1963).

8. My search for the attitudinal variables governing interest group participation was guided by the variables suggested in: Harry Eckstein, *Pressure Group Politics* (Stanford, Stanford University Press, 1960), pp. 15–39; and Joseph LaPalombara, "The Utilities and Limitations of Interest Group Theory in Non-American Field Situations," *Journal of Politics*, XXII (Feb., 1960), 29–49.

9. See David Truman, "Federalism and the Party System," in Arthur MacMahon, ed., *Federalism: Mature and Emergent* (New York, Doubleday, 1955), pp. 115–36.

10. In attributing and gauging influence, I have been guided by the ground rules and warnings presented by Robert Dahl in "A Critique of the Ruling Elite Model," *American Political Science Review*, LII (June, 1958), 463–69; *Who Governs?* (New Haven, Yale University Press, 1961), particularly pp. 89–90; and *Modern Political Analysis* (Englewood Cliffs, N.J., Prentice-Hall, 1963), pp. 39–54.

11. The issues involving clearcut group influence are numbers 34 and 40 in Table 6.1. The issues where group influence was possibly important are numbers 28, 29, 31, 36, and 39.

12. Pressure-group explanations of the Spadina expressway and Bloor subway decisions were presented by the Toronto *Star*'s columnist, Ron Haggart.

13. For a sample of the recentralization literature, see Editors of *Fortune, The Exploding Metropolis* (New York, Doubleday, 1958); and Edward Higbee, *The Squeeze* (New York, John Morrow, 1960).

CHAPTER 7

The Social Context of Metro Politics (continued)

1. The structured–unstructured distinction is developed in Oliver Williams and Charles Adrian, *Four Cities* (Philadelphia, University of Pennsylvania Press, 1963), particularly ch. 3. My references to particular American cities are based largely on descriptions contained in Edward Banfield and James Wilson, *City Politics* (Cambridge, Harvard and M.I.T. Press, 1963).

2. My remarks about Canadian city politics are based mainly on accounts presented in the Vancouver *Sun*, the Vancouver *Province*, the Montreal *Star*, *Le Devoir* (Montreal), the Winnipeg *Tribune*, and the Winnipeg *Free Press*.

3. "Friends and neighbors" is a pattern of voting analyzed by V. O. Key Jr., in *Southern Politics in State and Nation* (New York, Knopf, 1949), see particularly ch. 14.

4. The incumbency ratio is used in Charles Gilbert and Christopher Clague, "Electoral Systems in Large Cities," *Journal of Politics*, XXIV (May, 1962), 323–49; and Eugene Lee, *The Politics of Nonpartisanship* (Berkeley and Los Angeles, University of California Press, 1960), pp. 65–66. No exact comparisons between Metro and these studies can be made, since both studies dealt with city councilors. Nor do these studies produce any firm conclusion on the relation between unstructured politics and the security of incumbents. Lee found more security in partisan state elections than in nonpartisan city elections. Gilbert and Clague found security to be high in nonpartisan cities but highest in one-party cities.

5. For conflict between parties and nonpartisan reformers see A. T. Brown, *The Politics of Reform* (Kansas City, Community Studies, 1958); Robert Salisbury, "St. Louis Politics: Relationships among Interests, Parties, and Governmental Structure," *Western Political Quarterly*, XIII (June, 1960), 498–507; S. T. Gabis, "Leadership in a Large Manager City: The Case of Kansas City," *The Annals of the American Academy of Social and Political Science*, CXXXV (May, 1964), 52–63. See also Banfield and Wilson, *City Politics*.

6. A note on Canadian political parties might be in order for American readers. The two major parties in Canada are the Liberal

Party, an urban, middle-class, middle-of-the-road party, and the Progressive-Conservative Party, an amalgam of prairie farmers, the eastern business community, and small town residents throughout Canada. The most important minor party is the New Democratic Party (the Cooperative Commonwealth Federation before 1961), a left-of-center, urban party formally affiliated with labor unions but also drawing strong support from professional people and the intellectual community. The Social Credit Party and the *Ralliment des Creditistes* hold seats in the House of Commons, but neither is active in the Toronto area. For more on Canadian parties see Hugh Thorburn, ed., *Political Parties in Canada* (Toronto, Prentice-Hall of Canada, 1963); and Leon Epstein, "A Comparative Study of Canadian Parties," *American Political Science Review*, LVIII (March, 1964), 46–59.

7. Williams and Adrian examine the impact of electoral politics on policy-making politics in *Four Cities*, particularly pp. 284–85.

8. Apparently broker leadership can occur in cities with unstructured elections (e.g., Minneapolis) or structured elections (e.g., Chicago). See Edward Banfield, *Political Influence* (New York, The Free Press, 1961), ch. 8 and 9; Alan Altshuler, *The City Planning Process* (Ithaca, Cornell University Press, 1965), ch. 7; and R. L. Morlan, "The Unorganized Politics of Minneapolis," reprinted in Edward Banfield, ed., *Urban Government* (New York, The Free Press, 1961), pp. 220–26.

9. Since the Metro chairman's role bears some resemblance to that of a city manager, my speculations were aided by the literature on the political effectiveness of managers. See Banfield and Wilson, *City Politics*, ch. 13; Williams and Adrian, *Four Cities*, pp. 278–87; and Gladys Kammerer *et al.*, *City Managers in Politics* (Gainsville, University of Florida Monograph, 1962).

10. For rebellions by outsiders, see Murray Levin, *The Alienated Voter* (New York, Holt, Rinehart, and Winston, 1960); and J. E. Horton and W. E. Thompson, "Powerlessness and Political Negativism: A Study of Defeated Referendums," *American Journal of Sociology*, LXVII (March, 1962), 485–93.

11. Williams and Adrian relate electoral politics and access in *Four Cities*, pp. 80–85.

12. Robert Agger *et al.* point out some of the limitations of a decision-making approach to community power structure in *The Rulers and the Ruled* (New York, Wiley, 1964), pp. 66–68. For recent attempts to describe the social characteristics of local decision makers see Lee, *The Politics of Nonpartisanship*, pp. 50–59; Robert Dahl, *Who Governs?* (New Haven, Yale University Press, 1961),

pp. 11–84; and Theodore Lowi, *At the Pleasure of the Mayor* (New York, The Free Press, 1964). The only application of this technique to Canadian municipal decision makers can be found in Guy Bourassa, "Les Elites Politique de Montréal: de L'Aristocratie à La Démocratie," *Canadian Journal of Economics and Political Science*, XXXI (Feb., 1965), 35–51. More is said about the legislators' reference groups in ch. 8.

13. The BMR study was entitled *The Metro Politician: A Profile*, and appeared in June, 1963. Written questionnaires were sent to all the candidates in the 1962 municipal election, but only about half of the 407 candidates replied. School board candidates were included in the survey and are included in my tabulations.

14. For these good government ideals see Herbert Kaufman, *Politics and Policies in State and Local Governments* (Englewood Cliffs, N.J., Prentice-Hall, 1963), pp. 44–51; and Banfield and Wilson, *City Politics*, pp. 138–50. The notion of a middle-class ethos is critically scrutinized in Raymond Wolfinger and John Field, "Political Ethos and the Structure of City Government," *American Political Science Review*, LX (June, 1966), 306–26.

15. Agger and others make the point that an elite substantially agreed on major issues helps produce limited mass participation and dull politics. Agger *et al.*, *The Rulers and the Ruled*, pp. 662ff.

16. The evidence of lesser participation by lower-income groups and newcomers is summarized in Robert Lane, *Political Life* (New York, The Free Press, 1959), pp. 220–72. Such lesser participation, however, does not prevent lower-income groups from rising to positions of power in many American cities. See, for example, Dahl, *Who Governs?*, pp. 32–62.

17. The difficulties that Negroes have in penetrating unstructured electoral systems is described in James Wilson, *Negro Politics* (New York, The Free Press, 1960), pp. 41–44.

18. The large-ward–small-ward distinction and its ramifications are spelled out in Banfield and Wilson, *City Politics*, pp. 89–96 and 303–8.

19. The conservatism of working-class politicians is by no means unique to Metro. See Banfield and Wilson, *City Politics*, pp. 159–60. The conservatism of a working-class political machine was the major theme of a pioneering study, Harold Gosnell, *Machine Politics: Chicago Model* (Chicago, University of Chicago Press, 1937).

20. For political culture as a concept, see Samuel Beer *et al.*, *Patterns of Government* (New York, Random House, 1962), pp. 32–45; and Lucian Pye, *Politics, Personality, and Nation Building* (New Haven, Yale University Press, 1962), Part III. Various notions of

political culture are reviewed and criticized in Young C. Kim, "The Concept of Political Culture in Comparative Politics," *Journal of Politics*, XXVI (May, 1964), 313–36. The influence of Talcott Parsons on this concept can be clearly seen in Gabriel Almond, "Comparative Political Systems," *Journal of Politics*, XVIII (Aug., 1956), 391–406.

21. My discussion of Canadian political culture draws freely from personal impressions and from the following sources: S. D. Clark, "The Canadian Community," in George Brown, ed., *Canada* (Cambridge, Toronto, and Berkeley and Los Angeles, Cambridge University Press, University of Toronto Press, and University of California Press, 1953), pp. 375–89; Kaspar Naegele, "Canadian Society: Some Relections," in Bernard Blishen *et al.*, *Canadian Society* (New York, The Free Press, 1961), pp. 1–53. For the parent British culture, see Gabriel Almond and Sidney Verba, *The Civic Culture* (Princeton, Princeton University Press, 1963), pp. 455–56 and *passim.*; and Richard Rose, *England* (Boston, Little, Brown, 1964), ch. 2. The degree of deference to authority is cited as an important part of political culture in the Almond and Verba book.

22. Outside of a few stray remarks in Williams and Adrian and in Lockard, I know of no attempt to distinguish local systems from other types of political systems. See Williams and Adrian, *Four Cities*, p. 14; and Duane Lockard, *The Politics of State and Local Government* (New York, Macmillan, 1963), p. 276.

23. Scott Greer, *The Emerging City* (New York, The Free Press, 1962), ch. 5.

24. Lockard, *The Politics of State and Local Government*, p. 276.

25. That a homogeneous social structure may restrict the degree of political pluralism has been noted in many community studies. See, for example, William Form and Delbert Miller, *Industry, Labor, and Community* (New York, Harper, 1960), ch. 13; and Agger *et al.*, *The Rulers and the Ruled*, pp. 680–85.

CHAPTER 8

Roles in the Legislative Subsystem

1. My sources on roles, role definition, and referent points are listed in notes 28 and 29 to ch. 1.

2. The term "major" is defined in Table 3.1 and in the discussion at that point. The universe of votes in Table 8.2 (280 votes) equals the total number of major split votes (293) minus the number of votes (13) on which the Metro chairman took no position. In all my

statements and calculations concerning legislative voting, the period examined is July 1, 1953 (the first meeting of the Metro Council) to June 30, 1965.

3. An early attempt to see legislatures as social systems, or what the author called "groups," is contained in David Truman, *The Governmental Process* (New York, Knopf, 1951), pp. 343-46. This approach is pursued in other studies of the U.S. Congress. For example, Ralph Huitt, "The Morse Committee Assignment Controversy: A Study in Senate Norms," *American Political Science Review*, LI (June, 1957), 313-29; David Truman, *The Congressional Party* (New York, Wiley, 1959); Donald Matthews, *The U.S. Senators and Their World* (Chapel Hill, University of North Carolina Press, 1960), particularly pp. 92-117; Richard Fenno Jr., "The House Appropriations Committee as a Political System: The Problem of Integration," *American Political Science Review*, LVI (June, 1962), 310-24; and Ralph Huitt, "The Internal Distribution of Influence: The Senate," and Richard Fenno Jr., "The Internal Distribution of Influence: The House," both appearing in David Truman, ed., *The Congress and America's Future* (Englewood Cliffs, N.J., Prentice-Hall, 1965), pp. 52-101.

4. For the norms of the U.S. Congress see the studies cited in note 3.

5. The sociologists' definition of "norm" may be seen in Robert Merton, "Social Structure and Anomie," in *Social Theory and Social Structure* (rev. ed.; New York, The Free Press, 1957), pp. 131-60. See also A. Paul Hare, *Handbook of Small Group Research* (New York, The Free Press, 1962), pp. 23-48.

6. Hare, *Handbook of Small Group Research*, pp. 24-29 and the studies cited therein.

7. The index of cohesion is applied to a session of the U.S. Congress by David Truman in *The Congressional Party*, p. 48 and *passim*. Frank Sorauf discusses the application of this index to state legislatures in *Party and Representation* (New York, Atherton, 1963), pp. 121-46.

CHAPTER 9

A Functional Assessment of the Metro System

1. Talcott Parsons' emphasis on survival can be seen in his discussion of functional imperatives; see *The Social System* (New York, The Free Press, 1951), pp. 26-36. Amitai Etzioni contrasts the "effectiveness" criterion with the functionalists' "survival" cri-

terion in *A Comparative Analysis of Complex Organizations* (New York, The Free Press, 1961), pp. 78–79. More recently Parsons has turned his attention to problems of change and development; "Evolutionary Universals in Society," *American Sociological Review,* XXIX (June, 1964), 339–57.

2. My notions of "development" are largely derived from the Parsons article cited in note 1 and from Paul Diesing, *Reason in Society* (Urbana, University of Illinois Press, 1962), particularly ch. 3; S. N. Eisenstadt, "Bureaucracy and Political Development," and Bert Hoselitz, "Levels of Economic Performance and Bureaucratic Structures," both appearing in Joseph LaPalombara, ed., *Bureaucracy and Political Development* (Princeton, Princeton University Press, 1963), pp. 96–119 and 168–98; S. N. Eisenstadt, "Social Change, Differentiation and Evolution," *American Sociological Review,* XXIX (June, 1964), 375–85; and Karl Deutsch, *The Nerves of Government* (New York, The Free Press, 1965), particularly ch. 14.

3. Deutsch presents some indices of integration in Philip Jacob and James Toscano, eds., *The Integration of Political Communities* (Philadelphia and New York, Lippincott, 1964). I use Deutsch's Indices of "growth" as indices of adaptive development; see *The Nerves of Government,* pp. 245–63.

4. I have not used all of Deutsch's indices, some of which are more relevant to national than metropolitan systems; see *The Nerves of Government,* pp. 245–63.

5. The need for coordination to develop along with differentiation is emphasized by Diesing and Eisenstadt in the studies cited in note 2 of this chapter.

RESEARCH PROCEDURES
AND SOURCES
ON METRO TORONTO

This study is based largely on written sources, supplemented by personal interviews. The most important written sources were the three Toronto newspapers, the *Globe and Mail*, the *Star*, and the *Telegram*. The Association of Women Electors' observer reports on meetings of the Metro Council, the Toronto City Council, the Metro School Board, and the Toronto Board of Education are invaluable sources for anyone seeking to understand policy making in the Metro area. I also had access to miscellaneous documents—letters, memoranda, briefs—in the files of Bureau of Municipal Research, the Municipal Reference Branch of the Toronto Public Library, and the libraries of the *Globe* and the *Star*. Frederick Gardiner kindly permitted me to examine a file he had maintained while serving as Metro chairman. The *Minutes of the Metropolitan Toronto Council* do little more than record the votes and present the text of bylaws; but the committee reports, contained in the appendix to these minutes, often provide important background information on issues. The briefs submitted to the Goldenberg Commission—the Royal Commission on Metropolitan Toronto—and the hearings of that commission are also important sources of data.

My interviews and formal conversations were held with four types of actors: Metro councilors, interest group leaders, public administrators, and knowledgeable observers. These interviews were most important as sources in my description of relations between the chairman and the cabinet (chapters 3 and 4), the chairman's relations with certain independent commissions (chapter 5), the attitudes of interest group leaders (chapter 6), the role of parties in civic elections (chapter 7), and the Metro councilor's image of his appropriate legislative role (chapter 8). In addition a number of participants submitted written comments on an earlier version of this essay.

The reader may be interested in knowing why some but not all of my assertions were supported with quantitative evidence. Such a policy was *not* dictated by the view that certain kinds of generalization did not lend themselves to quantitative statement. It seems to me that any of my qualitative generalizations could have been stated more precisely in quantitative terms or could have been demonstrated more convincingly if supported with quantitative evidence. My decisions about when to resort to statistics were guided by the following considerations.

1. In some cases, a statement or generalization involving the terms "sometime" or "usually" was sufficient to my purpose. Although such generalizations could have been stated more precisely in quantitative form, only a rough qualitative statement seemed necessary to the point I was making. The same might be said about comparative statements. Whether one uses a vague statement about "more" or "less," or a precise measurement of difference, should depend on one's purpose. In other words, I acted on the assumption that, though all generalizations *could* be stated in quantitative fashion, not all generalizations *should* be so stated. To seek precision in all generalizations would scatter too widely the energies and resources of the researcher.

2. In some cases, like those dealing with the cabinet and the independent commissions, quantification was desirable but not feasible. Information on intra-administrative politics may be extracted only with great difficulty, and rarely does one obtain sufficient information to deal with such behavior in quantitative terms. The use of indices based on behavior reported in the press, like breaks in cabinet unity, can carry one only so far. I made greater use of quantitative data in chapter 8 simply because the legislators regularly and publicly cast votes.

3. In other cases, the securing of more extension quantitative data would have clarified some problem; but the cost of assembling this data would have been considerable, and the problem or generalization was not central to the overall purpose of the study. Thus, obtaining reliable survey data on public opinion in Metro would have greatly facilitated my discussion in chapter 7, but the expense of such survey research did not seem justifiable. In a study of policy making, the central problem is how the policy makers see public opinion. What public opinion in the area really is may have little impact on policy outcomes.

The following written sources contain useful information on various aspects of Metro Toronto government, although none of the authors is explicitly concerned with Metro as a political system:

1. Studies That Refer to the Metro Toronto System

Callard, K. "Montreal and Toronto" in W. A. Robson, ed., *Great Cities of the World*. Rev. ed. London, Allen and Unwin, 1957.

Keith-Lucas, B. "Metropolitan Local Government in Canada," *Public Administration Review*, XXXIX (Autumn, 1961), 251–62.

Commonwealth of Massachusetts. Legislative Research Council. "Metropolitan Government in Canada." 1959.

Plunkett, T. J. "Metropolitan Government in Canada," *University of Toronto Law Journal*, XIV, No. 1 (1961), 29–51.

Rowat, D. *Your Local Government*. Toronto, Macmillan, 1955.

——"Planning and Metropolitan Government," *Canadian Public Administration*, I (March, 1958), 14–21.

——"The Municipal System." Talk prepared for presentation on the CBC French Network, 1965.

2. Descriptions and Evaluations of the Metro Toronto System

Crouch, W. "Metropolitan Government in Toronto, *Public Administration Review*, XIV (Spring, 1954), 85–95.

Grumm, J. G. *Metropolitan Area Government: The Toronto Experience*. Lawrence, University of Kansas Publication, 1959.

Hardy, E. "Federated Toronto: A 'Half Measure' of Progress," *National Civic Review*, XLVII (Oct., 1958), 445–50.

Milner, J. B. "The Metropolitan Toronto Plan," *University of Pennsylvania Law Review*, CV (Feb., 1957), 570–87.

Rose, A. *The Case Against Total Amalgamation in Metro Toronto*. Berkeley, Institute of Governmental Studies, University of California, 1963.

——"A Decade of Metropolitan Government in Toronto," *Buffalo Law Review*, XIII (Spring, 1964), 539–56.

Silcox, P. "The Metropolitan Council and Toronto's Metropolitan Problem, 1953–1961." Unpublished masters dissertation, University of Toronto, 1962.

Smallwood, F. *Metro Toronto: A Decade Later*. Toronto, Bureau of Municipal Research, 1963.

3. Government Documents and Quasi-Official Sources

Allen, W. "Address at Inaugural Meeting of the Metropolitan Toronto Council," 1962–1965.

——"A Tenth Birthday." Address delivered to the Canadian Club of Toronto, 1963.

City of Toronto Planning Board. *Urban Renewal: A Short Statement*, 1957.

——*The Changing City*. 1959.

——*A Report on the Ethnic Origins of the Population of Toronto*. 1961.

——*Plan for Downtown Toronto*. 1963.

Civic Advisory Council of the City of Toronto, Committee on Metropolitan Problems. *First Report*, 1949–1950; and *Final Report*, 1951.

Gardiner, F. "Address at Inaugural Meeting of the Metropolitan Toronto Council," 1953–1961.

——"Organizing the Metropolitan Administration in Toronto," in *Proceedings of the Institute of Public Administration of Canada*. 1954.

——"Metropolitan Toronto Government." Address delivered at York University, 1964.

Lascelles, G. A. "Financing Metropolitan Toronto," *Canadian Tax Journal*, III (Jan.-Feb., 1955), 16–24.

McCordic, W. "Metro's Dilemma in Public Education," *Canadian Public Administration*, VII (Dec., 1964), 464–78.

Metropolitan Toronto Planning Board. "Draft Official Plan." 1959.

Municipality of Metropolitan Toronto. *Annual Report*, 1958–1963, 1965.

Province of Ontario. *Revised Statutes*. Chapter 260 (the "Metro Toronto Act").

——Department of Economics. *A Report on Metro Toronto*. 1961.

——Metropolitan Toronto Commission of Inquiry. *Report to the Lieutenant Governor of Ontario in Council*. 1958.

——Ontario Municipal Board. *Decisions and Recommendations of the Board in the Matter of Sections 20 and 22 of "the Municipal Act."* 1953. (Urging the creation of Metro.)

——Royal Commission on Metropolitan Toronto. Briefs submitted to the Commission and transcript of the public hearings, 1964.

———*Report*, 1965.

Toronto Transit Commission. *Annual Report*, 1953–1965.

4. Nonofficial Sources on Specialized Aspects of the Metro System

Bureau of Municipal Research. *A Statement on the Subway Controversy*. 1958.

——*Reorganization of Public Transit.* 1960.
——*Financing Hospital Construction.* 1962.
——*Metro Welfare Costs.* 1963.
——*New Hope for Public Housing.* 1963.
——*The Metro Politician: A Profile.* 1963.
——*Financing Metro: Additional Sources of Revenue.* 1965.
——*Metro Toronto: Proposals for Reform.* 1965.
Feldman, L. "A Housing Project Wends Its Weary Way," *Canadian Public Administration*, VII (June, 1963), 221–32.
Hardy, E. *Fire Protection Services.* Toronto, Bureau of Municipal Research, 1957.
Ontario Association of Housing Authorities. *Good Housing For Canadians.* 1964.
Rose, A. *Regent Park: A Study in Slum Clearance.* Toronto, University of Toronto Press, 1958.
——"The Changing City," *Canadian Welfare*, XXXIX (Jan.-Feb., 1963), 6–11.
——"Services for the Changed City," *Canadian Welfare*, XXXIX (March-April, 1963), 64–71.
Social Planning Council of Metropolitan Toronto. "Brief Submitted to the Royal Commission on Metropolitan Toronto." 1964.

INDEX

Access to decision makers, 197–98

Activist style in Metro Council: newspaper endorsement of, 193; and legislative role definition, 217; and legislative styles, 222–23; Metro councilors' attitude toward, 234; suburban bloc's view of, 239–40; and Toronto bloc, 242–43

Activities in electoral process, 182–83

Activities in policy-making process: defined, 28–31; and influence, 30–31; in urban political systems, 34–37; and Metro's formal structure, 57; performed by administrators, 60–61, 76; largely within formal institutions of government, 157; *see also* Policy-making process; *and specific activities, e.g.,* Interest articulation; Majority building

Actor analysis: defined, 21–23; applied to Metro councilors, 40, 215–45; need for, 64

Adaptation: defined, 24–28; and functional differentiation, 25, 28; and systemic development, 26–28, 248–49; and policy-making process, 29–31; in urban political systems, 36–37; and functional assessment of systems, 37–39, 246–47; adaptive needs of provincial government, 49–50; and Metro's formal structure, 57; and role differentiation, 59–64, 82; performed by administrators, 61–64; and Metro integration, 62–64; Metro's adaptive performance, 65–69, 251–53; gaps in adaptive performance, 68–69, 123, 180; and structural strain, 72–73; and dif-

fuse support, 85, 88; contribution of independent commissions to, 87–88; and construction programs, 117; and Metro reorganization issues, 118; of administrative systems, 129–30; of TTC, 142, 145; of independent sub-systems, 148–49; of regulatory commissions, 150–51; of independent commissions and line departments, 152–53; of Metro School Board, 153–55; probable impact of party government on, 195–96; of political systems, 253; effect of 1966 reforms on, 257–58, 263; *see also* Systems

Administrative organizations: functional approach to, 129–30; policy equilibrium in, 130; *see also* Administrators; Cabinet, Metro

Administrative politics, *see* Politics of administration

Administrators: in policy-making process, 3; in urban political systems, 33–38; relation to Metro Council, 51, 57–58; professionalization and civil service recruitment, 90–91, 169, 171, 201, 206; advantage over interest groups, 213; *see also* Cabinet, Metro

Affective, *see* Expressive orientations

Agger, Robert, 273, 274, 286, 287, 288

Aggregation, *see* Majority building

Air-pollution control program: politics of, 94, 100, 104, 112–14; transfer to Metro level, 114; evolution of, 119–20; interest group involvement in, 160

Alderfer, Harold, 265

Aldermen, Toronto: position defined,

tion, 23; and role differentiation, 28–31; and individual decision making, 64; and Metro system, 64, 82; *see also* Adaptation; Contributions; Integration; Tasks

Gabis, S. T., 285
Garceau, Oliver, 271
Gardiner, Frederick, 279, 291, 294; appointment as Metro chairman, 49, 52; role in Executive Committee, 57, 59; view of Bill 80, 57; expands role of chairman, 58–59; secures role differentiation, 59–62, 64; and origins of cabinet, 60–61; pivotal role of, 62, 154; style, performance, and effectiveness, 62, 67, 121–25, 141, 146; emphasizes adaptive problems, 63–64; and functional needs of system, 64; and Council deference to leadership, 66–67, 95–96; views on major policy programs, 68–74, 107–10, 116–20; as chief administrator, 69–76, 78–80, 91, 152–53; and Metro reorganization issues, 74, 118; views on independent commissions, 74–75, 87, 112, 118; and Metro integration, 82, 85–92, 257; relations with Metro Council, 82–89, 90; view of parity, 85; view of chairman's formal powers, 89; and manipulation of affect, 91–92; and extralegislative groups, 92–93; influence at provincial level, 110, 127, 150–51; and Metro's policy outputs, 116–20; and gradualist strategy, 120–21, 126, 236; selection of a successor to, 122, 190; defends TTC, 134; relations with TTC commissioners, 137, 138–39; view of TTC tasks, 145; and independent regulatory commissions, 149–51; his TTC reorganization plan, 165; interest group views on, 170, 174; interest group influence on, 177; impact of newspapers on, 180; and unstructured legislatures, 194; and political culture, 211; interaction of personality and political structure, 245; and Metro's impasse, 256; *see also* Metro chairman
Gilbert, Charles, 285
Givens, Philip: endorsed by Labor,

191; as good government candidate, 202; legislative style of, 227, 231
Globe and Mail, Toronto: involvement in Metro policy making, 160–66; as part of good government bloc, 169–72; and Metro reorganization issue, 172; endorses candidates, 192; *see also* Newspapers
Goals: Parsons' treatment of, 15; of modern political systems, 16; in Metro system, 17–19; of urban political systems, 19–20; and contributions, 24; *see also* Systems
Goldenberg Commission, *see* Ontario Royal Commission on Metropolitan Toronto
Good government groups: hostile to TTC, 139; and Metro policy-making process, 160–66; views of, 169–72; and Metro reorganization issues, 172; satisfaction with Metro outputs, 173; and Gardiner, 197
Good government values: Gardiner as advocate, 69; and long-range capital planning, 70; and metropolitan federation, 80; opposed to patronage, 91; and Metro political elite, 200–1; and Toronto elections, 202; and ethnic leaders, 207; and legislative role definition, 217; in Toronto political system, 230
Goodhead, N., 226
Gosnell, Harold, 287
Gould, J., 227
Government officials: in urban political systems, 34–36; as major influentials in Metro, 157; interest group pressures on, 173; conflict among, 174–75; group access to, 197–98; and interest group involvement, 251; *see also* Administrators; Metro councilors, Metro political elite
Gradualist strategy: in Metro and international systems, 120, 236; failure of, 250
Grant, Daniel, 275
Grass-roots groups, *see* Neighborhood groups
Grayson, M., 227
Great Britain, *see* British political culture

Greenstone, J. D., 265
Greer, Scott, 213, 276, 288
Griggs, H., 226
Grossman, A., 227
Grossman, L. S., 276
Groups, *see* Interest groups; Subsystems

Haas, Ernst, 26, 267, 271, 272, 278, 279, 282, 283
Haggart, Ron, 284
Hague, Dorothy, 187, 226
Hall, Fred, 150, 226
Hamilton, Douglas: as TTC commissioner, 135, 140; appointment to TTC, 161, 163
Hamilton, Ont.: board of control system in, 55; elections in, 184
Hardy, Eric., 293
Hare, A. P., 289
Harkness, R., 284
Harris, A., 226
Hauser, Philip, 284
Health, *see* Fluoridation of water; Public health program
Herring, Pendleton, 268, 269, 276
Higbee, Edward, 285
Hiscott, C., 226
Hodgins, A., 227
Holden, Matthew, 282
Holley, J., 226
Holt, Robert, 268
Homans, George, 262, 270, 272, 273, 278
Home rule, *see* Municipal-provincial relations; Municipal-state relations
Homes for the aged, 164
Horkins, R., 227
Horton, J. E., 286
Hoselitz, Bert, 290
Hospital construction grants: as nonissue, 68; and Metro Council politics, 94, 104, 107; compared to public housing politics, 109; and interest group involvement, 160
Housing, *see* Public housing program; Urban redevelopment and renewal program
Huitt, Ralph, 289
Hunter, Floyd, 274, 278
Huntington, Samuel, 283

Ideologies, *see* Conservatism; Good government values; Liberal-welfare values; Recentralization ideology
Independent boards and commissions: in municipal and Metro government, 55–57; appointments to, 66, 95, 97; legislative deference to, 67; as threat to administrative unity, 67; views of cabinet and Gardiner on, 74–75; contribution to Metro system, 87–88; legislative control of, 112, 156; views on continued independence of, 118; functional differences among, 147–48; compared to line departments, 151–53; as good government ideal, 169–70, 201
Independent regulatory commissions, 147–51
Individual, and role, 5
Influence: as currency of transactions, 13; approach to study of, 15; and activities in policy-making process, 30–31; pervasive and specific, 31, 178–80, 219; to be discussed, 40; of Metro government officials, 157; of interest groups, 175–78; of newspapers, 192–93, 225, 241; and access, 197; in legislative role definition, 217–18, 231–32; within Metro Council, 233; within suburban bloc, 238, 240; within Toronto bloc, 241
Institutionalization, *see* Integration
Instrumental orientations: in systems, 16, 21; in Metro system, 18; in urban political systems, 19–20
Integration: of social system, 5–6, 15–17, 21–23, 24; Merton on, 11; uses of concept, 11; and power, 12–15; in Metro system, 17–19, 57, 63–64, 80–85, 249–53, 257–58, 263; of urban political systems, 19–20, 35–37, 211; and equilibrium, 21; redefined, 24–28; of international organizations, 24; the Haas-Deutsch approach to, 24; and policy-making process, 29–31; and functional assessment of systems, 37–39, 246–47; integrative needs of provincial government, 49–50; and role differentiation in Metro system, 59–63; and Metro adaptation, 62–64; and structural strain, 71–72; and parity,

Metro Council (*Continued*)
pattern emerges, 123; hiatus in achievements, 126–27; future relations with chairman, 127–28; relations with TTC, 133–34, 138–41, 143–46; structure compared to Metro School Board's, 154; preoccupied with federal issues, 158; interest group pressures on, 173; Allen's control of, 174; interaction with chairman and interest groups, 175–78; and Spadina Expressway, 177; impact of newspapers on, 180; party intervention in, 189–90; impact of elections on, 193; pattern of voting in, 193–94; probable impact of party government on, 195–96; consequences of ethnic ascendance for, 206, 207–8; as a social system, 218, 231–36; Toronto aldermen in, 221; militancy in, 223; support for chairman, 224–25, 226–27; consensus within, 233–34, 250; norms and social control in, 233–35; cohesion in, 235–36, 237; integration of, 236; compared to other legislative systems, 236; blocs in, 236–45; appointments to Executive Committee, 240; Toronto bloc's view of, 243; impasse in, 252–53; proposed reforms in, 254; direct elections to, 258–59; under new Metro Act, 261; future of, 262–63

Metro councilors: role definition by, 22–23, 40, 215–45; and legislators in other systems, 37; role to be described, 39–40; basic orientation to Metro system, 59, 61, 82, 83–85, 193–94; defer to leadership, 61, 85, 95–97, 174, 201; and integrative function, 62–63; and adaptation, 62–63; as issue initiators, 66, 69; Gardiner's relations with, 75, 119, 124; weak involvement in Metro issues, 78, 95; image of cabinet, 79; indirect elections of, 80–82, 83, 115, 218, 257–59; and parity, 84–85, 158; views of Metro chairman, 89, 92, 115; moderates and militants, 90, 223–25; and appointments to Executive Committee, 90; attitudes on construction programs, 106–10, 116–17; and service programs, 110–12, 119; and reg-

ulatory programs, 112–13, 119–20; and Metro reorganization issues, 114–16, 119, 158; views on independent commissions, 118, 148, 153; and spillover, 120–21; relations with Allen, 122–25, 127–28; and Metro's policy impasse, 125–26, 252–53, 263; views on transit and TTC, 132–33, 139–41, 144–45; and independent regulatory commissions, 147–48, 150–51; compared to Metro School Board members, 154; views on interest groups, 157–58, 175; pervasive influence over, 178–80; and newspapers, 180; reelection of, 186; and interest group pressures, 188; view of elections, 194–95; probable impact of party government on, 195–96; as Metro's political elite, 198; policy views of, 200–2; and political culture, 209; exert little influence on each other, 217–18, 231–32, 233–36; pressures on, 220–21; roles and styles of, 215–25; activists, 222–23; support for chairman, 224–25, 226–31, 236; style and group pressures, 225, 228; style and constituency, 228–31; consensus among, 233–34; and Council norms, 234–35; and legislative integration, 236; loyalty to bloc, 236–38; changes in role definition, 250, 262–63; recent view of Metro, 253–55; direct election of, 257–59

Metro Executive Committee: and board of control, 57; powers and composition, 58–59; appointments to, 90, 242; relations with department heads, 124, 127; defeats transit plan, 125; and social control in Council, 234; and suburban bloc leadership, 238–40; and Toronto bloc leadership, 241, 242–43; proposed reforms in, 254; under new Metro Act, 261

Metro Licensing Commission, 146–51, 163; *see also* Licensing program

Metro-municipal relations: distribution of powers, 52–55; Gardiner's and cabinet's views on, 70; proposals for shift in powers, 114–16, 257, 260–61; and fluoridation, 115–16, 158; Allen's views on, 122; and indirect election of Metro councilors, 217

Metro school superintendent, 154

Metro Separate School Board, 153–54

Metro Toronto Act: terms of, 50–57; gaps in, 57–58; emphasized construction programs, 68–69; and public transit, 132–33; and Metro School Board, 153; and election of Metro councilors, 218; revised, 256

Metro Toronto and Region Conservation Authority, 153

Metro works commissioner, and air-pollution control, 113–14

Meyerson, Martin, 274

Miami, metropolitan federation plan in, 42, 80, 81–82

Middle class, 39; representation in Metro political elite, 199–200, 203; values of, 200, 201, 203; and unstructured electoral politics, 204; and large-ward system, 206; and political culture, 209–10; and City of Toronto politics, 230; see also Class; Good government groups

Militant style in Metro Council: described, 217, 223–31; and legislative integration, 233; Metro councilors' view of, 234

Miller, Delbert, 274, 288

Milner, J. B., 293

Mimico: population changes in, 44; legislative behavior of reeves, 226, 229; merged with Etobicoke, 261; see also Suburban bloc in Metro Council; Suburban political systems

Minneapolis, electoral politics in, 184

Mitchell, William, 267, 269, 274–75

Modelski, George, 267

Moderate style in Metro Council: described, 217, 223–31; and legislative integration, 233; Metro councilors' view of, 234; and Executive Committee appointments, 240

Modern political systems, 15–16

Montreal: as Toronto's rival, 105; elections in, 182; ethnic conflict in, 208

Morlan, R. L., 286

Mould, J., 226

Munger, Ralph, 274, 275

Municipality of Metropolitan Toronto, see Metro political system

Municipal political systems: relations with Metro system, 39, 80–82, 127, 249–50, 258; structure of government, 55–56; rearrangement of boundaries, 115, 261; and Metro School Board, 153–54; deal with neighborhood issues, 172–73; elections in, 184–98; parties in, 189–90; Labor in, 190–92; newspapers' role in, 192–93; relations with Metro councilors, 193–94, 200–1, 216–21, 223, 225, 228–29, 236, 238, 258; elections and access, 197–98; and political elites, 198–99; not executive-directed systems, 211; activists in, 222–23; see also Metro-municipal relations; Suburban political systems; Toronto political system

Municipal-provincial relations: and distinctive features of urban political systems, 17–19, 24, 212–13; and home rule, 47–48; and municipal contributions to provincial system, 49–50; and organization of municipal government in Ontario, 55–57; responsibilities for service and regulatory programs, 105–6; and Metro's performance, 252

Municipal school boards, 148, 153–55, 262; see also Metro School Board

Municipal-state relations (United States): and distinctive features of urban political systems, 17–19, 24, 212–13; compared to municipal-provincial relations, 47–50

Naegele, Kaspar, 288

Nagel, Ernest, 265

Nash, F., 227

Nashville, metropolitan federation plan in, 42, 80

Natanson, Maurice, 270

Nation-building, and functionalist approach, 12

Nealson, B., 226

Negotiation, see Bargaining

Negroes, 38

Neighborhood groups: and legislative roles and styles, 61, 216, 217, 223, 225; and construction programs, 105, 108, 177; and transit service, 132; and independent subsystems, 148; and policy-making process, 159–66; special-

cept defined, 209; Canadian, British, and American compared, 210–11

Political development, *see* Development of systems

Political elite, *see* Metro political elite

Political parties, 3, 39; in urban political systems, 35–36; as links between system and environment, 159; and policy-making process, 159; partisan municipal government as an issue, 169, 171, 206, 259–60; in urban elections, 181–84, 187; in Canadian city politics, 182–84, 191; in Metro area elections, 188–90, 192–93, 195–96; and local legislative politics, 189–90; in Winnipeg and Vancouver, 191; and Metro policy making, 193; and political culture, 201; and ethnic groups, 203–4; difficulty in defining local issues, 212; as reference groups for legislators, 217, 223, 239; and Metro's impasse, 256–57; *see also* Electoral factions

Political science: and functionalism, 11–17, 20; and sociology, 11–12; and concept of power, 13–15; and urban political systems, 156

Politics: as study of political systems, 4, 7–8, 11–15; war theory of, 13–15; *see also* Systems

Politics of administration: literature on, 60; in Metro, 60–62; Metro compared to New York City, 76–80; new pattern in Metro, 127

Polsby, Nelson, 274, 284

Power: and normative integration, 11–15; and war theory of politics, 13–14; productive and allocative aspects of, 14–15

Pressure groups, *see* Interest groups

Problem solving, *see* Adaptation; Integration

Progressive-Conservative Party, *see* Conservative Party

Property tax, *see* Assessment of property; Taxes

Protestants, 199–200, 203

Provincial government, *see* Municipal-provincial relations; Ontario cabinet

Public assistance program: Metro and municipal powers in, 53–54, 114–15,

125; as a nonissue, 68, 69; compared to construction programs, 105; Allen's views on, 122; and interest groups, 163, 167, 171, 172; and liberal-welfare bloc, 170; Metro's achievements in, 252, 255; and new Metro Act, 263

Public finance, *see* Budgets, operating; Capital expenditures and finance; Taxes

Public health program: municipal control of, 52, 54; as a nonissue, 68, 69; politics of fluoridation, 115–16; Metro's achievements in, 255

Public housing program: Metro and municipal powers over, 53–54, 74, 115, 125; vested in independent board, 56; views of Gardiner and cabinet on, 72–74; and Metro Council, 94, 104, 106–7; politics of, 109–10; Allen's views on, 122–23; interest group involvement in, 161, 162, 163, 164, 167, 170, 172; newspapers' influence on, 179; as issue in elections, 185; as obnoxious intrusion, 216; Metro's achievements in, 255

Public opinion: and Metro councilors, 157–58; and fluoridation referendum, 158; and Metro elections, 196–97; and defense of municipal rights, 219

Public policy: as system outputs, 8, 16; as outcome of conflict, 13; Parsons' approach to, 15; outputs and integration, 26; outputs in urban political systems, 32–34; Metro policies to be described, 39–40; approach to study of, 99–103; policy programs as subsystems, 99–100; emergence of new programs, 101–3; political attitudes on various programs, 105–16, 153; Metro's outputs, 116–21; evolution of Metro's program, 118–20; output, integration, and adaptation, 248–50, 252–53, 256, 259, 263; *see also* Policy-making process; *and specific policy programs, e.g.,* Public transit; Police protection

Public transit program: Metro and municipal powers over, 52, 54; vested in independent commission, 56, 71, 87–88; and comprehensive transpor-

Scarborough: postwar development, 44, 45; legislative behavior of reeves, 224, 226, 229–30; under new Metro Act, 261–62; *see also* Suburban bloc in Metro Council; Suburban political systems

Schindeler, F. F., 276

Schlesinger Jr., Arthur, 280

Schmandt, Henry, 276

Schools, *see* Education; Metro School Board

Scythes, J. A., 135–36

Seagrave, R., 226

Secord, G., 135

Segmental system, defined, 18–20

Selznick, Philip, 276–77, 283

Service programs: and suburbs, 45, 168, 228; and parity, 84; and Metro Council, 94, 100, 104, 105; compared to construction programs, 105, 106, 110–11; politics of, 110–12; and regulatory programs, 113; Metro and municipal power over, 114; policy outputs, 117–18, 120, 125–26; evolution of, 119; and interest groups, 149, 168; need strong Metro chairman, 153; as divisive issue in suburban bloc, 241; Metro achievement in, 255–56

Sewer construction program: Metro control over, 53, 54; emphasized in early capital budgets, 70, 71, 111; and Metro Council, 94, 104, 106–7; and interest groups, 160, 164

Shils, Edward, 266, 271

Silcox, Peter, 293

Silverman, Corinne, 271

Simon, Herbert, 269, 270, 277, 281, 282, 283

Simonsky, L., 226

Simpson, H., 226

Sinclair, Clive, 135

Singer, J. D., 271

Singer, V., 226

Slack, defined, 18

Slater, P. E., 272

Smallwood, Frank, 277, 293

Smelser, Neil, 266, 267, 268, 272, 273

Social change, and functionalism, 12; *see also* Development of systems

Social context of political systems, 64, 156–59, 181, 193–94, 197–98, 201, 208–9, 214; *see also* Class; Ethnic groups; Interest groups; Political parties

Social control: in systems, 6, 10, 11; and political systems, 16, 24; in Metro system, 17–19, 82; in urban political systems, 18–19; and integration of systems, 25, 248; not available to Metro chairman, 90; in Metro Council, 234; and index of cohesion, 236; and bloc loyalty, 238; in Toronto bloc, 241–42

Socialism, in Canadian city politics, 184, 191–92

Socialization, 7; and political systems, 16, 24; in Metro system, 17–19, 82; in urban political systems, 19; and integration of systems, 25

Social Planning Council: and policy-making process, 160–67; stands between two blocs, 171; and elections, 188

Social work, *see* Public assistance program; Social Planning Council

Sociology: and political science, 11–12; and urban political systems, 156; definition of "role" and "norm," 233, 234

Sofen, Edward, 275

Soft programs, *see* Nonconstruction programs

Sorauf, Frank, 272, 289

Spadina Expressway, 106–7, 161, 165, 177

Specific support, *see* Support, diffuse and specific

Spillover, and Metro integration, 120–121, 126

Star, Toronto: and policy-making process, 160–66; as part of liberal-welfare bloc, 169–71; as rival of *Telegram*, 170–71; and Metro reorganization, 172; on transportation policies, 177; view of Metro system, 179; conflicts with cabinet, 180; translates liberal values, 190; endorses candidates, 192

Strains: in cabinet, 71–75; in TTC, 140; in Toronto bloc in Metro Council 243–44

Strategic behavior, in war theory of politics, 13; *see also* Instrumental orientations

Strath, J., 226

Structural-Functionalism, *see* Functionalism

Structured electoral politics, *see* Elections; Electoral factions; Political parties

Style, 23, 217, 222; *see also* Activist style in Metro Council; Metro councilors; Militant style in Metro Council; Moderate style in Metro Council

Subsystems: hierarchic arrangement of, 6; and functional requisites, 7–8; in relation to larger system, 7–8, 12; exchanges among, 8–9; and level-of-analysis problem, 9, 11; pursue self-interest, 16; and multiple loyalties, 19; Metro subsystems to be described, 39; policy areas as, 99–100; spillover between, 120–21; independent agencies as, 129; development and decline of, 144; performance and form of organization, 151–53

Suburban bloc in Metro Council: views on public housing, 73–74; views on Metro-municipal relations, 74; views on parity, 84; Gardiner's relations with, 86, 89; views on water rates, 87, 111–12; as a voting bloc, 90; and TTC appointments, 91; and factional voting in Council, 93–95, 103–4, 118; views on construction programs, 106; on expressways, 107–8; on subways, 108–9; and police protection, 111; on Metro service programs, 111–12; on Metro reorganization issues, 114–16; relations with Allen, 121–23, 125; views on public transit, 132–33; opposition to TTC, 134–35, 141; and independent subsystems, 148; on fluoridation, 158; in policy-making process, 160–66; and interest groups, 169, 175, 176; newspaper influence on, 179; and Metro's policy output, 180; as obstacle to party government, 196; and ethnic group ascendance, 206; support for Metro chairman, 224–25, 226–27, 229–30; militancy of, 225, 228; influence within, 231–33; norms of, 234; and legislative integration, 236; as a source of loyalty, 236–38; internal structure of, 238–40; cohesion compared to Toronto bloc, 241–

42, 243; recent views on Metro, 253–55; and Metro's impasse, 256–57; and 1966 reforms, 257, 261; future of, 262–63

Suburban political systems: socio-economic context of, 42–44; view of metropolitan problems and reform, 45–46; response to federation, 47; representation on Metro Council, 50, 56; structure of government, 55–56; representation on Executive Committee, 59; representation on TTC, 110, 132–33, 137; and suburban bus service, 133–35, 137, 138–39, 142; and Metro School Board, 155; seen as middle class, 170; interest groups in, 172; control growth of, 178; elections in, 185–88; parties in, 188; Labor in, 191; newspaper influence in, 192; suburban reeves as activists, 223, 224; and Metro councilors' militancy, 225; and styles in Metro Council, 228, 230; loss of activists, 240, 243; alter view of Metro, 250; under new Metro Act, 254, 261–63

Subway construction program: controversies over planning, 67, 72, 138–39; cabinet views on, 71; and Metro Council, 87, 94, 104; political popularity of, 105, 106, 107; politics of, 108–9, 138–40; versus expressways, 111; Allen's plan for, 125; and TTC strategies, 131–34, 138–39; TTC deadlocked on, 142, 143, 145; and interest groups, 160–63, 165, 169–72, 177; and recentralization ideology, 178–79; newspaper influence on, 179, 180; as election issue, 185; *see also* Public transit program

Summerville, Donald: endorsed by Labor, 191; legislative style of, 227, 231

Sum-zero game, 14–15, 106, 111–12

Support, diffuse and specific: and Metro integration, 18, 85; in urban political systems, 19; and integration of systems, 25–26, 248; and Metro's adaptive development, 88; for particular policy programs, 108, 109

Support-securing activities: in policy-making process, 28–29; in urban political systems, 34–37

Swansea: postwar changes in, 44, 45;

Working class, 39; in American city politics, 169; and Metro's political elite, 201–2; factors governing entrance into elite, 202–6; and unstructured electoral politics, 204; future representation in elite, 206; and political culture, 209–10; as reference group, 221

Wrong, Dennis, 276

York: postwar changes in, 42, 44, 45; electoral politics in, 185; legislative behavior of reeves, 226, 229; under new Metro Act, 261–62; *see also* Suburban bloc in Metro Council; Suburban political systems

Yorkdale shopping center, 177

Zoning: Metro and municipal powers over, 53; and neighborhood groups, 168; *see also* Land-use planning

N

Cε